E. M. FORSTER

Modern Critical Views

Henry Adams
Edward Albee
A. R. Ammons
Matthew Arnold
John Ashbery
W. H. Auden
Jane Austen
James Baldwin
Charles Baudelaire
Samuel Beckett
Saul Bellow
The Bible
Elizabeth Bishop
William Blake
Jorge Luis Borges
Elizabeth Bowen
Bertolt Brecht
The Brontës
Robert Browning
Anthony Burgess
George Gordon, Lord
   Byron
Thomas Carlyle
Lewis Carroll
Willa Cather
Cervantes
Geoffrey Chaucer
Kate Chopin
Samuel Taylor Coleridge
Joseph Conrad
Contemporary Poets
Hart Crane
Stephen Crane
Dante
Charles Dickens
Emily Dickinson
John Donne & the Seven-
   teenth-Century Meta-
   physical Poets
Elizabethan Dramatists
Theodore Dreiser
John Dryden
George Eliot
T. S. Eliot
Ralph Ellison
Ralph Waldo Emerson
William Faulkner
Henry Fielding
F. Scott Fitzgerald
Gustave Flaubert
E. M. Forster
Sigmund Freud
Robert Frost

Robert Graves
Graham Greene
Thomas Hardy
Nathaniel Hawthorne
William Hazlitt
Seamus Heaney
Ernest Hemingway
Geoffrey Hill
Friedrich Hölderlin
Homer
Gerard Manley Hopkins
William Dean Howells
Zora Neale Hurston
Henry James
Samuel Johnson and
   James Boswell
Ben Jonson
James Joyce
Franz Kafka
John Keats
Rudyard Kipling
D. H. Lawrence
John Le Carré
Ursula K. Le Guin
Doris Lessing
Sinclair Lewis
Robert Lowell
Norman Mailer
Bernard Malamud
Thomas Mann
Christopher Marlowe
Carson McCullers
Herman Melville
James Merrill
Arthur Miller
John Milton
Eugenio Montale
Marianne Moore
Iris Murdoch
Vladimir Nabokov
Joyce Carol Oates
Sean O'Casey
Flannery O'Connor
Eugene O'Neill
George Orwell
Cynthia Ozick
Walter Pater
Walker Percy
Harold Pinter
Plato
Edgar Allan Poe
Poets of Sensibility & the
   Sublime

Alexander Pope
Katherine Ann Porter
Ezra Pound
Pre-Raphaelite Poets
Marcel Proust
Thomas Pynchon
Arthur Rimbaud
Theodore Roethke
Philip Roth
John Ruskin
J. D. Salinger
Gershom Scholem
William Shakespeare
   (3 vols.)
   Histories & Poems
   Comedies
   Tragedies
George Bernard Shaw
Mary Wollstonecraft
   Shelley
Percy Bysshe Shelley
Edmund Spenser
Gertrude Stein
John Steinbeck
Laurence Sterne
Wallace Stevens
Tom Stoppard
Jonathan Swift
Alfred, Lord Tennyson
William Makepeace
   Thackeray
Henry David Thoreau
Leo Tolstoi
Anthony Trollope
Mark Twain
John Updike
Gore Vidal
Virgil
Robert Penn Warren
Evelyn Waugh
Eudora Welty
Nathanael West
Edith Wharton
Walt Whitman
Oscar Wilde
Tennessee Williams
William Carlos Williams
Thomas Wolfe
Virginia Woolf
William Wordsworth
Richard Wright
William Butler Yeats

These and other titles in preparation

Modern Critical Views

E. M. FORSTER

Edited and with an introduction by
Harold Bloom
Sterling Professor of the Humanities
Yale University

CHELSEA HOUSE PUBLISHERS
New York ◊ Philadelphia

© 1987 by Chelsea House Publishers, a division
of Main Line Book Co.

Introduction © 1987 by Harold Bloom

Printed and bound in the United States of America

10 9 8 7 6 5 4 3 2

∞ The paper used in this publication meets the minimum
requirements of the American National Standard for Permanence
of Paper for Printed Library Materials, Z39.48–1984.

Library of Congress Cataloging-in-Publication Data
E. M. Forster.
   (Modern critical views)
   Bibliography: p.
   Includes index.
   1. Forster, E. M. (Edward Morgan), 1879–1970—
Criticism and interpretation.   I. Bloom, Harold.
II. Series.
PR6011.O58Z6524   1986   823'.914   86–14783
ISBN 0–87754–643–6 (alk. paper)

Contents

Editor's Note

This book gathers together a representative selection of the best critical essays devoted to the writings of E. M. Forster, arranged in the chronological order of their original publication. I am grateful to Jennifer Wagner for her erudition and judgment in helping me to locate and choose these essays.

My introduction centers upon Forster's spiritual stance in *A Passage to India,* which is related to his experience of life in modern Alexandria, and to his book on the spirit and history of ancient Alexandria. Lionel Trilling, the most eminent of Forster's critics, begins the chronological sequence with an analysis of Forster's own literary criticism, characterized as being marked by a relaxed will, akin to Hinduism, as opposed to T. S. Eliot's New Criticism, with its Christian intensification of the will.

George H. Thomson considers the narrative voice of Forster's Italian novels, *Where Angels Fear to Tread* and *A Room with a View,* finding them unique in Forster's canon, in that "the object of vision is apprehended more fully and the moment of ecstasy is participated in more wholeheartedly by the narrator than by his characters." In an exegesis of *The Longest Journey,* which Forster considered one of his best novels, John Colmer sees the book as one that unsettles all accepted critical categories. Alan Wilde explores the subtle "injunctions and disjunctions" that fuse and defuse sex and love in Forster's fiction in an overview of the author's work that extends from the earliest fiction to *Maurice* and the posthumously published homosexual short stories.

Howards End, perhaps Forster's strongest novel, is the subject in the essay by Barbara B. Rosecrance, which reinterprets the novel as a searching critique of Forster's own liberalism, even as that liberalism still receives its most comprehensive expression. *A Passage to India,* Forster's most widely read and influential novel, properly concludes this book, as we are given three remarkable studies of its perpetual relevance to us. Martin Price subtly expounds the novel's subtlety, which for him "lies in its unrelieved tension of flesh and spirit, exclusion and invitation, the social self and the deeper impersonal self." A sensitive account of Forster's friendship with Syed Ross Masood leads Rustom Bharucha into his exegesis of *A Passage to India*, where Masood served as the model for Aziz, who is for Bharucha an emblem of Forster's love for India. In this volume's closing essay, printed here for the first time, Sara Suleri brilliantly describes the role of Adela Quested in the novel as "a passageway for the aborted eroticism between the European Fielding and the Indian Aziz," and so as another emblem, one that represents India's refusal to yield to any Western mode of representation, even a mode as affectionate and subtle as the narrative art of E. M. Forster.

Introduction

I

E. M. Forster's canonical critic was Lionel Trilling, who might have written Forster's novels had Forster not written them and had Trilling been English. Trilling ended his book on Forster (1924) with the tribute that forever exalts the author of *Howards End* and *A Passage to India* as one of those storytellers whose efforts "work without man's consciousness of them, and even against his conscious will." In Trilling's sympathetic interpretation (or identification), Forster was the true antithesis to the world of telegrams and anger:

> A world at war is necessarily a world of will; in a world at war Forster reminds us of a world where the will is not everything, of a world of true order, of the necessary connection of passion and prose, and of the strange paradoxes of being human. He is one of those who raise the shield of Achilles, which is the moral intelligence of art, against the panic and emptiness which make their onset when the will is tired from its own excess.

Trilling subtly echoed Forster's own response to World War I, a response which Forster recalled as an immersion in Blake, William Morris, the early T. S. Eliot, J. K. Huysmans, Yeats: "They took me into a country where the will was not everything." Yet one can wonder whether Forster and Trilling, prophets of the liberal imagination, did not yield to a vision where there was not quite enough conscious will. *A Passage to India,* Forster's most famous work, can sustain many rereadings, so intricate is its orchestration. It is one of only a few novels of this century that is *written-through,* in the musical sense of thorough composition. But reading it yet again, after twenty years away from it, I find it to be a narrative all of whose principal figures—Aziz, Fielding, Adela Quested, Mrs. Moore, Godbole—lack conscious will.

Doubtless, this is Forster's deliberate art, but the consequence is curious; the characters do not sustain rereading so well as the novel does, because none is larger than the book. Poldy holds my imagination quite apart from Joyce's *Ulysses,* as Isabel Archer does in James's *The Portrait of a Lady,* or indeed as Mrs. Wilcox does in Forster's *Howards End,* at least while she is represented as being alive. The aesthetic puzzle of *A Passage to India* is why Aziz and Fielding could not have been stronger and more vivid beings than they are.

What matters most in *A Passage to India* is India, and not any Indians nor any English. But this assertion requires amendment, since Forster's India is not so much a social or cultural reality as it is an enigmatic vision of the Hindu religion, or rather of the Hindu religion as it is reimagined by the English liberal mind at its most sensitive and scrupulous. The largest surprise of a careful rereading of *A Passage to India* after so many years is that, in some aspects, it now seems a strikingly *religious* book. Forster shows us what we never ought to have forgotten, which is that any distinction between religious and secular literature is finally a mere political or societal polemic, but is neither a spiritual nor an aesthetic judgment. There is no sacred literature and no post-sacred literature, great or good. *A Passage to India* falls perhaps just short of greatness, in a strict aesthetic judgment, but spiritually it is an extraordinary achievement.

T. S. Eliot consciously strove to be a devotional poet, and certainly did become a Christian polemicist as a cultural and literary critic. Forster, an amiable freethinker and secular humanist, in his *Commonplace Book* admirably compared himself to Eliot:

> With Eliot? I feel now to be as far ahead of him as I was once behind. Always a distance—and a respectful one. How I dislike his homage to pain! What a mind except the human could have excogitated it? Of course there's pain on and off through each individual's life, and pain at the end of most lives. You can't shirk it and so on. But why should it be endorsed by the schoolmaster and sanctified by the priest until   ·
>
> the fire and the rose are one
>
> when so much of it is caused by disease or by bullies? It is here that Eliot becomes unsatisfactory as a seer.

One could add: it is here that Forster becomes most satisfactory as a seer, for that is the peculiar excellence of *A Passage to India.* We are reminded that Forster is another of John Ruskin's heirs, together with Proust, whom

Forster rightly admired above all other modern novelists. Forster too wishes *to make us see,* in the hope that by seeing we will learn to connect, with ourselves and with others, and like Ruskin, Forster knows that seeing in this strong sense is religious, but in a mode beyond dogmatism.

II

A Passage to India, published in 1924, reflects Forster's service as private secretary to the Maharajah of Dewas State Senior in 1921–22, which in turn issued from his Indian visit of 1912–13 with G. Lowes Dickinson. It was not until 1953 that Forster published *The Hill of Devi,* utilizing letters he had written home from India, both forty and thirty years before. *The Hill of Devi* celebrates Forster's Maharajah as a kind of saint, indeed as a religious genius, though Forster is anything but persuasive when he attempts to sustain his judgment of his friend and employer. What does come through is Forster's appreciation of certain elements in Hinduism, an appreciation that achieves its apotheosis in *A Passage to India,* and particularly in "Temple," the novel's foreshortened final part. Forster's ultimate tribute to his Maharajah, a muddler in practical matters and so one who died in disgrace, is a singular testimony for a freethinker. *The Hill of Devi* concludes with what must be called a mystical apprehension:

> His religion was the deepest thing in him. It ought to be studied— neither by the psychologist nor by the mythologist but by the individual who has experienced similar promptings. He penetrated into rare regions and he was always hoping that others would follow him there.

What are those promptings? Where are those regions? Are these the questions fleshed out by *A Passage to India*? After observing the mystical Maharajah dance before the altar of the God Krishna, Forster quotes from a letter by the Maharajah describing the festival, and then attempts what replies seem possible:

> Such was his account. But what did he feel when he danced like King David before the altar? What were his religious opinions?
> The first question is easier to answer than the second. He felt as King David and other mystics have felt when they are in the mystic state. He presented well-known characteristics. He was convinced that he was in touch with the reality he called Krishna. And he was unconscious of the world around him. "You can

come in during my observances tomorrow and see me if you like, but I shall not know that you are there," he once told Malcolm. And he didn't know. He was in an abnormal but recognisable state; psychologists have studied it.

More interesting, and more elusive, are his religious opinions. The unseen was always close to him, even when he was joking or intriguing. Red paint on a stone could evoke it. Like most people, he implied beliefs and formulated rules for behaviour, and since he had a lively mind, he was often inconsistent. It was difficult to be sure what he did believe (outside the great mystic moments) or what he thought right or wrong. Indians are even more puzzling than Westerners here. Mr. Shastri, a spiritual and subtle Brahmin, once uttered a puzzler: "If the Gods do a thing, it is a reason for men not to do it." No doubt he was in a particular religious mood. In another mood he would have urged us to imitate the Gods. And the Maharajah was all moods. They played over his face, they agitated his delicate feet and hands. To get any pronouncement from so mercurial a creature on the subject, say, of asceticism, was impossible. As a boy, he had thought of retiring from the world, and it was an ideal which he cherished throughout his life, and which, at the end, he would have done well to practise. Yet he would condemn asceticism, declare that salvation could not be reached through it, that it might be Vedantic but it was not Vedic, and matter and spirit must both be given their due. Nothing too much! In such a mood he seemed Greek.

He believed in the heart, and here we reach firmer ground. "I stand for the heart. To the dogs with the head," cries Herman Melville, and he would have agreed. Affection, or the possibility of it, quivered through everything, from Gokul Ashtami down to daily human relationships. When I returned to England and he heard that I was worried because the post-war world of the '20's would not add up into sense, he sent me a message. "Tell him," it ran, "tell him from me to follow his heart, and his mind will see everything clear." The message as phrased is too facile: doors open into silliness at once. But to remember and respect and prefer the heart, to have the instinct which follows it wherever possible—what surer help than that could one have through life? What better hope of clarification? Melville goes on: "The reason that the mass of men fear God and at bottom dislike Him, is because they rather distrust His heart." With that too he would have agreed.

With all respect for Forster, neither he nor his prince is coherent here, and I suspect that Forster is weakly misreading Melville, who is both more ironic and more Gnostic than Forster chooses to realize. Melville too distrusts the heart of Jehovah and consigns the head to the dogs precisely because he associates the head with Jehovah, and identifies Jehovah with the Demiurge, the god of this world. More vital would be the question: what does Professor Godbole in *A Passage to India* believe? Is he more coherent than the Maharajah, and does Forster himself achieve a more unified vision there than he does in *The Hill of Devi*?

Criticism from Lionel Trilling on has evaded these questions, but such evasion is inevitable because Forster may be vulnerable to the indictment that he himself made against Joseph Conrad, to the effect that

> he is misty in the middle as well as at the edges, that the secret casket of his genius contains a vapour rather than a jewel; and that we need not try to write him down philosophically, because there is, in this particular direction, nothing to write. No creed, in fact. Only opinions, and the right to throw them overboard when facts make them look absurd. Opinions held under the semblance of eternity, girt with the sea, crowned with the stars, and therefore easily mistaken for a creed.

Heart of Darkness sustains Forster's gentle wit, but *Nostromo* does not. Is there a vapor rather than a jewel in Forster's consciousness of Hinduism, at least as represented in *A Passage to India*? "Hinduism" may be the wrong word in that question; "religion" would be better, and "spirituality" better yet. For I do not read Forster as being either hungry for belief or skeptical of it. Rather, he seems to me an Alexandrian, of the third century before the Common Era, an age celebrated in his *Alexandria: A History and a Guide* (1922), a book that goes back to his happy years in Alexandria (1915–19). In some curious sense, Forster's India is Alexandrian, and his vision of Hinduism is Plotinean. *A Passage to India* is a narrative of Neo-Platonic spirituality, and the true heroine of that narrative, Mrs. Moore, is the Alexandrian figure of Wisdom, the Sophia, as set forth in the Hellenistic Jewish Wisdom of Solomon. Of Wisdom or Sophia, Forster says: "She is a messenger who bridges the gulf and makes us friends of God," which is a useful description of the narrative function of Mrs. Moore. And after quoting Plotinus (in a passage that includes one of his book's epigraphs): "To any vision must be brought an eye adapted to what is to be seen," Forster comments:

> This sublime passage suggests three comments, with which our glance at Plotinus must close. In the first place its tone is religious, and in this it is typical of all Alexandrian philosophy. In the second place it lays stress on behaviour and training; the Supreme Vision cannot be acquired by magic tricks—only those will see it who are fit to see. And in the third place the vision of oneself and the vision of God are really the same, because each individual *is* God, if only he knew it. And here is the great difference between Plotinus and Christianity. The Christian promise is that a man shall see God, the Neo-Platonic—like the Indian—that he shall be God. Perhaps, on the quays of Alexandria, Plotinus talked with Hindu merchants who came to the town. At all events his system can be paralleled in the religious writings of India. He comes nearer than any other Greek philosopher to the thought of the East.

Forster's Alexandria is in the first place personal; he associated the city always with his sexual maturation as a homosexual. But, as the book *Alexandria* shrewdly shows, Forster finds his precursor culture in ancient Alexandria; indeed he helps to teach us that we are all Alexandrians, insofar as we now live in a literary culture. Forster's insight is massively supported by the historian F. E. Peters in the great study *The Harvest of Hellenism,* when he catalogs our debts to the Eastern Hellenism of Alexandria:

> Its monuments are gnosticism, the university, the catechetical school, pastoral poetry, monasticism, the romance, grammar, lexicography, city planning, theology, canon law, heresy, and scholasticism.

Forster would have added, thinking of the Ptolemaic Alexandria of 331–30 B.C.E., that the most relevant legacy was an eclectic and tolerant liberal humanism, scientific and scholarly, exalting the values of affection over those of belief. That is already the vision of *A Passage to India,* and it opens to the novel's central spiritual question: how are the divine and the human linked? In *Alexandria,* Forster presents us with a clue by his account of the Arian heresy:

> Christ is the Son of God. Then is he not younger than God? Arius held that he was and that there was a period before time began

when the First Person of the Trinity existed and the Second did not. A typical Alexandrian theologian, occupied with the favourite problem of linking human and divine, Arius thought to solve the problem by making the link predominately human. He did not deny the Godhead of Christ, but he did make him inferior to the Father—of *like* substance, not of the *same* substance, which was the view held by Athanasius, and stamped as orthodox by the Council of Nicaea. Moreover the Arian Christ, like the Gnostic Demiurge, made the world;—creation, an inferior activity, being entrusted to him by the Father, who had Himself created nothing but Christ.

It is easy to see why Arianism became popular. By making Christ younger and lower than God it brought him nearer to us—indeed it tended to level him into a mere good man and to forestall Unitarianism. It appealed to the untheologically minded, to emperors and even more to empresses. But St. Athanasius, who viewed the innovation with an expert eye, saw that while it popularised Christ it isolated God, and he fought it with vigour and venom. His success has been described. It was condemned as heretical in 325, and by the end of the century had been expelled from orthodox Christendom. Of the theatre of this ancient strife no trace remains at Alexandria; the church of St. Mark where Arius was presbyter has vanished: so have the churches where Athanasius thundered—St. Theonas and the Caesareum. Nor do we know in which street Arius died of epilepsy. But the strife still continues in the hearts of men, who always tend to magnify the human in the divine, and it is probable that many an individual Christian to-day is an Arian without knowing it.

To magnify the human in the divine is certainly Forster's quest, and appears to be his interpretation of Hinduism in *A Passage to India*:

Down in the sacred corridors, joy had seethed to jollity. It was their duty to play various games to amuse the newly born God, and to simulate his sports with the wanton dairymaids of Brindaban. Butter played a prominent part in these. When the cradle had been removed, the principal nobles of the state gathered together for an innocent frolic. They removed their turbans, and one put a lump of butter on his forehead, and waited for it to slide down his nose into his mouth. Before it could arrive, another stole up behind him, snatched the melting morsel, and swallowed

it himself. All laughed exultantly at discovering that the divine
sense of humour coincided with their own. "God si love!" There
is fun in heaven. God can play practical jokes upon Himself, draw
chairs away from beneath His own posteriors, set His own turbans on fire, and steal His own petticoats when He bathes. By
sacrificing good taste, this worship achieved what Christianity
has shirked: the inclusion of merriment. All spirit as well as all
matter must participate in salvation, and if practical jokes are
banned, the circle is incomplete. Having swallowed the butter,
they played another game which chanced to be graceful: the fon-
dling of Shri Krishna under the similitude of a child. A pretty red
and gold ball is thrown, and he who catches it chooses a child
from the crowd, raises it in his arms, and carries it round to be
caressed. All stroke the darling creature for the Creator's sake,
and murmur happy words. The child is restored to his parents,
the ball thrown on, and another child becomes for a moment the
World's desire. And the Lord bounds hither and thither through
the aisles, chance, and the sport of chance, irradiating little mor-
tals with His immortality. . . . When they had played this long
enough—and being exempt from boredom, they played it again
and again, they played it again and again—they took many sticks
and hit them together, whack smack, as though they fought the
Pandava wars, and threshed and churned with them, and later on
they hung from the roof of the temple, in a net, a great black
earthenware jar, which was painted here and there with red, and
wreathed with dried figs. Now came a rousing sport. Springing
up, they struck at the jar with their sticks. It cracked, broke, and
a mass of greasy rice and milk poured on to their faces. They ate
and smeared one another's mouths and dived between each other's legs for what had been pashed upon the carpet. This way and
that spread the divine mess, until the line of schoolboys, who had
somewhat fended off the crowd, broke for their share. The corridors, the courtyard, were filled with benign confusion. Also the
flies awoke and claimed their share of God's bounty. There was
no quarrelling, owing to the nature of the gift, for blessed is the
man who confers it on another, he imitates God. And those "im-
itations," those "substitutions," continued to flicker through the
assembly for many hours, awaking in each man, according to
his capacity, an emotion that he would not have had otherwise.
No definite image survived; at the Birth it was questionable

whether a silver doll or a mud village, or a silk napkin, or an intangible spirit, or a pious resolution, had been born. Perhaps all these things! Perhaps none! Perhaps all birth is an allegory! Still, it was the main event of the religious year. It caused strange thoughts. Covered with grease and dust, Professor Godbole had once more developed the life of his spirit. He had, with increasing vividness, again seen Mrs. Moore, and round her faintly clinging forms of trouble. He was a Brahman, she Christian, but it made no difference, it made no difference whether she was a trick of his memory or a telepathic appeal. It was his duty, as it was his desire, to place himself in the position of the God and to love her, and to place himself in her position and to say to the God, "Come, come, come, come." This was all he could do. How inadequate! But each according to his own capacities, and he knew that his own were small. "One old Englishwoman and one little, little wasp," he thought, as he stepped out of the temple into the grey of a pouring wet morning. "It does not seem much, still it is more than I am myself."

Professor Godbole's epiphany, his linkage of Mrs. Moore's receptivity toward the wasp with his own receptivity toward Mrs. Moore, has been much admired by critics, deservedly so. In this moment-of-moments, Godbole receives Mrs. Moore into Forster's own faithless faith: a religion of love between equals, as opposed to Christianity, a religion of love between the incommensurate Jehovah and his creatures. But though beautifully executed, Forster's vision of Godbole and Mrs. Moore is spiritually a little too easy. Forster knew that, and the finest moment in *A Passage to India* encompasses this knowing. It comes in a sublime juxtaposition, in the crossing between the conclusion of "Part II: Caves" and the beginning of "Part III: Temple," where Godbole is seen standing in the presence of God. The brief and beautiful chapter 32 that concludes "Caves" returns Fielding to a Western and Ruskinian vision of form in Venice:

Egypt was charming—a green strip of carpet and walking up and down it four sorts of animals and one sort of man. Fielding's business took him there for a few days. He re-embarked at Alexandria—bright blue sky, constant wind, clean low coast-line, as against the intricacies of Bombay. Crete welcomed him next with the long snowy ridge of its mountains, and then came Venice. As he landed on the piazzetta a cup of beauty was lifted to his lips, and he drank with a sense of disloyalty. The buildings of Venice, like the mountains of Crete and the fields of Egypt, stood in the right place, whereas in poor India everything was placed wrong. He had forgotten the beauty of form among idol temples and lumpy hills; indeed, without form, how can there be beauty? Form stammered here and there in a mosque, became rigid through nervousness even, but oh these Italian churches! San Giorgio standing on the island which could scarcely have risen from the waves without it, the Salute holding the entrance of a canal which, but for it, would not be the Grand Canal! In the old undergraduate days he had wrapped himself up in the many-coloured blanket of St. Mark's, but something more precious than mosaics and marbles was offered to him now: the harmony between the works of man and the earth that upholds them, the civilization that has escaped muddle, the spirit in a reasonable form, with flesh and blood subsisting. Writing picture post-cards to his Indian friends, he felt that all of them would miss the joys he experienced now, the joys of form, and that this constituted a serious barrier. They would see the sumptuousness of Venice, not its shape, and though Venice was not Europe, it was part of the Mediterranean harmony. The Mediterranean is the human norm. When men leave that exquisite lake, whether through the Bosphorus or the Pillars of Hercules, they approach the monstrous and extraordinary; and the southern exit leads to the strangest experience of all. Turning his back on it yet again, he took the train northward, and tender romantic fancies that he thought were dead for ever, flowered when he saw the buttercups and daisies of June.

After the muddle of India, where "everything was placed wrong," Fielding learns again "the beauty of form." Alexandria, like Venice, is part of the Mediterranean harmony, the human norm, but India is the cosmos of "the monstrous and extraordinary." Fielding confronting the Venetian churches has absolutely nothing in common with Professor Godbole confronting the God Krishna at the opposite end of the same strip of carpet upon which Godbole stands. Forster is too wise not to know that the passage to India is only a passage. A passage is a journey, or an occurrence between two persons. Fielding and Aziz do not quite make the passage together, do not exchange vows that bind. Perhaps that recognition of limits is the ultimate beauty of form in A Passage to India.

LIONEL TRILLING

Mind and Will: Forster's
Literary Criticism

No one is likely to take with perfect literalness, as representing Forster's actual belief, the religious ideas of the last part of *A Passage to India*. Yet certainly Forster has always had a strong tendency to "accept" the universe and in a way that has some affinity with Hindu religious thought. This tendency must be taken into account in any attempt to understand Forster's mind; it is especially relevant to an understanding of his literary criticism. Certainly it is easy enough, and true enough, to say that Forster is not a great critic. Yet so simple a judgment is not sufficient. It does not take into account the great disproportion between Forster's critical gifts and the use he makes of them. The gifts are great; the critical canon is not great. The disproportion is puzzling, yet we can begin to understand it if we understand something of the nature of Forster's "acceptance."

But first we must remember that all modern critics are judged under the aspect of a critical movement which is one of the most aggressive and hard-working the history of literature has known, the movement which took its beginnings in T. E. Hulme and has T. S. Eliot as its most notable exponent. No criticism has been so concerned to make distinctions and erect barriers, to separate thing from thing and to make salvation depend on the right choice. Yeats, in one of his autobiographies, says that the religious life consists in making all things equal, the intellectual life in saying, "Thou fool." No criticism has said "Thou fool" so firmly and finally as this modern movement, and in the light of Yeats's remark it is interesting that it has been

From *E. M. Forster: A Study.* © 1944 by Lionel Trilling. Hogarth Press Ltd., 1951.

allied with religion, that it has had the intention (and sometimes the effect) of making non-religious and non-theological thought and feeling seem foolish, unprincipled, and slovenly.

But Forster is impelled precisely in the direction of making all things equal rather than in the direction of "Thou fool," and although he frequently says the latter, he will usually follow it with a quick gesture of deprecation to imply the former. Exclusion pains him and the aptitude for exclusion is what he chiefly dislikes in most aspects of Christianity; the gesture of deprecation seldom follows when a representative of Christianity is the fool. Mr. Sorley, the younger of the two missionaries of *A Passage to India*—they appear but momentarily—considers that in his father's heavenly house there are many mansions and that "there alone will the incompatible multitudes of mankind be welcomed and soothed," and he thinks that the monkeys too will perhaps be included. Yet he balks at the inclusion of jackals, wasps, oranges, cactuses, crystals and mud, and, most of all, of the bacteria inside him—"We must exclude something from our gathering or we shall be left with nothing." And Forster can go so far as to set this down in irony.

But poor Mr. Sorley is right. We must indeed exclude something from our gathering or we shall be left nothing. Indeed, unless we do, we ourselves shall not be left at all. And Forster, after all, knows this and makes his exclusions. Still, deep in his mental life is an aversion to raising barriers and setting up categories. Although he never loses his sense of the difference between sheep and goats, as he grows into life he is far more aware of good-and-evil than of good and evil.

Above his essay, "The Perfect Critic," T. S. Eliot blazons a sentence from Rémy de Gourmont: "Eriger en lois ses impressions personelles, c'est le grand effort d'un homme s'il est sincère." For what it is worth the sentence may be taken as the motto of the critical movement to which I have referred; and although Mr. Eliot, after *The Sacred Wood*, would no doubt modify in the interests of tradition and dogma the arrogance of the personal emphasis, essentially it still describes his method. The effort to codify personal impressions is what gives weight and dignity to his work. But it is exactly weight and dignity that Forster fears; he rejects exactly the solemn unity of style that must inhere in the construction of law out of personal impressions. "The human mind is not a dignified organ," he says in *Aspects of the Novel*, "and I do not see how we can exercise it except through eclecticism." Then he continues with a characteristic modification: "And the only advice I would offer my fellow eclectics is: 'Do not be proud of your inconsistency. It is a pity, it is a pity that we should be equipped like this. It is a pity that man cannot be at the same time impressive and truthful.'"

Forster, then, is a critic with no drive to consistency, no desire to find an architectonic for his impressions. We might say of him that he is a critic without any desire for *success*. In short, he is an impressionistic critic. A few years ago the word impressionistic was the ultimate condemnation of the critic. But perhaps the long dull battle over Marxist criticism has shown us that one's personal impressions, whether or not one has an architectonic for them, are not things of chance and do not make a chaos. Even if they are not consciously erected into law, they follow the law of the personality, and of the personality shaped to greater or less degree by involvement with other laws than its own and by involvement with desires and intentions: the critic's personal impressions inevitably cohere into a structure.

But if between a critic like Forster and a critic like, say, Eliot, the difference is not so fundamental as at first appears, it is still considerable. For one thing, there is a great difference in aesthetic result. In Eliot the desire to make laws and the conscious effort for dignity have their unquestionable effect upon us. We respond to the effort; the form of dialectic gives us pleasure; we are connected with large issues. Literature thus acquires a magnificent importance, life seems more interesting. In such a critic we have met either an ally with whom we attack some enemy of the human spirit, or an opponent who gives us the satisfaction of conflict. Forster, on the contrary, asks us to relax. He can tell us, and very movingly, of the importance of literature, but he never intends to make any single literary work important. And the manner of his presentation of ideas is personal in a way that mocks the erection of laws. (To take a perhaps extreme example, this is the way Forster begins his essay on Virginia Woolf: "It is profoundly characteristic of the art of Virginia Woolf that when I decided to write about it and had planned a suitable opening paragraph, my fountain pen should disappear. Tiresome creature! It slipped through a pocket into a seam. I could pinch it, chivy it about, make holes in the coat lining, but a layer of tailor's stuffing prevented recovery. So near, and yet so far! Which is what one feels about her art." The essay does not succeed in bringing the art nearer; one perceives how useful rigour can be. Forster's Rede Lecture on Virginia Woolf is an act of commemoration rather than an effort of criticism, yet as criticism it is better than the essay; it is a great example of the art of compliment, the greater because it does not try to praise too much. It concludes: "And sometimes it is as a row of little silver cups that I see her work gleaming. 'These trophies,' the inscription runs, 'were won by the mind from matter, its enemy and its friend.'")

Eliot, of course, emerges as the better critic. Even if we grant Forster every possible virtue of his method—and it has virtues—he is never wholly satisfactory in criticism and frequently he is frustrating. For example, the essay *Anonymity,* issued as a pamphlet by the Hogarth Press, has a simple and important point. It protests the conception of personality used in the academic "study" of literature and it distinguishes between the superficial biographical personality and the deeper personality which is the actual source of literature. The latter, it says, has something in common with all other deeper personalities and is a "force that makes for anonymity," for great literature "wants not to be signed," but the academic "study" of literature—"only a serious form of gossip"—insists on underscoring every signature. This idea, so simple, sound and right, by a fatal paradox is expounded in a manner in which the superficial personality indulges all its whims: in consequence the idea is not properly developed, or even fully stated.

And not only does an excessive relaxation inadequately represent the ideas, it also leads them astray. In *Aspects of the Novel* there are many judgments that are wrong, not because they have travelled a wrong road but because they have not persevered far enough on the right road: they do not approach near enough to their objects. The estimate of Scott, for instance, is such a judgment; it does not continue through the obvious dullness to reach the rich and brilliant aspects of Scott's genius, nor does it see over the heads of the stuffy lordly characters to observe the fine humours of the humble characters. Or, in the comments on Dickens, it is a mere casual conventionality to say that Dickens deals with "types"; obviously people so eccentric as those that Dickens draws are not typical of anything, although their rich vitality may bring to mind other—and actual—people. The division of characters into "flat" and "round" is another and related conventionality, and an obfuscation of the actual facts of character-contrivance. Or again, the discussion of Gide's *Counterfeiters* is insufficient and even misleading. The analysis of Joyce is quite unworthy. Most disappointing of all from Forster is the treatment of Henry James, beginning with its stale joke about James's snobbery and his horror of being compared with the shopkeeping Richardson, concluding with an agreement with Wells's position in the famous *Boon* exchange of letters, and remarking incidentally that "most of human life has to disappear before [James] can do us a novel," that "maimed creatures can alone breathe in Henry James's pages—maimed yet specialized." Obviously not only energy has failed here, but with it intelligence.

And yet, on the other hand, *Aspects of the Novel* is full of the finest perceptions. There are, for example, the remarks on the aesthetic and moral effect of space in Tolstoy, or on the novelist's relation to beauty—"beauty at which a novelist should never aim, though he fails if he does not achieve it"—or the observation on the "voice" of the novelist, a matter which is never enough, if at all, discussed in the criticism of fiction, or the appreciation of the intermittent realism of Melville and Dostoevsky which gives their novels "what is always provocative in a work of art: roughness of surface"— these are the perceptions of a fine literary insight. Certainly none but a remarkable critical mind could have instituted the brilliant comparison between George Eliot and Dostoevsky which leads to the distinction between the novelist as preacher and the novelist as prophet. Only a critic truly sensitive to our cultural situation could so well understand the devices of the pseudo-scholar:

> This constant reference to genius is another characteristic of the pseudo-scholar. He loves mentioning genius, because the sound of the word exempts him from trying to discover its meaning. Literature is written by geniuses. Novelists are geniuses. There we are; now let us classify them. Which he does. Everything he says may be accurate but all is useless because he is moving around books instead of through them, he either has not read them or cannot read them properly. Books have to be read (worse luck, for it takes a long time); it is the only way of discovering what they contain. A few savage tribes eat them, but reading is the only method of assimilation revealed to the west. The reader must sit down alone and struggle with the writer, and this the pseudo-scholar will not do. He would rather relate a book to the history of its time, to events in the life of the author, to the events it describes, above all to some tendency. As soon as he can use the word "tendency" his spirits rise, and though those of his audience may sink, they often pull out their pencils at this point and make a note, under the belief that a tendency is portable.

Here, then, are the good and the bad. Our final estimate of *Aspects of the Novel* is not, however, the result of a balance of the good and the bad. Rather it is a response to the whole temper of the volume; and that response is genial, admiring, but not likely to be either strong or fertile.

In the same way we respond to Forster's occasional essays. Can we possibly not cherish this judgment of Joseph Conrad?

> These essays do suggest that he is misty in the middle as well as at the edges, that the secret casket of his genius contains a vapour rather than a jewel; and that we need not try to write him down philosophically, because there is, in this particular direction, nothing to write. No creed in fact. Only opinions, and the right

to throw them overboard when facts make them look absurd. Opinions held under the semblance of eternity, girt with the sea, crowned with the stars, and therefore easily mistaken for a creed.

And we respond to it the more when we go on to read, "One realizes . . . what a noble artist is here, what an austere character, by whose side most of our contemporary writers appear obsequious." Yet the essay on Conrad is not satisfying; it has said so much that it must say more, and it does not.

The combination of particular perception and general inadequacy continues. Ronald Firbank is not a likely occasion for great criticism and Forster's essay on him is far from important, but when it refers in passing to "a hundred other [of Firbank's] sentences or people (the two classes are not separable)," it touches not only Firbank but Ben Jonson and La Bruyère. The essay on Sinclair Lewis's development is not sufficiently firm or precise and its conclusion, "The longer one lives, the less important does 'development' appear," is not so much disarming as disarmed, yet when it speaks of literary "photography" as being a pursuit only for the very young, requiring to be supported by firmer intellectual interests than Lewis has, it is extraordinarily sound. Or the essay on Proust, inadequate as it is, contains the comparison of the ideas of Proust and Dante on love, Proust believing that the more we love the less we understand, Dante believing that the more we love the more we understand. The essay on T. S. Eliot is better than admirers of Eliot make it out to be. Its chief fault—apart from its not pursuing the subject far enough—is the simplicity with which it views the obscurity of Eliot's verse, its failure to see that the obscurity is a form of communication. Yet the description of Eliot's prose is admirable—it "conveys something, but is often occupied in tracing the boundaries of the unsaid." There is perceptive malice in the comparison of *The Waste Land* with *Prometheus Unbound,* in the suspicion that Eliot believes that "the muses are connected not so much with Apollo as with the oldest county families," or in the reference to the "several well-turned compliments to religion and divine grace" in *For Lancelot Andrewes,* and there is sympathetic understanding of the horror which Eliot perceives and which Forster symbolizes in the cheery milkman who so casually announced the news of England's entrance into the war in 1914. This essay contains one of the best possible statements of how literature works to "help" us:

> Huysman's *À Rebours* is the book of that blessed period [of the war] that I remember best. Oh, the relief of a world which lived for its sensations and ignored the will—the world of des Esseintes! Was it decadent? Yes, and thank God. Yes; here again

was a human being who had time to feel and experiment with his feelings, to taste and arrange books and fabricate flowers, and be selfish and himself. The waves of edifying bilge rolled off me, the newspapers ebbed; Professor Cramb, that profound philosopher, and Raemaekers, that inspired artist, floated out into an oblivion which, thank God, has since become permanent, and something resembling reality took their place. Perhaps it was not real, but it was helpful, and in 1917 that was enough to make me repeat after the muezzin in my minaret "Thank God."

And five years later, in 1934, Forster comments on Arnold's line, "Who prop, thou ask'st, in these bad days, my mind?" and takes up this theme again:

> The people I really clung to in the days [of the war] were those who had nothing tangible to offer: Blake, William Morris, the early T. S. Eliot, J. K. Huysmans, Yeats. They took me into a country where the will was not everything.

All this is fine, yet the total effect is not really impressive. For the fact is that a good critic, as we now judge, is made not only by perception but by belief. It is not that he erects his personal impressions into a law, but rather that he attaches his personal impressions to an extrinsic faith, a framework of tradition and intention which keeps them together and advantageously exposes them to view. But Forster's critical method is precisely the announcement of his reluctance to accept a faith. "I do not believe in Belief," he wrote in 1939 in the essay contributed to the series, *What I Believe,*

> Faith, to my mind, is a stiffening process, a sort of mental starch, which ought to be applied as sparingly as possible. I dislike the stuff. Herein I probably differ from most people, who believe in Belief, and are only sorry that they cannot swallow even more than they do. My law givers are Erasmus and Montaigne, not Moses and St. Paul. My temple stands not upon Mount Moriah, but in that Elysian Field, where even the immoral are admitted. My motto is: "Lord, I disbelieve—help thou my unbelief."

For belief he would substitute "tolerance, good temper and sympathy—they are what matter really, and if the human race is not to collapse they must come to the front before long."

An inadequate view of things, certainly—the questions and objections that would destroy it will be apparent at once. Here is a liberalism which

seems to carry itself to the extreme of anarchy, a liberalism shot through
with a sentimentally-literal Christian morality. It is laissez-faire to the ultimate. In its casual anarchism it is an affront to the Western mind.

But in the odd way that we have, we will feel better and more respectful
of it if we understand that it is an entirely intentional affront. The laxness
of the critical manner in which Forster sets forth his literary insights is no
doubt the expression of a temperament—even of the fault of a temperament—but it is also the expression of an intention. It is *consciously* a contradiction of the Western tradition of intellect which believes that by making
decisions, by choosing precisely, by evaluating correctly it can solve all difficulties. In our day it is to be found in such antithetical personalities as T. S.
Eliot and H. G. Wells. What Forster thinks of Eliot's Christian Society we
may guess from a remark or two in the early essay on Eliot; what he thinks
of Wells we know from an essay of 1941: "Each time Mr. Wells and my
other architectural friends anticipate a great outburst of post-war activity
and world-planning my heart contracts. To me the best chance for future
society lies through apathy, uninventiveness and inertia."

The vital mess of Gino's room rises to view again—the casual disorder
that nourishes life. Forster has many times written with a kind of intense
wistfulness of the slovenly East or the blooming tropics or the primitive,
non-progressive community. The great description of the birth of Krishna
in the last part of *A Passage to India* is a glorification of mess and relaxation,
of the mind that does not precisely distinguish. For Forster at many moments
a cycle of Cathay is better far than twenty years of Europe. Possibly even
twenty years of Cathay is better than a cycle of Europe.

Perhaps no one in our time has expressed so simply as Forster the
weariness with the intellectual tradition of Europe which has been in some
corner of the European psyche since early in the nineteenth century. The
young Matthew Arnold felt, a hundred years ago, much of what Forster feels
today. It was the perception of the dangers of a rigid intellectualism, a fierce
conscience, the everlasting research of the mind into itself that made the
young Arnold keep his distance from his Oxford friends and be aggressively
gay, arrogant, frivolous, dandified, at the very time that he was writing some
of his best and saddest verse. He feared their nagging, rigorous intellects; he
wanted the life of acceptant calm—he never said the life of simple instinct,
but perhaps it was that, too—into which the discriminating judgment did
not always enter. And in connection with Forster, it is interesting to observe
that Arnold found something of what he wanted in the Bhagavad Gita.

In the first chapter of [*E. M. Forster*] I have spoken of Forster as one of
the best representatives of the intellectual tradition of Europe. Is it a contra-

diction or is it a paradox that he should be wearied of that tradition? Neither: it is a modification. In *A Passage to India,* writing of the Indian heat, Forster says that "in Europe life retreats out of the cold, and exquisite fireside myths have resulted—Balder, Persephone—but here the retreat is from the source of life, the treacherous sun . . ." To Forster, who has so often spoken of the saving virtues of intellect, the intellect, which can be a source of life, can also, at certain intensities, be treacherous. Still speaking of the heat, Forster says, "Men . . . desire that joy shall be graceful and sorrow august and infinity have a form, and India fails to accommodate them. The annual helter-skelter of April, when irritability and lust spread like a canker, is one of her comments on the orderly hopes of humanity. Fish manage better; fish, as the tanks dry, wriggle into the mud and wait for the rains to uncake them. But men try to be harmonious all the year round, and the results are occasionally disastrous. The triumphant machine of civilization may suddenly hitch and be immobilized into a car of stone . . ." To retreat from the fierce sun of the intellect, to abandon the strictness of order and law may at certain times be the best means of asserting the intellect and order and law.

But even if it is put in this light, there will surely be but few to cheer Forster's retreat from what we think the best aspect of our tradition and the only hope for our future. It is defeatist, it is passive. And certainly if it were generally shared, our situation would be a bad one. Forster knows this, for he is a worldly man. "Tolerance, good temper and sympathy," he says in the pamphlet *What I Believe,* "are no longer enough in a world which is rent by religious and racial persecution, in a world where ignorance rules, and science, who ought to have ruled, plays the subservient pimp." So fighting comes to take their place, and faith turns out to be a necessary "starch." But the weariness remains, and as one watches it in unwearied action, its strange virtue begins to appear.

Part of the principle of the "weariness" is an abiding suspicion of the idea of progress as conceived by historical judgment. In historical judgment itself, as it is usually exercised, Forster has no confidence whatever and the essay "The Consolations of History" represents it, with some bitterness, as but a pleasant academic game.

> Yet sweet though it is to dally with the past, one returns to the finer pleasures of morality in the end. The schoolmaster in each of us awakes, examines the facts of History, and marks them on the result of the examination. Not all the marks need be bad. Some incidents, like the Risorgimento, get excellent as a matter of course, while others, such as the character of Queen Elizabeth,

get excellent in the long run. Nor must events be marked at their
face value. Why was it right of Drake to play bowls when he
heard the Armada was approaching, but wrong of Charles II to
catch moths when he heard that the Dutch Fleet had entered the
Medway? The answer is "Because Drake won." Why was it right
of Alexander the Great to throw away water when his army was
perishing, but wrong of Marie Antoinette to say "Let them eat
cake?" The answer is "Because Marie Antoinette was executed."
... We must take a larger view of the past than of the present,
because when examining the present we can never be sure what
is going to pay. As a general rule, anything that ends abruptly
must be given bad marks; for instance, the fourth century B.C.
at Athens, the year 1492 in Italy, and the summer of 1914 everywhere. A civilization that passes quickly must be decadent, therefore let us censure those epochs that thought themselves so bright,
let us show that their joys were hectic and their pleasures vile,
and clouded by the premonition of doom. On the other hand, a
civilization that does not pass, like the Chinese, must be stagnant,
and is to be censured on that account. Nor can one approve
anarchy. What then survives? Oh, a greater purpose, the slow
evolution of Good through the centuries—an evolution less slow
than it seems, because a thousand years are as yesterday, and
consequently Christianity was only, so to speak, established on
Wednesday last. And if this argument should seem flimsy (it is
the Bishop of London's, not our own—he put it into his Christmas sermon) one can at all events return to an indubitable
triumph of evolution—oneself, sitting untouched and untouchable in the professorial chair, and giving marks to men.

In *What I Believe* Forster gave a reluctant and qualified assent to the
notion of human improvement—for it is a generous faith. But clearly he has
no confidence in it. And that lack of confidence did its useful work when
Forster spoke to the P.E.N. Club in 1941 and said that "the past is merely
a series of messes, succeeding one another by discoverable laws no doubt,
and certainly marked by an increasing growth of human interference; but
messes all the same." He was countering the feeling of remorse which at-
tacked so many intellectuals at the beginning of the war, the feeling that if
we "had all played less in the twenties and theorized less in the thirties, the
jelly of civilization would have slid out of its mould and stood upright in a
beautiful shape." He stood out against the mind's harsh rigour to itself which

allowed so many intellectuals to acquiesce when *The Times* announced the "Eclipse of the Highbrow." By a certain reserve in his opinion of the powers of the intellect, he could defend the intellect when it was condemned for failure to do what it cannot do unaided.

The impulse toward "acceptance," toward relaxation, had found its useful expression a year earlier when Forster spoke of the intense morality, the exacerbated sense of responsibility which he found to blame for the rise of Nazism in Germany. In 1940, in the pamphlet *Nordic Twilight,* he commented on Germany's extreme serious-mindedness as being one of the cultural habits that made Nazism possible.

> Incidentally (and I think this has been part of her malady) [Germany] had a deeper sense than ourselves of the Tragic in life. Seriously minded, she felt that there must lie ahead for herself or for someone an irreparable disaster. That was the mentality of Wagner, and perhaps the present war may be considered as a scene (we do not yet know which) out of the *Nibelung's Ring.* I listen to Wagner to-day with unchanged admiration and increasing anxiety. Here is a world in which someone must come to grief, and with the maximum of orchestration and scenery. The hero slays or is slain, Hunding kills Siegmund, Siegfried kills the dragon, Hagen Siegfried, Brunnhilde leaps into the flames and brings down the Halls of Earth and Heaven. The tragic view of the universe can be noble and elevating, but it is a dangerous guide to daily conduct, and it may harden into a stupid barbarism, which smashes at problems instead of disentangling them.

Still earlier, in an essay in *The New Statesman and Nation* of June 10, 1939, with war more and more certain, Forster warned of the danger of the tragic attitude, of the danger of trying to meet the situation with all one's energy.

> The decade being tragic, it seems at first obvious that our way of living should correspond. How can we justify our trivialities and hesitations? Ought we not to rise to the great dramatic conception which we see developing around us? . . . Ought we not, at such a moment, to act as Wagnerian heroes and heroines who are raised above themselves by the conviction that all is lost or that all can be saved, and stride singing into the flames?
>
> To ask such a question is to answer it. No one who debates whether he shall behave tragically can possibly be a tragic char-

acter. He may have a just sense of the stage; . . . but he is not
properly cast as an actor. . . . He will not even pay the tribute of
unalloyed terror.

For the effort to meet the situation with what seems all one's perception will
actually prevent perception:

> We are worried rather than frantic. But worry is terribly insidi-
> ous; besides taking the joy out of life, it prevents the victim from
> being detached and from observing what is happening to the
> human experiment. It tempts him to simplify, since through sim-
> plification he may find peace. Nagging and stinging night and
> day, it is the undying worm, the worst of our foes. The only
> satisfactory release, I think, is to be found in the direction of
> complexity. The world won't work out, and the person who can
> realize this and not just say it and lament it, has done as well as
> can be expected in the present year. Perhaps the crisis is a tem-
> porary one, and now nearing its end. 1940 may bring personal
> danger and physical pain and new standards.

Personal danger and physical pain will involve the whole of the human or-
ganism, will require a more direct, a more organic response than any the
conscientious intellect can give.

Forster, then, has no faith in what order the intellect can bring. Many
have risen to say that romanticism—by which they mean undisciplined emotion—is to blame for the Nazi ideology. If such futile accusations are being
made, someone might well point out that the extreme and fantastic belief in
intellect, in logic, in rationality is to blame for the conception of the New
Order. Yet Forster, whose first allegiance was to Greece, has a belief in one
sort of order—the order of art. The order of art he sets against the order of
force. In *What I Believe* he accepts, as any worldly man must, the order of
force, and his defence of democracy—the two cheers he gives it—is based
on the tendency of democracy to conceal its force more than do other forms
of government, and on the permission democracy gives to variety and criticism. The intervals between its displays of force are more frequent and it is
in these intervals that the true life of man gets lived and the true work of
man gets done. For Forster the truest work of man is art; the order of art
stands beside the order of the universe, the best testimony man can give of
his dignity. In "The New Disorder" (the P.E.N. speech published in *Horizon*,
December, 1941) he says:

> [A work of art] is the only material object in the universe which

may possess internal harmony. All the others have been pressed into shape from outside, and when their mould is removed they collapse. The work of art stands by itself, and nothing else does. It achieves something which has often been promised by society but always delusively. Ancient Athens made a mess—but the Antigone stands up. Renaissance Rome made a mess—but the ceiling of the Sistine got painted; Louis XIV made a mess—but there was Phèdre; Louis XV continued it, but Voltaire got his letters written. Art for Art's sake? I should think so, and more so than ever at the present time. It is the one orderly product which our muddling race has produced. It is the cry of a thousand sentinels, the echo from a thousand labyrinths, it is the lighthouse which cannot be hidden; *c'est le meilleur témoignage que nous puissions donner de notre dignité.*

In the pertinacity of art to assert order, Forster says, "there seems to me, as I grow older, something more and more profound, something which does in fact concern people who do not care about art at all." Art is the sign of man's latent ability eventually to make even the right social order. But the paradox is that art which testifies to our worthiness by its order, cannot be produced by social order—for the order of society, however good, is the order of force. And Forster declares the necessity of the artist's being, as the nineteenth century conceived him, an outsider and a Bohemian. "Order" does not produce order—only the vital mess does that.

The paradox is greater still: in Forster's belief in the relaxed will, in the deep suspiciousness of the rigid exercise of the intellect, there lies the deepest faith in the will and the intellect. [The] introductory chapter [to *E. M. Forster*] has spoken of Forster's refusal to be great. It is a refusal that is often disappointing and sometimes irritating. We admire his novels so fully that we want to say that he is a great novelist: somehow he slips from under the adjective and by innumerable gestures—of which the actual abandonment of the novel is not least—signals to us that he is not a great novelist. He is not a great critic, not a great "thinker." He has shirked the responsibility, we feel, and that is wrong in a day in which each man must bear his share. His refusal of greatness is a refusal of will and that is bad. . . .

We judge thus as we see his refusal of greatness quite by itself. But when we see it beside the postures that greatness assumes we find another meaning in the refusal. It speaks to us of a world where the will is not everything and it suggests that where the will is not everything it will be a better and a more effective will. We can see that Morton Dauwen Zabel was right when he said of Forster that "he has no stylistic followers and perhaps few disciples in thought, yet if one were fixing the provenance of Auden's generation, Forster's name—whatever the claim of James, Lawrence, or Eliot—would suggest the most accurate combination of critical and temperamental forces, the only one stamped by the peculiarly English sceptical sensibility that survived the war with sanity and prepared the day for reassessment of the tradition and delusion that made our war possible."

There is a little and quite casual piece that Forster wrote for *The New Statesman and Nation* of November 4, 1939. It was called "The Top Drawer But One." It was about Mrs. Miniver (of the book, not the moving-picture), about whom it expressed a gentle but fatal opinion. *The Times* had written editorials about her, she delighted all middle-class England, and middle-class America even more. Delighted and defeated all of us, for Mrs. Miniver, with all her charm, is the complex expression of the modern will.

Forster begins by comparing her with a certain parson who always had the right cheery word to say to the villagers, who was genial and affable and able to win general esteem. But whenever he left a group of his parishioners after one of his successful conversations, the simple men began to utter smut in order to keep their self-respect.

> Mrs. Miniver . . . invites a similar reaction. She, too, has the right word for every occasion. What answer can the villagers make to a lady who is so amusing, clever, observant, broad-minded, shrewd, demure, Bohemian, happily married, triply childrened, public spirited and at all times such a lady. No answer, no answer at all. They listen to her saying the right thing, and are dumb. . . . Even if they disgrace themselves by spluttering smut in her hearing, she is not to be put out, for the class to which she and the parson belong has grown an extra thickness of skin in the last thirty years. "Touchée" she would exclaim, with her little ringing laugh, and pass on untouched. She is too wonderful with the villagers, she has them completely taped. Taximen, too. One day she overhears two ridiculous, fat, bottle-nosed taximen talking about the subconscious sense. She takes the absurdity back to her husband, whose sense of humour corresponds with her own, and if the taximen had turned the tables and ridiculed *her,* she would have taken that back, too. She has learnt the defensive value of honesty.

Mrs. Miniver is a lady but not an aristocrat; socially she is not top drawer, only top drawer but one. Her ancestry is good, she is very well-connected, but she is not wealthy, she even believes that she is poor and bravely assumes "that she can create the atmosphere of Madame de Sévigné by behaving like Mrs. Carlyle." Like all "the class to which she and most of us belong, the class which strangled the aristocracy in the nineteenth century, and has been haunted ever since by the ghost of its victim," she must assert her class by her will: she lives by the shadow of the past, past manners, past ideals, and her husband, her children, her humour, her intellect, and her Bohemian gaiety are the expressions of her subtle will. She represents the way of life, the special hidden vice of the modern cultivated middle class.

It is the insight of the relaxed will that has called the turn on Mrs. Miniver. That, perhaps, describes the limits of what the intelligence of the relaxed will can do—for all the world loves Mrs. Miniver, all the world that can possibly hope to be Mrs. Miniver, or marry her, or be given tea by her. But Forster knows that Mrs Miniver can defeat anything. He probably even knows that she has read the novels of E. M. Forster and that something of her manner has been learned from their mockery of other manners. In this knowledge he is perhaps sustained by the thought that if the moral intelligence of art does no more than drive Mrs. Miniver from manner to manner, making her not quite easy, it has done its work. Not much to do, perhaps, yet if it did less the world would be impossible.

One has no notion what influence the moral intelligence of any artist has had on the world; such men, for instance, as Dante, Chaucer, Shakespeare, Calderón, and Milton—it is with these that Shelley begins a long and famous list—have never effected conversions or made revolutions yet, with Shelley, we know that "it exceeds all imagination to conceive what would have been the moral condition of the world" if they had never existed. The stories they tell drop deep into the mind of man, so deep that they are forgotten, so deep that they work without man's consciousness of them, and even against his conscious will. A world at war is necessarily a world of will; in a world at war Forster reminds us of a world where the will is not everything, of a world of true order, of the necessary connection of passion and prose, and of the strange paradoxes of being human. He is one of those who raise the shield of Achilles, which is the moral intelligence of art, against the panic and emptiness which make their onset when the will is tired from its own excess.

GEORGE H. THOMSON

The Italian Romances

To any vision must be brought an eye adapted to what is to be seen.
—PLOTINUS

The narrator is always, in Forster's novels, the more or less omniscient author. And he is always immensely important because it is his role to imply or represent to the reader the whole image of man. Forster is writing romance in which the conflicting forces of our inner life are given external representation. Life and death, good and evil, spring and fall contend with each other. The characters embodying these forces are of necessity partial. The whole image of man comes through to us only at the end of the novel when all elements are in place and all conflicts have been resolved. Here is the goal toward which the narrator has been moving all along. But from the beginning his perfect command of every detail and every moment in the fiction has been our guarantee that he was in possession of and would bring us to the integrated vision, the whole image.

Forster has said that the author's personality is conveyed through such noble agencies as "the characters or the plot or his comments on life." We may take *A Room with a View* as our first text for a study of how Forster's personality is conveyed to the reader and how that personality controls the reader's response to the fiction.

There are three principles of narration in *A Room with a View* and in all the novels up to *A Passage to India.* One, dialogue and bits of incisive description and information are the main constituent. Two, normally each chapter offers access to the thoughts and inner life of one character. Three,

From *The Fiction of E. M. Forster.* © 1967 by George H. Thomson. Wayne State University Press, 1967.

of the various characters whose inner life offers a perspective on events, one emerges as dominant. (Lucy Honeychurch in *A Room with a View*, Philip Herriton in *Where Angels Fear to Tread*, Rickie Elliot in *The Longest Journey*, and Margaret Schlegel in *Howards End*.)

Each of these principles of narration is qualified by the intervention of the narrator. One, description and information often turn into commentary and judgment. Two, the perspective offered by the inner life of a character very often changes to that of Forster, or the two perspectives become inextricably blended. Three, though one of the several characters whose inner life offers a perspective on events emerges as dominant, his point of view does not dominate the narrative as a whole.

The intervention of the narrator at its most extreme can be illustrated from the well-known scene at the end of chapter 6 of *A Room with a View* in which Lucy Honeychurch and the hero, George Emerson, unexpectedly meet and, under the spell of the Italian spring, not so unexpectedly kiss. The chapter in parody of the picaresque is entitled "The Reverend Arthur Beebe, the Reverend Cuthbert Eager, Mr. Emerson, Mr. George Emerson, Miss Eleanor Lavish, Miss Charlotte Bartlett, and Miss Lucy Honeychurch, Drive out in Carriages to see a View: Italians Drive Them." In keeping with its picaresque nature the chapter permits the point of view of several characters but allows no one point of view to dominate. The fact that it is an exception to Forster's usual practice is explained by the nature of the scene toward which the whole chapter builds. After the ascent into the hills above Florence, Lucy is separated from her spinsterish cousin, Miss Bartlett, and seeks the "good man," by which term she means the Reverend Arthur Beebe.

> The view was forming at last; she could discern the river, the golden plain, other hills. . . .
>
> At the same moment the ground gave way, and with a cry she fell out of the wood. Light and beauty enveloped her. She had fallen on to a little open terrace, which was covered with violets from end to end. . . .
>
> From her feet the ground sloped sharply into the view, and violets ran down in rivulets and streams and cataracts, irrigating the hill-side with blue, eddying round the tree stems, collecting into pools in the hollows, covering the grass with spots of azure foam. But never again were they in such profusion; this terrace was the well-head, the primal source whence beauty gushed out to water the earth.
>
> Standing at its brink, like a swimmer who prepares, was the

good man. But he was not the good man that she had expected, and he was alone.

George had turned at the sound of her arrival. For a moment he contemplated her, as one who had fallen out of heaven. He saw radiant joy in her face, he saw the flowers beat against her dress in blue waves. . . . He stepped quickly forward and kissed her.

Before she could speak, almost before she could feel, a voice called, "Lucy! Lucy! Lucy!" The silence of life had been broken by Miss Bartlett, who stood brown against the view.

Time after time we seem about to enter Lucy's mind, about to participate fully in her point of view. And for a moment near the end we seem to see with George Emerson's eyes. But in fact we only stand in the same position he does, just as an instant before we stood in Lucy's position when "George had turned at the sound of her arrival." In this way Forster brings us close to the characters while yet maintaining his and our detachment. The detachment is apparent in other ways. The beautiful description of the violets is not an account of Lucy's impression of them; it is a statement about their ultimate reality: "But never again were they in such profusion; this terrace was the well-head, the primal sourse whence beauty gushed out to water the earth." Caught up in a moment of ecstasy, everything is transformed, everything is touched by greatness and completeness and becomes archetypal. The violets appear as the type of springtime glory; the characters as the type of lovers. The lovers, buoyed up by the sea of violets, appear as the image of youth and beauty and vitality. They have transcended the personal and individual.

To convey this universal quality of the lovers Forster avoids any intimate handling of their experience. Without losing immediacy or vividness he stands off and catches them in so commanding a perspective that their archetypal nature is apparent. And so we come back to Forster the narrator, for this supreme typicality is an expression of the commanding perspective of his personality.

I turn now to a second scene from A Room with a View, a scene much longer than the first. It is not well-known. It has no special qualities. It is strictly bread-and-butter Forster, and exemplifies perfectly all the principles of narration outlined earlier.

The scene belongs to the last half of the novel and takes place at Windy Corner where Lucy, back from her Italian trip and her stay in Florence at the Pension Bertolini, is living with her good-natured mother and brother.

Her memory of that ineradicable moment on the Italian hillside when George
Emerson appeared to her suddenly like a hero out of romance is now obscured by the presence of Cecil Vyse, her Sir Willoughby Patterne style fiancé.
But her past as represented by Italy is pursuing her. The Reverend Arthur
Beebe has become the local rector and the Emersons, father and son, have
moved into the neighborhood. The Emersons are to Lucy like the grain of
sand to the oyster, a persistent irritant. She tells her mother and Cecil a story
about old Mr. Emerson and is disturbed to find herself telling a silly lie and
saying that the name is Harris. She is upset by Mr. Beebe's story about old
Miss Alan at the Pension Bertolini and how her room was filled with violets
by the Emersons because they knew she loved violets. She is annoyed by a
letter from Charlotte saying how unfortunate it is that the Emersons have
moved into the neighborhood. And she is embarrassed at coming upon
George Emerson swimming with Mr. Beebe and her brother Freddy in the
Sacred Lake. In this, her first meeting with George since the kiss on the
hillside, she is not prepared for a frank and happy greeting from a half-
naked young man of possibly god-like appearance. To make things worse,
Lucy at this moment finds her mother especially sympathetic to Charlotte
because poor Charlotte is just now having the plumbers to clean her cistern
and replace her boiler. (One trusts these details are not symbolic.) At the
same time Freddy has invited the Emersons for tennis the following Sunday.

Lucy is haunted by George Emerson and by all the ramifications of her
brief acquaintance with him. But she will not admit—indeed she cannot on
account of her engagement to Cecil—that he is anything more to her than
an annoyance. This then is her situation. Its difficulty is heightened by the
tension between Cecil on the one side and her mother and Freddy on the
other.

The scene, constituting the last four pages of chapter 13, is too long to
quote here, but I hope the reader can turn to it before going on. It begins:
"Dinner was at half-past seven." It ends with the veiled insolence of Cecil's
plea: "We don't want no dessert."

All the more typical narrative principles of Forster's fiction are illustrated by the scene. The importance of dialogue is obvious, as is its conjunction with description and information which tend to become the
comment and judgment of the narrator. We have significant access to the
mind and motives of one character, Lucy, but her perspective often shifts to
or blends with that of the narrator: When Lucy hopes that her remark about
seeing Emerson in Florence will pass for a reply, we have both an account
of her unexpressed thought and a comment on it; and when we read the
paragraph beginning "But Lucy hardened her heart. It was no good being

kind to Miss Bartlett," we are seeing the matter from Lucy's point of view but her view is being summarized and presented in the words of the narrator, and it is the narrator's quality of mind that is apparent, not Lucy's. Finally we can see in miniature how, among the characters, Lucy's point of view is the dominant one and yet it does not dominate the scene, for the scene like the novel is controlled by the perspective of the narrator.

It is not my primary object to establish that Forster is a great novelist. But I must say that this everyday example of his work seems to me first-rate. Moreover, its excellence seems to me to depend on our sense of the command and poise, the perceptiveness and wit of the narrator whose presence is unobtrusive but at all times decisive. It is he who judges that Freddy "gabbled" a grace. It is he who deems it fortunate the men were hungry. It is he who sets up the little trap for Lucy when Freddy asks if Emerson is the clever sort or a decent chap. Before Lucy can say "Ask Cecil" we have already thought of Cecil as an example of the clever sort. It is he who rushes into a relatively long and breathless account of Mrs. Honeychurch's views on lady novelists in imitation of Mrs. Honeychurch and then adds—is it information or judgment?—that Lucy "artfully" fed the flames. It is he who says that "Cecil laid his hand over his eyes" and that "Cecil crumbled his bread," representing these actions not as Lucy would see them but as Cecil would hope them to be seen by a detached observer if such were present. Full justice is done to Cecil's half-despairing, half-satirical intent. At the same time by juxtaposition with the good-natured simplicity of the Honeychurches his superciliousness is justly exposed.

Again, when Lucy opposes inviting Charlotte and resorts to an argument of the most appalling triviality, it is the narrator who says "Alas!" in a tone we may guess to be a compound of humor, despair, and sarcasm. Finally it is he who blends his view with that of Lucy in describing the ghosts which plague her, so that we seem to be given at one and the same time an inner and outer perspective on her experience.

This scene is mainly dramatic. If we allowed ourselves the distinction it would be a case of showing rather than telling. What is shown is a discussion among a group of lively and convincing individuals. Yet at every turn the presence of the narrator is obvious. It is he who allows us to have a unified and commanding perspective on the whole scene.

The perfect economy of the scene may also be attributed to the narrator. Though there is a quite elaborate body of material here, including many references to past events, not a single detail is irrelevant or without value in the context. Even Mrs. Honeychurch's outburst against lady novelists is neatly illustrative of her ingenuous character and highlights by contrast the artfulness of Lucy. Besides, Miss Lavish as novelist deserves emphasis at this point for her novel is soon to play a decisive role in the story. What is most to be admired, however, is the way the trivialities—eggs and boilers, guest rooms and maids—are used not simply as realistic talking points for the revealing of character but as an important part of the Honeychurch way of life. The apparent subject of the scene is what happened to Lucy at dinner. The less apparent subject is the grounds for the tension between Cecil and the Honeychurches and the futility of Lucy's hope that she can have a foot in both worlds. Thus while she is contending with one phase of her confusion, another phase is pressing in upon her. Here again we become aware of the transcendent perspective of the narrator.

It is not especially difficult to get at the ways the author-narrator's personality is conveyed through his comment and interpretation and through our awareness of his guiding presence. But it is very difficult to get at the ways his personality is conveyed through his characters. The obvious way is by his attitude to them as implied or stated in his descriptions and comments. The less obvious way, though much the more important, is by his relationship to his characters. This relationship is not easy to define. Indeed, the attempt can be dangerous for it may lead one into the labyrinth of biographical speculation. There is, alas, no precise line separating those matters which pertain to the artist's character as a man and those which pertain to his character as a narrator. All one can do is proceed with what one hopes is discretion.

Thus I will go so far as to imagine Forster at the turn of the century saying to himself: How, in an age increasingly introspective, how after George Eliot and all her intimate involvement with the character, can I treat man's psychological nature as objectively as his moral nature was treated by Pope or Jane Austen? How, without seeming inhuman, can I achieve a detachment that will let me judge and evaluate without the emotional harassment of extreme involvement? Had Forster been born a generation later his answer to the question might have been that of Robbe-Grillet: you cannot achieve objectivity, therefore eliminate the psychology; or that of Samuel Beckett: reduce man's psychological nature to so elementary a level that it is almost beyond pathos. In fact his answer is that of romance: you can treat the inner life objectively by objectifying it, by giving it an outward representation. If life and death, good and evil contend for the soul of man, let these forces have separate representation and let them contend openly. Under such circumstances the narrator can be uninhibited in his attitude to the characters representing these forces. He can approach them with detachment and irony, with wit and playfulness, with the sense that at every moment he has the right to laugh, to ridicule, to judge. This is precisely the approach we have observed in Forster's treatment of the dinner scene. But to appreciate more fully his relationship to his characters, we must scrutinize them carefully.

It is easy to see the romance division of characters in *A Room with a View*. Since Lucy's family are on the side of light, the evils of society must be found elsewhere. In part 1 they are found at the Pension Bertolini and in the person of the Reverend Cuthbert Eager. In part 2 the Reverend Arthur Beebe takes Mr. Eager's place as a source of darkness, though the meaningless sterility of society is mainly represented by Cecil Vyse. On the side of good are Mrs. Honeychurch and Freddy, though they are hardly aware of being on a side, and Mr. Emerson, a philosophical type who quotes Samuel Butler and is very much aware of being on a side. Then there is George Emerson whose good character is complicated by the fact that too severe a knock may once for all deprive him of the will to live.

Lucy Honeychurch's character is also complicated. As the scene of springtime and violets makes clear, she is by nature on the side of goodness and light. But society teaches her to flee from Florence and George Emerson and to rush off to Rome and Cecil Vyse. Society teaches her to be dishonest with herself, and the result is the artful, ghost-haunted young lady we see at dinner.

Lucy combines two roles in *A Room with a View*. As a *romance* heroine her character is fixed; she stands for the forces of life and light. As a *romantic* heroine, that is as the ingénue in a romantic plot, we would expect her character to be in the process of formation and to become formed or fixed only when she achieves happiness and marriage. But Forster has modified her romantic role in order to avoid seriously disrupting the romance pattern of the novel. We do not get the impression that Lucy's character is being formed. Her nature is already established and the only question is whether it will triumph or go under. When she deceives herself the darkness comes on. She is not changing so much as moving toward nothingness. And when Mr. Emerson rescues her, more through his voice, his seriousness and his age than through any words, she finds as he speaks that the darkness is withdrawn "veil after veil," and she can see to the bottom of her soul. "It was as if he had made her see the whole of everything at once."

Essentially Lucy remains a romance heroine. This same pattern is obvious in the characterization of George Emerson whose role as *romantic* hero is decisively subordinated to his role as *romance* hero. What concerns us about these young people is not their psychology but their fate. Forster is not interested in the inwardness of their experience. For instance the first five chapters of part 2, which take us from Lucy's engagement up to the dinner scene and which include the first meeting of George and Lucy since Italy, offer little insight into the heroine's mind and feelings. Forster implies that confusion and darkness reign—what more is there to be said? Then in the dinner scene which comes after Lucy's meeting with George, that is to say, after she has been disturbed by contact with reality, her inner life begins again to take on significance. But in discussing it, Forster repeatedly uses images of ghosts and darkness to dramatize the starkness of the issue. "The ghosts were returning." They invade and usurp all the places Lucy has valued: Italy, the Sacred Lake, Windy Corner. The juxtaposing of that which suggests death with that which suggests life is striking and gives a kind of public quality to Lucy's thoughts.

The reader may justly observe at this point that had Lucy gone under she would not on that account have entirely ceased to exist and that if we are to see adequately the issue that confronts her we should have some idea of what might become of her. We are given a very good idea of the dark side of her fate in the character of Miss Bartlett. In keeping with Forster's economy of means in this novel she has several other roles in addition to that of Lucy's double. She is a Jamesian *ficelle,* a representative of the triviality and evil restrictiveness of society, and unconsciously she is a promoter of the romance between George and Lucy. But of course her great interest is as a model of what Lucy will be thirty years from now if she denies the life force—and her love for George Emerson.

And what, the impatient reader may ask, does all this tell us about the personality of the narrator? It tells us, in the first place, that he is interested not in psychological processes but in the great forces that make or break a character. It tells us, too, that he is a strenuously committed moralist who sees the conflict between fulfillment and negation as a conflict between life and death, good and evil. And it tells us that he is uncompromising in his attitude to both sides in this struggle, being ready at all times to satirize and mock the representatives of darkness and evil and to honor at all times the representatives of goodness and light. He never hesitates to evaluate and judge his characters.

We are now in a position to sum up Forster's relationship to his characters. He is not, like George Eliot, the careful analyst who scrupulously weighs every detail before reaching a judgment. He is not, like Henry James, the equally careful analyst who scrupulously maneuvers every detail into place in an attempt to do justice to his heroine. Indeed, he is a narrator who has no responsibility to his characters. This is the remarkable fact about his relationship to them. But however remarkable it may be, it should not surprise us. We have already established in the earlier discussion of romance that Forster's negative characters are not morally accountable for the evil that attends them and that his positive characters have not quite earned the given moments of their deepest insight and highest goodness. Forster's non-responsibility to his characters is the corollary of their own non-responsibility.

Only the whole image of man—not the aspects of his nature as symbolized by romance characters—can be thought of as morally responsible. Hence the narrator is responsible not to his characters but to a whole image of man which he bears within himself and which, being implicit throughout his narrative, must in some sense be made explicit before the story ends. The narrator is responsible to the values and the total vision for which he stands. He is responsible to himself in the sense that he must at all times judge according to his vision, and he is responsible to the reader for he must at all times help the reader to judge also according to the vision. It follows from this that he must be responsible *about* his characters but not *to* them. He must make sure that they subserve his values and forward the development of his total image of man; there his obligation ends.

To fulfill this obligation will require skill and ingenuity in the manner of presentation. Romance characters are by nature fixed and unchanging. But the narrator is free to withhold knowledge about their true natures and to reveal this knowledge progressively or suddenly at such times as will be most effective. Thus in part 1 Mr. Beebe appears in a favorable light, but in part 2 we more and more see that he stands against life. *He* has not changed. But the hidden springs of his nature have been exposed by events and the comments on events. An example of a different kind is to be seen in the potential likeness of Lucy and her cousin. This is not at first apparent to the reader. Indeed, even later it comes as a kind of revelation. From these illustrations we see that the presentation of fixed characters leaves the narrator a great deal of freedom; and further that the exercise of this freedom, because it is so obviously a part of the strategy of telling the story, shows us the interests and moral intentions of the narrator.

It is not possible to keep in separate compartments the treatment of plot and character. But insofar as it is possible we will now go on to look at how the ordering of events reveals the same decisive moralist apparent in the presentation of character.

It is true, of course, that at first glance *A Room with a View* looks like having a thoroughly romantic plot. The heroine is unexpectedly kissed by the young man for whom she is obviously intended. She thinks herself insulted and runs away. In time she thinks herself in love with another man, a man very unlike the first and one for whom she is just as obviously not intended. Having got over this error in judgment by seeing the two men together, she is still deluded enough to think she must uphold her reputation and must refuse to admit her love. Through the kindly intervention of an old wise man she is able to recognize the truth of her own feelings. And so she marries the young man and lives happily ever after. It is obvious that the central interest of such a plot, if it is indeed romantic, must be the development of the mind and character of the heroine.

When we look more closely at Forster's plot, however, we see that its central interest is the development of a series of contrasts. In part 1, Lucy moves toward light and the fulfillment of her nature, but at the last moment she is overcome by darkness—and flees. In part 2 she moves towards darkness and the denial of her nature, but at the last moment she sees the light. This parallel with contrast is also represented in the detailed plotting. Lucy, having been kissed by George, confides in Charlotte who dismisses George and arranges Lucy's departure for Rome. Charlotte confides in Miss Lavish, who in turn confides in the readers of her novel, including George and Lucy. As a result George kisses Lucy again, and Lucy confides in Miss Bartlett again. But this time her former chaperone is helpless and Lucy must herself dismiss George. Now Charlotte confides in Mr. Beebe and the two of them help Lucy in her plan to go to Greece which is in fact a plan to run away from George for the second time. The difference here is that her plan fails.

Forster also provides contrasts and parallels at a more detailed level. Thus for example the expedition of the tourists to the Italian hills (chapter 6) is echoed in the expedition of Lucy, Mrs. Honeychurch, and Cecil to the garden-party (chapter 9: "Lucy as a Work of Art"). Again we have a social outing, including a carriage ride. Again the party breaks up, but this time the lovers are openly and deliberately together. They walk through woods. Lucy appears to Cecil as a work of art rather than as flesh and blood. George, you will recall, saw "the flowers beat against her dress in blue waves"; Cecil, whose taste inclines to the artificial and exotic, sees her as "some brilliant flower that has no leaves of its own, but blooms abruptly out of a world of green." They are in a small clearing, the view is restricted, and the Sacred Lake (reminiscent of the sea of violets) is now a puddle. Cecil, deliberate and passionless, asks Lucy for a kiss. Here no Miss Bartlett roams the woods to threaten interruptions, yet Cecil suffers from the fear of being observed. In case anyone should miss the parallel between the two scenes, Lucy's first words after the kiss are about the Emersons.

Forster's tendency to construct his plot by juxtaposing related but contrasting episodes and blocks of material is powerfully reinforced by his handling of setting. Here and elsewhere Forster designs his settings with such economy and relevance that they may be interpreted as extensions of character and plot.

"Windy Corner lay, not on the summit of the ridge, but a few hundred feet down the southern slope, at the springing of one of the great buttresses that supported the hill. On either side of it was a shallow ravine, filled with ferns and pine-trees. . . . Whenever Mr. Beebe crossed the ridge and caught sight of these noble dispositions of the earth, and, poised in the middle of them, Windy Corner—he laughed. The situation was so glorious." Earlier the scene is described from Lucy's point of view. "Seated on a promontory herself, she could see the pine-clad promontories descending one beyond another into the Weald. The farther one descended the garden, the more glorious was this lateral view." There can be no doubt Windy Corner is intended to parallel the violet-covered terrace overlooking Florence. And this is as it should be, for Windy Corner is on the side of light.

Then there is darkness. Forster's handling of light and dark is the most significant feature of the settings in this novel. In part 1, after experiencing the glorious sun-drenched slopes of the Italian mountains, Lucy descends into storm and darkness. In part 2, after encountering George at the Sacred Lake in a setting of sunshine, clear water, and happiness, she finds during the dinner scene that the Sacred Lake and Windy Corner, formerly the world of life and light, are being usurped by ghosts and darkness. Again, when George comes for tennis the Sunday following, the day is glorious. And again Lucy is kissed. She dismisses George, but going outdoors becomes aware of the approach of autumn and darkness. That same night she dismisses Cecil and determines never to marry. "The night received her, as it had received Miss Bartlett thirty years before."

The next chapter (18), much of it from Mr. Beebe's point of view, reinforces the pattern. It is a blustering, windy day, autumn has come and the flowers are being broken down. Mr. Beebe and Miss Bartlett, returning from tea, "hurried home through a world of black and grey," while Mrs. Honeychurch "still wrestled with the lives of her flowers. 'It gets too dark,' she said hopelessly." When Mr. Beebe leaves, he sees Windy Corner poised below him—"as a beacon in the roaring tides of darkness." It has been agreed that Lucy may go to Greece. Thus she will be leaving this one point of light in a dark world. The following chapter is one of rain and dismalness. Up the dark hill stands the dark church. In Mr. Beebe's study, Lucy and Mr. Emerson are surrounded and pressed in upon by books—"black, brown, and that acrid, theological blue." And Mr. Beebe himself appears as a "long black column."

But at this moment, the blackest in Lucy's life, Mr. Emerson points the contrast: "Now it is all dark. . . . I know. But remember the mountains over Florence and the view." The recurring movement from light to dark is halted and reversed. Yet the mountains and the view appear only as a memory; the returning light is more subdued.

And so George and Lucy, again in Florence and in the spring, are aware of the dying evening and the roar of the river Arno. At the novel's end passion is requited, love attained. "But they were conscious of a love more mysterious than this. . . . they heard the river, bearing down the snows of winter into the Mediterranean." Their love is related to the cycle of nature and to the related cycle of life and death. When there is life, when there is light and spring and fulfillment, then darkness and winter and death can be accepted and integrated into the total vision. Here the simplified romance characters attain wholeness.

Character, plot, setting, and commentary unite to dramatize and enforce a decisive moral outlook. That outlook is embodied from the beginning in the personality of the author-narrator. He is the center which emanates outward in a perfect circle of inclusiveness.

A briefer treatment of *Where Angels Fear to Tread* will be sufficient to show how it differs from *A Room with a View* and how its narrator differs. Unlike George and Lucy, the principal characters in this novel no longer bear even a superficial resemblance to those of romantic convention. Gino, the Italian antagonist-protagonist, shares in the paradoxical qualities of his country, in its energy and reality, its brutality and mystery. He may be a possible hero of romance, but as a romantic hero he is quite out of the question. The same is true of Lilia Herriton, the English woman whom he marries. She is no ingénue, but a thirty-five-year-old widow, vulgar, superficial, and fun-loving. It is true that her brother-in-law Philip Herriton is the right age for a romantic lead, but he is content to be a spectator of the world's comedy. And it is true that Caroline Abbott is the right age to play opposite a romantic lead, but she is of a matronly disposition. Besides, by the time Philip has stopped being a spectator and fallen in love with her, she has developed a helpless passion for Gino. The world of romance is more bizarre than that of romantic comedy but even by the freer standards of romance, these characters are an odd lot.

The plot too is an extraordinary and melodramatic affair. Many writers of fiction have—in Richard Chase's words—excelled in the skillful use of melodrama: "They have known . . . how to take advantage of the abstractness of melodrama and its capacity to evoke ultimates and absolutes, in order to dramatize theological, moral, and less frequently political ideology." This capacity to evoke ultimates explains melodrama's great appeal to the romance writer and its prominent role in the romance tradition.

Romance narratives, especially of the quest type, sometimes take the form of an apparently endless sequence of adventures. More frequently, as the result of thematic commitment, they are highly structured. Forster is not much interested in the capacity of romance to encompass adventures, but he is intensely interested in its capacity to dramatize moral confrontations. Hence his plots, exploiting the direct appeal of melodrama, tend to be highly ordered, though by Jamesian standards the ordering falls short of tidiness. It is true, of course, that in *Aspects of the Novel* he shows himself to be thoroughly modern in his "oh dear yes" attitude to plot. That is because his symbols and his vision of life came to him through people and places and the inwardness of his own experience and could best be expressed in fiction through character and setting. Thus his low opinion of plot does not stem from the realist objection that it is arbitrary and unmimetic but from the simple fact that it was not central to his vision of life. On the other hand, when he needed plot to bring out the implications of his vision, he used it with a casual boldness which can still agitate and astound the realistic brotherhood of critics. The daring and rigorous use of plot pattern is especially notable in *Where Angels Fear to Tread* which falls neatly into two parallel parts, the first part (chapters 1 to 4) being much the shorter.

The opening chapter, after showing us Lilia's departure for Italy, offers a detached survey of the Herriton family and their typical suburban life in Sawston. We do not see events from the point of view of the characters nor do we get a look at their inner lives except incidentally in the way of necessary information. Thus the chapter is more than usually rich in brief comments and judgments by Forster. Chapter 2 brings Philip Herriton to Monteriano to prevent the marriage of Lilia and Gino. He leaves when he finds he has come too late. Chapters 3 and 4 describe the breakdown of the marriage, the birth of a son, and the death of Lilia.

Chapter 5 is like chapter 1. Lilia's death is like Lilia's departure. Everyone in Sawston can now settle down into an orderly and undisturbed existence. Then Caroline Abbott makes an issue of the baby; and Philip, this time accompanied by his stiff-necked sister Harriet, is despatched to Monteriano on another rescue operation. The remaining chapters, fully half the novel, show the catastrophic failure of that operation.

Contained within this orderly framework is a series of dramatic and melodramatic episodes: in part one, Lilia's hasty marriage to Gino, her attempt to flee from Monteriano, and her sudden death in childbirth; in part two, the exciting visit to the Monteriano opera, the kidnapping of the baby, the intervention of the grotesque idiot who assists Harriet, the collision of the carriages in the darkness and the wet—with the consequent death of the baby—and the weird scene also in the dark in which Gino, frenzied on account of the loss of his son, tortures Philip by alternately twisting his broken arm and compressing his windpipe. Philip faints and the scene takes another extraordinary turn. As he comes to, he hears a voice saying to Gino that his son is dead. "The room was full of light, and Miss Abbott had Gino by the shoulders, holding him down in a chair. She was exhausted with the struggle, and her arms were trembling." Yet this like all the other melodramatic moments is thoroughly convincing.

The odd assortment of characters and exceptional incidents are credible because the story is furnished with a narrator whose tone is consistently serious and, when satire is in order, biting. This mature and almost somber nature of the storyteller is especially obvious in the presentation of setting and in some of the descriptions and commentary.

The settings are symbolic, the object of the symbolism being to sharpen the contrasts between Sawston and Monteriano. Here to begin with is a Sawston scene from the opening chapter of the novel. Mrs. Herriton, assisted by her daughter Harriet, is planting the kitchen garden; she is practical, we may suppose. She says, "We will save the peas to the last; they are the greatest fun," thereby evincing her "gift of making work a treat." When they come to the peas, Harriet holds the string "to guide the row straight" as is appropriate for a person strict, narrow, and lacking pliancy, while her mother "scratched a furrow with a pointed stick," an act suggestive of the injurious decisiveness of her interfering nature. She sows the peas evenly and well—then the letter arrives from Lilia with the shocking announcement of her engagement to an Italian—and Harriet forgets to cover the peas. Before nightfall the sparrows have taken every one. "But countless fragments of the letter remained, disfiguring the tidy ground." The best laid plans come to nought and what would be wished away persists, disrupting and disfiguring ordered existence.

Mrs. Herriton has three successive plans for her daughter-in-law: to cultivate Lilia and make a lady of her, to save her from the Italian marriage, and finally to rescue the child of that marriage from its Italian father. In each, Harriet is her assistant. Each plan fails. In the last, Harriet is directly responsible for the death of the child. So the kitchen garden has weighty implications. As a functioning symbol, however, it is light-weight. It appears once only, it comes early in the novel, and it lacks archetypal reference. In other words it is perfectly suited to the spiritual dimensions of Mrs. Herriton and life in Sawston.

At the heart of Monteriano is the Piazza with its three great attractions—the Palazzo Pubblico, the Collegiate Church of Santa Deodata, and
the Caffè Garibaldi: "the intellect, the soul, and the body. . . . For a moment
Philip stood in its centre . . . thinking how wonderful it must feel to belong
to a city, however mean." Here then is a symbol of the self, of the complete
man, which in turn is a symbol of and is symbolized by the city, the image
of a complete society. The tower commanding the Siena gate reaches up to
heaven and down to hell. Philip, looking at it with Miss Abbott, and seeing
the summit of the tower radiant in the sun while the base is in shadow and
pasted over with advertisements, asks "Is it to be a symbol of the town?"

The symbolism of the complete city, contrasting with the triviality of
Sawston, is the narrator's device for enlarging our understanding of the
characters and of the issues confronting them. But more than that, the symbolism greatly assists him in achieving an overmastering perspective. It is
true that at the end of the novel Philip believes himself to have seen all round
the sequence of events and to have got hold of its meaning. "And to see
round it he was standing at an immense distance." It is true too that he has
a fuller grasp of the symbolism than any other character and that he has
been helped by it in arriving at his whole and distanced view of things. In
this sense he may be thought of as dramatizing the experience of the reader.
But the reader in his turn is helped by the symbolism and by the narrator
to attain a perspective more complete and more immense than Philip's.

The symbolic settings are only one of the narrator's means of putting
himself and us in a commanding position with reference to the action. Of
even more importance are a series of comments and descriptions which obviously go beyond the knowledge, observation, or interest of the characters.
Here, for example, is a comment inspired by Gino's intense love for his son:
"For a wonderful physical tie binds the parents to the children; and—by
some sad, strange irony—it does not bind us children to our parents. For if
it did, if we could answer their love not with gratitude but with equal love,
life would lose much of its pathos and much of its squalor, and we might
be wonderfully happy. Gino passionately embracing, Miss Abbott reverently
averting her eyes—both of them had parents whom they did not love so very
much." As the last sentence shows, this commentary places the experience
in a perspective greater than the characters in their involvement can command.

The most impressive descriptions of this kind relate to Monteriano and
its legends. One of these legends concerns Santa Deodata. She is not an
important saint and during her lifetime she did not achieve much, yet a
church has risen over her grave. Her strength was in her denial of the world,

in her determination not to participate. In this she is both a parallel and a contrast to Philip. Like her, he refuses to participate; but he remains a spectator for personal and trivial reasons whereas Santa Deodata, however misguided she may have been, was deeply serious in her refusal to take part in life. This implied analogy gives us an added perspective on Philip's character.

But of all the descriptions relating to Monteriano and its legends, the most extraordinary is the following exercise in historical imagination (Philip and Miss Abbott are looking out from their hotel which was once a castle):

> She removed a pile of plates from the Gothic window, and they leant out of it. Close opposite, wedged between mean houses, there rose up one of the great towers. It is your tower: you stretch a barricade between it and the hotel, and the traffic is blocked in a moment. Farther up, where the street empties out by the church, your connections, the Merli and the Capocchi, do likewise. They command the Piazza, you the Siena gate. No one can move in either but he shall be instantly slain, either by bows or by crossbows, or by Greek fire. Beware, however, of the back bedroom windows. For they are menaced by the tower of the Aldobrandeschi, and before now arrows have struck quivering over the washstand. Guard these windows well, lest there be a repetition of the events of February 1338, when the hotel was surprised from the rear, and your dearest friend—you could just make out that it was he—was thrown at you over the stairs.

These moments in the narrative have almost an autobiographical quality. By this I do not mean that in any way we know them to be autobiographical. Nor do I mean that if we did know them to be autobiographical our perception of their literary quality would be altered. We know Philip Herriton is somewhat like Forster but there is scarcely a hint of autobiographical quality in Forster's presentation of him. Rather I mean that at these moments the narrator seems to look through or over the heads of his characters and their situations and to speak directly to us about his own experience of the situation or place or legend. But he does not seem to speak to us intimately or privately, and for this reason I judge the effect not to be autobiographical. Indeed, even in *The Longest Journey*, an admittedly personal novel, the narrator seldom strikes an autobiographical note. What we have in *Where Angels Fear to Tread*, and to a lesser degree in *A Room with a View*, is a narrator who can be thoughtful and imaginative beyond the range of his characters and a narrator who wishes to share with the reader an enriched and commanding perspective. This is not incompatible with what we also have, a narrator capable of a large measure of detachment and objectivity. The ability to untie the two roles of presiding genius and detached observer gives a very distinct character to the personality of Forster the narrator.

At the same time the narrator's personality has its own distinct character in each novel. In *Where Angels Fear to Tread* his personality has a certain somber and mature quality; in *A Room with a View* it has a witty and urbane exuberance. The difference in personality may be related to the order of composition. The Italian part of *A Room with a View* was first written in 1903. The story, though not completed for publication until 1908, was obviously carried through very much in the spirit of its beginning. For this reason it is justifiable and indeed right to treat it as Forster's first novel. The high-spirited youthfulness of the narrator, contrasting as it does with the graver insight of the narrator of *Where Angels Fear to Tread*, is a decisive indication of the correctness of such an order.

I now turn to a more general way of regarding the presence of the author's personality in his work, a way of regarding it which applies to all Forster's novels equally and indeed to all successful fiction whatsoever. Charles Morgan has put the case admirably with reference to drama:

> Form is *in itself* valuable only in those works of art into which the time-factor does not enter, and which, therefore, come to us whole. Painting, sculpture and architecture come to us whole; they are directly formal arts. An epic poem does not come to us whole, but a short lyric or a particular line therein may almost be said to do this, so slight, by comparison with an epic, is the time-factor involved. A play's performance occupies two or three hours. Until the end its form is latent in it. It follows that during the performance we are not influenced by the form itself, the completed thing, but by our anticipations of completion. We are, so to speak, waiting for the suspended rhyme or harmony, and this formal suspense has the greater power if we know before-hand, as the Greeks did, what the formal release is to be.

This same principle applies to the novel. But in the novel much of our sense of anticipated form will relate to the narrator and to our confidence in him. This is what Forster is saying in *Aspects of the Novel* when he tells us that "a character in a book is real . . . when the novelist knows everything about it. He may not choose to tell us all he knows—many of the facts, even of the kind we call obvious, may be hidden. But he will give us the feeling that though the character has not been explained, it is explicable, and we get from this a reality of a kind we can never get in daily life." In a similar way the form, though incomplete, is assured and real and meaningful. Such a sense cannot be attributed to anything abstract, it must be attributed to the personality of the author-narrator. In some works the personality may be detached or invisible. In Forster's works it is strikingly present in the form of a narrator who, as the more or less omniscient author at the center of the fiction, expands outward to include all in a formal unity which is from the first anticipated and at the last fulfilled.

The author-narrator is the ultimate man of order, the ultimate source of the reader's experience of the work as a totality. But this is not in itself sufficient grounds for speaking of the narrator as archteype. To this way of speaking it must be objected that such a conception of the narrator is applicable to all fiction, or at least to all fiction successful enough to create a sense of unity, and that logically a narrator so defined as archetypal belongs to a category different from that of archetypal objects or characters or moments of vision within a fiction. The force of this objection is demonstrable in the short stories. There the ecstatic moment of identity with nature gives rise to the sense of a living totality. The author-narrator exists in or behind the fiction, but in the reader's actual experiencing of the story he appears as a secondary source of totality; the moment, or the character participating in the moment, appears as the primary source. It is the moment which is archetypal. Similarly, in the later novels, archetypal characters and objects are primary in the reader's experience of a subsuming mythic order and unity.

Here the Italian romances reveal their unique character. In them, the object of vision is apprehended more fully and the moment of ecstasy is participated in more wholeheartedly by the narrator than by his characters. George and Lucy are transformed in each other's eyes, but our vision of the two of them as the type of young lovers caught up in an eternal springtime of violets goes beyond their own comprehension. It is finally the vision of the narrator. In like manner, the presentation of Monteriano is one of abiding visionary insight into the permanent reality of the archetypal city. This ecstatic insight, transcending the characters and their individual moments of experience, adheres to the author-narrator.

Such a situation is unique in Forster's fiction (always leaving *A Passage to India* aside). In every one of the short stories at least one character fully apprehends the object of vision or fully experiences the moment of ecstasy. The same is true of the characters in the later novels, though every reader will be able to detect examples of vision which belong essentially to the author-narrator. In *The Longest Journey*, . . . the splendid account of the Wiltshire downs as the center of England begins as Rickie's view, but ends as the narrator's. Even so, we come to understand this vision as the conscious expression of what Stephen Wonham experiences unconsciously. And Stephen, in his turn, assumes the role of hero in our eyes because that is the way he is seen by other characters in the novel.

It will be understood, in view of what has already been said about romance, that the total order in each of Forster's works transcends the individual characters and their moments of ecstatic experience. And it will be understood that this total order, though it embodies the visionary, is not itself visionary. Even in the Italian romances, where the narrator is a visionary center, the vision does not touch all, for which reason its all-inclusiveness is limited to those areas where it does touch. Only the narrator with respect to order is a center expanding outward to include all.

But within this total order, the narrator as a focus of vision, as a personality directly related to moments of ecstatic experience, creates in his own person an awareness of visionary totality and mythic unity. Accordingly he takes on a status closely resembling that of archetypal characters within the fiction. For this reason *A Room with a View* and *Where Angels Fear to Tread,* alone among Forster's works, may justify a conception of the narrator as archetype.

JOHN COLMER

The Longest Journey

In *A Room with a View* and *Where Angels Fear to Tread* the juxtaposition of Italy and England serves as a major structural principle for contrasting two approaches to life: the instinctive and the conventional. In the three English novels, *The Longest Journey* (1907), *Howards End* (1910), and *Maurice* (written 1913–14), the structure rests on contrasts within English society; consequently communities and houses serve a more important symbolic role than in the Italian novels. Thus the tripartite division of *The Longest Journey* into Cambridge, Sawston, and Wiltshire corresponds to three different responses to life; it also marks the main stages in the development of the hero, who—we are told—was sensitive to places and "would compare Cambridge with Sawston and either with a third type of existence, to which for want of a better name, he gave the name 'Wiltshire.'" In *Howards End* there is no similar formal division; but Mrs Wilcox's house Howards End is contrasted with London to symbolize the conflict between continuity and change in English society in the Edwardian period. The spirit of place, previously associated in the short stories and Italian novels with classical myth and Mediterranean culture, now assumes a distinctly English form; moreover, the individual's moments of truth, the symbolic moments in his spiritual development, are now presented in relation to a larger, public theme.

This theme is England, the continuity of the English tradition, the question of who shall inherit England, which all three novels specifically ask.

From *E. M. Forster: The Personal Voice*. © 1975 by John Colmer. Routledge & Kegan Paul Ltd., 1975.

Each attempts to convey an answer in a final pastoral coda: the scene in which Stephen Wonham, who guides "the future of the race," takes his daughter into the woods to sleep; the scene in which Helen Schlegel and her baby assume the role of inheritors in the hay field in *Howards End*; and the escape to happiness "in the greenwoods" for Maurice and Alec at the end of *Maurice*. The nature of the answer is not very convincing, particularly in the light of later historical development, as Forster admitted towards the end of his life, saying that the English countryside had lost its plausibility and so too had the established home as a symbol of continuity. It is not only the concern with the relationship between the individual and the spirit of England that these three novels have in common, however. They also assert the supremacy of imaginative vision; they explore the possibilities of man living in harmony with the earth; they are centrally concerned with the sanctity of personal relations, with the need "to connect"; and they all show that ultimately "the inner life pays," an ironic reversal of the commercial ethics of the day.

The Longest Journey is Forster's most autobiographical novel. In the introduction which Forster wrote in 1960 for the World's Classics edition of the novel, he confesses that although it has proved the "least popular" of his novels, it was the one he was "most glad to have written."

> For in it I have managed to get nearer than elsewhere towards what was on my mind—or rather towards that junction of mind with heart where the creative impulse sparks. Thoughts and emotions collided if they did not always co-operate.

As the story of a young man who struggles to retain his human and artistic integrity, *The Longest Journey* makes an illuminating comparison with James Joyce's *A Portrait of the Artist as a Young Man* (1916) and Lawrence's *Sons and Lovers* (1913); and, as the story of the painful initiation of a young man into life, with Butler's *The Way of All Flesh* (1902). In Forster's Italian novels, it will be recalled, there is a strong antithesis between two kinds of young men and consequently two responses to life, between aesthetes, such as Philip Herriton, and the embodiments of natural passion, Gino or George Emerson. *The Longest Journey,* because it is closely autobiographical, offers a direct insight into the original sources of this duality: salvation through culture and salvation through nature. And since it is longer and more complicated than either of the Italian novels and is moreover wholly set in England, it renders more fully the forces in English society that make it peculiarly difficult for anyone to be both cultured and natural at the same time.

The basic story of *The Longest Journey* is simple but there is the inevitability of Greek tragedy and of Ibsen's still-topical *Ghosts* in the complex interaction of past and present that leads to the denouement. In the first section, Cambridge, we meet the hero, Rickie Elliot, an undergraduate with the hereditary defect of a lame foot; he is not particularly clever, but is full of high ideals and intent on learning to love and understand everyone. This part of the novel expresses a radiant vision of human fellowship. In the Sawston chapters, we watch the progressive deterioration of Rickie's character under the influence of his wife Agnes, an unimaginative and untruthful woman, and of her brother Mr Pembroke, a housemaster at Sawston school where Rickie has become a teacher. The ideals of human fellowship and the pursuit of reality are replaced by the worthless ideals of the school, by a life of compromise and deceit and the acceptance of the second best. In this novel Rickie is faced with a symbolic moment of choice. He learns that the coarse, virile young man, Stephen Wonham, who lives on his aunt's farm, is his own illegitimate brother. Although he longs to grasp the moment and greet Stephen as a brother, he is prevented from doing so by Agnes, who is more concerned with saving face in society than with truth and salvation. The moment passes and Rickie becomes muddled. When he discovers that Stephen is the son not of his detested father but of the mother he had loved, he regards Stephen as a symbol of her frailty and needs to learn painfully that he is a symbol of his mother's love. Throughout these later sections, Rickie's transformation of experience into abstractions expresses the victory of Sawston over Cambridge, the triumph of life lived at second-hand over the fearless immediate grasp of reality. In the last section of the novel, Wiltshire, Rickie loses his own life in saving Stephen from being run over by a train. After Rickie's death, Stephen thinks of him lying in the earth. "The body was dust. . . . The spirit had fled, in agony and loneliness, never to know that it had bequeathed him salvation."

Clearly another story about salvation, yet equally important is the theme of illusion and reality. Indeed, the novel opens with a group of undergraduates grappling with one of the central problems of European philosophy: is reality in the object or in the mind of the perceiver? Is the cow really there? From this point, the word reality recurs repeatedly. Stewart Ansell, with all the pedantic integrity of the undergraduate pholosopher, a pedantry that nevertheless "lay close to the vineyards of life," refuses to recognize the existence of Agnes Pembroke, whose entrance interrupts the discussion, even though she bounds in with the brash confidence of someone who has just got herself engaged to a handsome young soldier, Gerald. By Ansell's standards, she has no reality; she is a figment of Rickie's diseased imagination.

Subsequently, Rickie tells Agnes that she must mind such a "real thing" as Gerald's death and much later that Stephen must be told such a "real thing" as his parentage. At Sawston he prays to be delivered "from the shadow of unreality that had begun to darken his world." When he has finally left his wife and turned back to literature he finds happiness, "because, as we used to say at Cambridge the cow is there. The world is real again." But the sceptical, mocking Mrs Failing tries to discredit his discovery of happiness and reality.

Forster has admitted that when he wrote *The Longest Journey* he had several different ideas of reality in his mind.

> There was the metaphysical idea of Reality ("the cow is there"): there was the ethical idea that reality must be faced (Rickie won't face Stephen); there was the idea, or ideal of the British Public School; there was the title exhorting us in the words of Shelley not to love one person only; there was Cambridge, there was Wiltshire.

With so many different ideas "whirling around" in his mind, it is hardly surprising that the novel operates on many levels and is not entirely free from confusion. Moreover, in developing these various conceptions of reality, the novelist was very conscious of forces tugging him in opposite directions. On the one hand, he felt inspired by the spirit of place, which seemed to offer him authentic insights into reality. On the other hand, he felt the "spirit of anti-literature" making him go "deliberately wrong." By the spirit of anti-literature he means the tug towards artificial and self-conscious writing. It has been suggested that the element of literary self-consciousness, opposed as it was to the inspirational, may have been a device for covering up "scandal," a contrivance to divert attention from the "authorial self-portrait." But it seems simpler to assume that it sprang primarily from a youthful compulsion to achieve fine effects through literary imitation, especially imitation of writers who celebrated the spirit of the earth, for example, Meredith, Richard Jefferies, and W. H. Hudson. Moreover, the evidence of a cancelled passage imitating Meredith and other changes made in the manuscript lend weight to this simpler stylistic explanation.

The first idea of *The Longest Journey,* "that of a man who discovers that he has an illegitimate brother," came to the author as early as 18 July 1904; then, between 1904 and 1907, "other ideas intervened to confuse or enrich the original theme." But it was the spirit of place which "fructified" his meagre conceptions of the "half-brother," as Forster's Introduction to the novel in 1960 and the essay "Three Countries" make clear. In them, he explains that the dry bones of the story were "vivified by the sudden irruption of the Wiltshire countryside" at Figsbury Rings, an ancient encampment five miles outside Salisbury consisting of an "outer circle of embankment and an inner circle, and in the centre . . . one tree." The site became Cadbury Rings in the novel. Speaking of their influence, in the essay "Three Countries," he writes:

> There's no case here of the direct inspiration which Italy gave me. But sitting upon the Rings several times and talking to the shepherds who frequented them, I had an emotion appropriate to the work in hand and particularly to the creation of one of the characters in it. Stephen Wonham. This rustic hero is not to everyone's taste. He can be boorish and a bore and when he gets drunk it is not upon wine. But he belongs to the countryside, he faces reality and he is the inheritor.

Forster's imagination caught fire on the Rings, just as it had caught fire in response to the spirit of Cambridge, "the fearless, uninfluential Cambridge that sought reality and cared for truth." From this compound *The Longest Journey* is created.

In this novel about the quest for truth each of the main characters represents a different approach to reality. For Rickie it is the way of imagination, reflected most obviously in his short stories, the visionary qualities of which satisfy neither his wife nor his potential publisher. For Stephen Wonham, it is the way of instinct; for Stewart Ansell it is the way of the intellect. The novel as a whole suggests that no one approach is sufficient but that all are necessary. Plot, characterization and imagery establish a series of confrontations and contrasts between the three different approaches which are defined and illustrated in a variety of ways: through the young men's families, the houses they inhabit, their response to money, friendship, love, and nature. The rather awkward flashback in the Madingley Dell when Rickie tells his friends the story of his life establishes him not only as the product of a loveless marriage but as a lonely city-dwelling child. "He had opened his eyes to filmy heavens, and taken his first walk on asphalt. He had seen civilization as a row of semi-detached villas, and society as a state in which men do not know the men who live next door." In his loneliness he would sob and ask "Shall I ever have a friend?" (compare Maurice's quest for the elusive friend). The flashback also establishes that Rickie hated his mocking father, adored his mother, who "was afraid of intimacy, in case it led to confessions," and felt remorsefully responsible for her death because he wilfully disobeyed her order to put on his overcoat on the day she died.

Rickie has no permanent home. He is dependent for hospitality on relations and friends: his cousins, the money-conscious Silts, "who combine to a peculiar degree the restrictions of hospitality with the discomforts of a boarding house"; and the Pembrokes, Herbert who teaches at Sawston and his sister Agnes who keeps house for him, a house in which "neither the cry of money nor the cry for money shall ever be heard." This is an index of their gentility and that unreal attitude to money common in their class, which Forster had encountered in his great-aunt Marianne Thornton. In fact to exclude the topic from polite conversation was a convenient device for ignoring economic privilege in the late Victorian and Edwardian period. And Agnes's silent but single-minded legacy-hunting illustrates how hypocritical the convention was.

Stewart Ansell's harmonious background is a complete contrast to Rickie's rootlessness and the Pembrokes' dissociation of culture from money. Ansell, who is a composite picture of Forster's Cambridge friends H. O. Meredith and the brilliant scholar Alfred Ainsworth, is the son of a successful suburban draper. Although his father knows nothing about philosophy, he loves his son and believes that he should be free to do what he wishes. The family, consisting of the father and two sisters, live over the shop. When Rickie visits Ansell, he contrasts the "live" money that rattles through their tills with the "dead" money that comes silently to him through the death of others. The Ansell family background, while acting as an obvious symbol for the wholeness of life that is attained through frankness and love and the union of money and culture, serves as an effective counterweight to Stewart Ansell's own somewhat pedantic separation of philosophy from life. In contrasted but related fashion, Stephen Wonham's coarse animal nature, his simple instinctive response to the earth and the local peasantry is set against the gentler and more civilized background of ideas provided in an unpublished book by his uncle, Mr Failing. These ideas, a combination of abstract nature worship and Utopian Socialism are strongly reminiscent of the thought of Edward Carpenter, author of *Civilisation: Its Cause and Cure* (1889), a once popular critique of the coming machine age. By placing the representatives of the three approaches to reality in such fully and appropriately realized settings, Forster increases the social and symbolic resonance of the novel and prevents it from becoming either thinly allegorical or overtly didactic.

Poets and novelists sometimes see their "intentions" more clearly in retrospect than at the time of writing, especially when provoked or given a nudge by subsequent criticism, as Forster was nudged by Lionel Trilling's book to see *Howards End* in Trilling's terms. Caution is therefore required in interpreting their remarks. Yet Forster's Introduction, written more than fifty years after the novel, offers a suggestive and succinct account of the quest for truth and the struggle between opposed characters and forces for possession of Rickie. Having spoken of Cambridge as the place where truth and reality are worshipped, he writes:

> Ansell is the undergraduate high-priest of that local shrine, Agnes Pembroke is its deadly debunker. Captured by her and by Sawston, Rickie goes to pieces, and cannot even be rescued when Ansell joins up with Stephen and strikes.

The account is especially interesting since it defines the conflict in the simplest possible terms and assigns to Ansell a role that he does not quite fulfil in the novel. At one time Forster gave him a more active part in bringing Stephen and Rickie together, but omitted it from the published novel. In reading the author's simple outline we need to remember that the conflict is a sex battle as well as a battle for truth. The Cambridge ideal of male friendship—and by implication the ideal of personal relations—excludes heterosexual love; the woman becomes an object of suspicion and is regarded either as an intruder or as something unreal. When Lytton Strachey went through the records of the Cambridge Apostles it became clear that most were homosexuals though not practising ones.

Agnes, on entering the magic Cambridge circle, instinctively recognizes Stewart Ansell as the enemy who must be won over or defeated. The ensuing conflict springs from sexual jealousy as much as from different standards of truth. One scene establishes clearly the intimate bond that exists between Stewart Ansell and Rickie (chapter 7). Rickie gives Ansell a garland of flowers, he speaks of "a kind of friendship office, where the marriage of true minds could be registered," and Ansell pulls him down affectionately by the ankles. Returning to this chapter after reading *Maurice* and the homosexual short stories, one sees immediately that the relationship is essentially homosexual. The two places that Rickie comes to associate with happiness are his rooms in Cambridge and the Dell at Madingley. He would like to extend this happiness to all, but both places are in fact places of seclusion (though not necessarily symbolic "wombs"), open only to the elect, with Stewart Ansell occupying a central place. Agnes breaks into both magic circles. Her first victory is complete when she calls Rickie into the Dell at Madingley and enfolds him as her lover: her second at Cadbury Rings. When Mrs Failing informs Rickie that Stephen Wonham is his step-brother, and Rickie, in a moment of understanding not horror, calls out "Stephen," it is Agnes, not Stephen who answers and who "caught him to her breast." Agnes, like Miss

Bartlett in *A Room with a View,* blots out the distant view, and therefore reality.

A further example of the way the struggle for truth is supported and qualified by overtones of sexual possession lies in the tentative hint that Agnes's opposition to Stephen Wonham arises partly from his similarity to her dead fiancé, Gerald. In chapter 31 of the published text, the fact that Agnes identifies Stephen with Gerald is only hinted at. Stephen tells Rickie that "She looked at me as if she knew me, and then gasped 'Gerald,' and started crying." But, in an earlier manuscript version the identification is made dramatic. Agnes throws herself into Stephen's arms when she calls him Gerald. This unconscious dimension in Agnes's character, stronger in the manuscript than in the published version, casts a sympathetic light on her inner conflict and hidden motives. Yet the chill analysis of her as someone who was not "conscious of her tragedy" in the printed text, someone from whom "the inner life had been withdrawn," firmly relegates her to the ranks of "the benighted."

When Agnes and Rickie announce their engagement, before Stephen Wonham enters the action, the philosopher Stewart Ansell sums up the situation.

> She is happy because she has conquered; he is happy because he has at last hung all the world's beauty on to a single peg. He was always trying to do it. He used to call the peg humanity. Will either of these happinesses last? His can't. Hers only for a time. I fight this woman not only because she fights me, but because I foresee the most appalling catastrophe. She wants Rickie, partly to replace another man whom she lost two years ago, partly to make something out of him. He is to write. In time she will get sick of this. He won't get famous. She will only see how thin he is and how lame. She will long for a jollier husband, and I don't blame her. And, having made him thoroughly miserable and degraded, she will bolt—if she can do it like a lady (chapter 8).

The prediction of this born misogynist proves accurate—except that it is Rickie who bolts. Stewart Ansell's objections to Agnes are simple and fundamental, as he explains in a letter to Rickie. They are "(1) She is not serious. (2) She is not truthful." The action of the novel endorses this analysis.

The change of scene from Cambridge to Cadover—"the perilous house"—is important in a variety of ways. It introduces two new characters who are to play vital parts in the novel: Mrs Failing, a spiteful sardonic old woman, who is Rickie's aunt; and Stephen Wonham. The change marks a

crucial stage in the development of the theme of brotherhood. It also introduces the first of the many references to the railway-crossing, thus prefiguring
Rickie's death there. And it brings a new spirit into the novel, the spirit of
Wessex: pagan, natural, and instinctive, a manifestation of the continuity of
rural England, a spirit embodied to some extent in Stephen. Mrs Failing,
who invites the newly engaged couple to Cadover, suggests another kind of
continuity. In her is continued the heartlessness of Rickie's dead father: his
sterile aestheticism, his delight in playing cruel tricks on people. Mrs Failing
begins by playing a trick on Agnes by pretending that the unshaven Stephen
is a peasant. In the older woman, Agnes meets her match: the two women,
adept in the art of compromise, form a truce in deceit. Agnes connives in
Mrs Failing's scheme to send Stephen away after the aunt's revelation that
he is Rickie's brother; they thus prevent Rickie from greeting him and acknowledging the relationship. When Agnes discovers that Mrs Failing has
not told Stephen, she announces triumphantly to Rickie, "Dear, we're
saved!" Her complicity in this scheme of false salvation is complete. And
Rickie is pained and shocked.

The description of Rickie's and Stephen's ride to Salisbury brings together the theme of brotherhood and the theme of the continuity of England
in a deeply moving fashion; it conveys a sense of some ultimate reality lying
behind favoured spots of English countryside; and it offers authentic intimations of infinity. The occasional lapses into religiosity of phrase—they
"were approaching the Throne of God"—are counterbalanced by the comedy of Rickie's failure to manage his mount and by the coarse humour of
the soldier they meet who sings rhymes about Aunt Emily, until Stephen
topples him in the mud. In this whole section much is made of settling one's
differences by physical contest, but without the sadistic overtones that accompany Gerald's bullying, or Mrs Failing's delight in cruelty, or Agnes's
repeated talk of horsewhipping. Rather this part establishes the value of
personal conflict, the reality of which is finally confirmed by Stephen's frank
contest with Mr Pembroke over the division of the profits from Rickie's
short stories and by the contrast made by Stephen between the sham values
represented by Mr Pembroke and the earthy reality of riding on Salisbury
Plain by night (chapter 35). Stephen, who serves to link the ideals of frater-
nity and the English spirit, is not merely a healthy animal, "with just enough
soul to contemplate its own bliss," in touch with nature, completely at home
with the morals and manners of the local peasants. In his simple fashion, he
is, like Stewart Ansell, a philosopher in search of truth, absurd as his six-
penny rational tracts may be. He is also imaginative, like Rickie; a child of
poetry and rebellion, although his imagination expresses itself more naturally

and in a less literary form: "he lived too near the things he loved to seem poetical." Since the novel is to end with Stephen as the "inheritor" of England, it is important that he should not appear as a crude embodiment of the primitive, but should contain within him the potentialities, at least, for intellectual and imaginative development. There is a world of difference too between his vital, good-natured, shambling confusion as he ignores social restraints and the spiritual muddle that overwhelms Rickie, a muddle that arises from social compromise and self-delusion.

Forster was wise to omit a long fantasy about the naked Stephen's encounter with the earth in the Salisbury ride episode, since it was a bad instance of the tug of "anti-literature" and disastrously lowered Stephen's potential as an inheritor instead of raising it. In his Introduction to the novel, he has given a not completely accurate summary of the deleted part. Near the beginning of the cancelled section, there is an invocation to the woodland deities to guard Stephen (at this stage called Harold Wonham). " 'O nymphs and woodland Fauns! O dryads and satyrs! O all ye hosts of earth whose deity I am compelled to greet! . . . Guard, O guard, this inefficient and most bumptious youth who advances without a talisman against your suspected powers.' " The young man feels that he is pursued by an unseen presence; and bumps into a huge grey shape (a tree): "his brain had been wiped clean, and he was a little child. Liking the smooth bark, he laid his cheek to it and kissed the living wood, again and again. Then he stood up smiling, but full of reverence." Meredith's account of Richard Feverel's night ride in the Rhineland forest was Forster's main model here, although the celebration of man's kinship with the earth could be found in a multitude of post-Darwinian writers. In the published novel, Stephen experiences a moment of panic fear when pursued by a flock of sheep, but the other elements connected with Pan disappear. Forster makes the point about his genuine contact with the earth more neatly and economically by picturing Stephen's contempt for one of Rickie's fanciful stories about getting in touch with nature when he reads it on the roof at Cadover. He exclaims, "In touch with Nature! What cant would the books think of next. His eyes closed. He was sleepy. Good, oh good! Sighing into his pipe, he fell asleep" (chapter 12). Stephen's faults are obvious, but they do not spring from the undeveloped heart. He is a genuine Pagan "who lives for the Now," the very opposite of Henry Wilcox in *Howards End,* who "lived for the five minutes that have passed, and the five minutes to come" and who "had the business mind" (chapter 29).

The central part of *The Longest Journey,* "Sawston," provides a convincing indictment of the system of education that produces the undeveloped heart in the English middle classes. Forster here draws on his own public school, Tonbridge, probably exaggerating little, as fellow sufferers at other schools testify. Recalling Goldsworthy Lowes Dickinson's miseries at Charterhouse, he once remarked "as generation after generation of sensitive boys record their experience in them, one marvels why the boarding house system continues at all, and why the middle classes still insist on so much discomfort for their children at such expense to themselves." Of course, the answer was that, in Forster's day, a public school education was both an assertion of economic status and an almost essential passport to administrative power in England and the British Empire. The end justified the means, even though the recognizable public school figure who was produced was damaged for life as a private individual. In the Sawston chapters, Forster connects the public and the private theme. His public theme is the education of an Englishman and the future of England: his private theme is the individual's quest for truth, love, comradeship, wholeness of being. It is appropriate that Rickie's moral deterioration should be set against a background of the shoddy second-hand values taught at Sawston. Although Rickie himself has suffered as a boy at a public school and is determined to spare others similar suffering, he is powerless to do so. He becomes enmeshed in a network of petty intrigue and deceit that culminates in a painful case of bullying. Sawston is the exact antithesis of Cambridge. It worships success, not truth; it believes in "personal influence," not "personal relations"; it seeks to develop *esprit de corps,* not brotherhood; it claims to be the "world in miniature," to speak for the world and not just for itself. "'The good societies [Stewart Ansell tells his listeners] say, "I tell you to do this because I am Cambridge." The bad ones say, "I tell you to do that because I am the great world." ' . . . They lie'" (chapter 7). Sawston is an enclosed, self-sufficient world in which spiritual muddle and unreality flourish. The fogs blot out the light. Rickie's marriage brings not the looked-for vision but phantoms and spectres as grey and ghastly as those that haunt the paintings of Eduard Munch or the plays of Ibsen and Strindberg. After the death of Agnes's child, the departure of the bullied Varden, and Rickie's total disenchantment with Agnes, those two very different apostles of truth, Stewart Ansell and Stephen Wonham, invade this unreal world and restore some sense of reality.

The dramatic climax of the Sawston chapters comes with Ansell's arraignment of Rickie and Agnes before the boys at Sunday dinner. Benjamin Britten has compared these recurrent big, rather melodramatic scenes in Forster's fiction to operatic set-pieces. This scene at Sawston comes nearer to the trial scene in *A Passage to India* than to the fight between Philip and Gino in *Where Angels Fear to Tread,* but the analogy with opera is appropriate to all three and comes as a useful reminder not to judge such set-pieces by purely realistic standards. The contrast between the isolated, accusing figure of Stewart Ansell, and the petty formality of the dining room, with its "imperial portraits," Union Jack, and figures at high table is a fine piece of theatre that dramatizes the actual clash of values. The success of the whole scene depends on multiple ironies. Ansell believes that Rickie knows nothing about having a brother; Rickie believes that he knows all. It is only when Rickie refers specifically to his "father's disgrace" that the secret is given to the world.

> "Please listen again," resumed Ansell. "Please correct two slight mistakes: firstly, Stephen is one of the greatest people I have ever met; secondly, he's not your father's son. He's the son of your mother."
>
> It was Rickie, not Ansell, who was carried from the hall, and it was Herbert who pronounced the blessing—
>
> *"Benedicto benedicatur."*
>
> A profound stillness succeeded the storm, and the boys, slipping away from their meal, told the news to the rest of the school, or put it in the letters they were writing home (chapter 27).

In the final section of the novel, "Wiltshire," the development of the different ideas of reality and of the relationships between the characters is complicated and confused. The question of ethical reality (will Rickie accept Stephen as a fellow man, a brother?) becomes inextricably mixed up with another notion of reality, psychological and spiritual in origin. The working out of the ethical theme requires that Rickie should cease to see Stephen as a symbol, either of his father's or his mother's frailty and see him as a man. But the working out of the psychological theme and the theme of continuity requires that Rickie should see his mother in Stephen and see him transfigured by the mother's love. When Pembroke tells Rickie that he should mind all the more on finding that it was his mother who was at fault, Rickie replies gently, "'I have been too far back,'" an evocative phrase, first used of the effect of Stephen's conversation with Ansell in a cancelled version of chapter 31, a phrase that foreshadows Forster's definition of prophecy in *Aspects of the Novel*. Rickie continues: "'Ansell took me a journey that was even new to him. We got behind right and wrong, to a place where only one thing matters—that the Beloved should arise from the Dead'" (chapter 31). It is clear that Stephen becomes transfigured and sanctified as a reincarnation of his mother's love. But the author cannot logically endorse both the ethical and the spiritual ideas of reality. Is it possible to ascribe the idea of the

Beloved rising from the grave as just one more of Rickie's illusions? Hardly, with the abundant evidence of the author's own belief in the influence of the dead in the other novels, and his stout defence of "ancestor worship" when challenged about this element: "'The present is so heavy and crude and so vulgar that something has to be thrown into the opposite scale. . . . This is not a private fancy of mine: all races who have practised ancestor worship know about it.'"

In the published version of *The Longest Journey*, the very Shelleyan incident when Rickie watches Stephen's "transfigured face" as he lights a paper boat that becomes a rose of flame and passes under one of the arches of the bridge, is the most striking visionary moment of the novel. It clearly carries the full weight of the author's imaginative approval; yet what it endorses is Rickie's acceptance of Stephen as a symbol, not a man. Moreover, a later passage that speaks of the "mystic rose and the face it illuminates" further clarifies Stephen's symbolic transfiguration into an image of the dead mother. In the cancelled sections that exist only in the manuscript, the theme of the mother's spirit living through Stephen is even more strongly stressed. An early version of chapter 32 includes two examples of the dead surviving in the living. One is Agnes's momentary identification of Stephen with her dead lover Gerald: he recalls "all the radiant possibilities that perished on a suburban football field." Stephen understands intuitively and is "transfixed with pity."

> "Poor girl—has it been like that—don't think I shall ever tell him—Ah poor girl!" Then the moment passed, the spirit returned to the grave, the lips were those of a stranger, and the memory of them an eternal shame.

Agnes's identification is clearly an illusory vision, the product of psychological guilt. The second survival from the dead is not illusory, however, although it, too, is connected with repressed guilt, Rickie's confused feeling that his failure to obey his mother's injunction to wear his overcoat was responsible for her death. In this version, the school is on fire. Stephen and Ansell urge Rickie to leave the burning house at Sawston,

> "No one's stopping!" they cried. "Come our way. Come back to the things you've forgotten."
> For a moment he murmured about duty.
> "But he must have a great coat!" said Stephen. "He can't go without a great coat."
> To Rickie also a mortal spirit was incarnate in immortal flesh.

Last time, when that voice had said those words, he had silenced
it fretfully [cf. end of chapter 2]. He obeyed it today, and the
three of them followed the course of the storm.

In the later published version, Forster still suggests that Rickie goes with
Stephen because he hears his mother's voice speaking through him and not
because he accepts Stephen's ethical argument, "'Come with me as a man
. . . Not as a brother; who cares what people did years back.'" But he no
longer makes the point dramatically but through commentary and he omits
the link with the overcoat.

Habit and sex may change with the new generation, features may
alter with the play of a private passion, but a voice is apart from
these. It lies nearer to the racial essence and perhaps to the divine;
it can, at all events, overleap one grave (chapter 31).

Ultimately the two approaches to brotherhood interweave and overlap but
are never satisfactorily reconciled. Rickie and the author appear to endorse
ideals of transfiguration, while Stephen appeals to a rough and ready ethical
ideal based on common humanity. As a further paradox the novel ends with
the triumph of Stephen's elemental qualities, but only because the dead Rickie
had "bequeathed him salvation."

Much of the awkwardness in the final section of *The Longest Journey*
also comes from the novelist's attempt to establish Stephen as someone fit
to be an "inheritor," first, in the sense of inheriting the qualities possessed
by his farmer father and his gentle mother, the qualities of "poetry and
rebellion" that brought them together; and second, in the sense of inheriting
the spirit of England's past, a past seen as essentially rural, associated with
ancient Wessex, pagan rather than Christian. At this late stage in the plot,
Forster suddenly switches to the past and relates the story of how the young
farmer Robert fell in love with Rickie's mother, waited patiently, and finally
ran away with her to Stockholm where Stephen was conceived. For the
reader, Robert achieves a symbolic rather than a real existence. He is clearly
intended to embody the spirit of the earth. "As he talked the earth became
a living being—or rather a being with a living skin—and manure no longer
dirty stuff, but a symbol of regeneration and of the birth of life from life"
(chapter 29). Certainly his practicality shows up old Mr Failing's shadowy
ideals of love and brotherhood, his firm grasp of the actual forms a healthy
contrast to Rickie's father's abstractions and cynicism. Even for Mrs Failing
the two lovers are no "ordinary people," but "forces of nature." And yet in
the midst of this overt celebration of love, nature, and the spirit of the earth,

there comes a chill qualifying passage. It is put in the mouth of the prosy Mr Failing certainly, but on the evidence of Forster's own eulogies elsewhere of "Love the Beloved Republic," it expresses the author's view that the republic "will not be brought about by love alone. It will approach with no flourish of trumpets, and have no declaration of independence. Self-sacrifice and—worse still—self-mutilation are the things that sometimes help it most." Mr Failing uses these sentiments to recommend an immediate rescue party to Stockholm; but they reverberate with a wider significance in the novel as a whole. After Rickie's brief vision of happiness and brotherhood at Cambridge, the emphasis falls on suffering, self-sacrifice, self-mutilation. Is Rickie's death at the railway-crossing to be seen as a necessary act of self-mutilation in the service of "Love the Beloved Republic"? And, autobiographically, a mutilation of one part of the self that another part may survive?

While Forster constantly emphasizes that Stephen inherits his parents' loving spirit, he places a quite extraordinary stress on his drunkenness and animality, especially in the final chapter. This may be partly to justify Rickie's sense of desertion and spiritual bankruptcy and partly to prevent the "inheritor" figure who represents the continuity of England from being refined away into a sentimental symbol. But the various sides of Stephen's character never come together as a whole. He is required to represent too many of the qualities Forster admired and to represent them in too simple and elemental a form. A good example of this oversimplification relates to the working out of the theme of personal relations. When Rickie reviews the watchwords that had ruled his life at Sawston, watchwords such as "Organize," "Systematize," "Fill up every moment," "Induce *esprit de corps,*" he sees that "they ignored personal contest, personal truces, personal love." Stephen, in his relations with the local peasants, exemplifies the importance of "personal contest," like Gino and Philip in *Where Angels Fear to Tread.* But he represents in a very rudimentary fashion the middle way between the preciosity of Cambridge's ideal of personal relations and the neglect of all personal relations at Sawston. Thematically, then, he contributes something to the ideal of wholeness, but there is little to suggest that Stephen was capable of wholeness of being himself, of uniting the monk and beast in man. There is altogether too much beast.

Why does Rickie save Stephen's life twice? First, he saves him from toppling over the banisters at Dunwood House; then, later, he saves him from being run over at the level-crossing. Why should the saving occur twice? And why should Rickie survive the first and die in the course of the second? The questions are not easily answered, but the attempt to answer them takes us to the heart of the novel. The first incident when Stephen throws a brick through the study window, wrecks the hall, lurches up the stairs, and nearly falls over the banisters, establishes Rickie's release from remorse and his consequent capacity for instinctive action. While Herbert Pembroke is calling for the police, Rickie has already saved Stephen. The simplicity of his greeting, "'Hello, Stephen!'" stresses his intuitive acceptance of his brother.

> Hither had Rickie moved in ten days—from disgust to penitence, from penitence to longing, from a life of horror to a new life, in which he still surprised himself by unexpected words. Hello, Stephen! For the son of his mother had come back, to forgive him, as she would have done, to live with him, as she had planned (chapter 31).

To Agnes, Stephen seems "a man of scandal"; to Rickie, he is "a symbol of redemption." Neither acknowledges him as a man "who would answer them back after a few hours' rest."

Forster's early attempts to imagine the confrontation and Rickie's decision to go with Stephen were sentimental and melodramatic. In the first of these Stewart Ansell accepts Rickie's invitation to Dunwood House, sleeps the night beside the drunken Stephen, and later prepares Stephen to accept a life shared with Rickie. A highly emotional scene between Stephen and Rickie follows in which Rickie constantly returns to the theme of his mother's resurrection in Stephen. In a later version Forster reduces the Ansell/Stephen explanation by condensing the essentials into dialogue at the beginning. The sentimental confrontation between the half-brothers follows. Rickie pleads for forgiveness. "'Son of my mother, kiss me; forgive me.'" He then speaks in prophetic vein of the dream he had after his child's death and of his newly gained vision of human continuity (Forster's master theme) as the result of seeing his mother resurrected in Stephen. "Rickie gazed at the pure stream to which he would never contribute and watched it broadening to the sea." Mawkish as this scene is, it does clarify Rickie's later action in the published novel in sacrificing his life for Stephen at the railway-crossing. At the end of this version storms gather; Agnes, who is terrified, throws herself into Stephen's arms; part of the school is struck by lightning; and Rickie follows the fleeing Stephen, obedient this time to the voice of his mother, as it speaks through Stephen and tells him to bring his great-coat. Forster was wise to omit most of the details in these two early versions and to retain only brief references to Ansell's intervention and the exact details of Rickie's dream. He showed a true craftsman's skill in combining both in a short semi-dramatized résumé of Rickie's moral and spiritual progress. This then leads up to his decision to leave Agnes and follow Stephen.

However, the confrontation at Sawston cannot mark the climax of the relations between Stephen and Rickie. Between this incident and the later one at the level-crossing, Rickie passes through stages of intense spiritual struggle. At Sawston he confesses to Stephen that ever since he failed to give himself up to the spirit of the ride to Salisbury, he has "taken the world at second-hand." He fights against Mrs Failing's cynicism, against her denial that the earth may "confirm" men's love, her denial that it will, in the words of her husband, "'suffer some rallying-point, spire, mound, for the new generation to cherish'" (chapter 34). The memory of Stephen sailing the paper boat, the "mystic rose," and the tunnel "dropping diamonds," comes back to Rickie as he drives away from Cadover. "He stood behind things at last, and knew that conventions are not majestic, and that they will not claim us in the end." Indeed, his liberation seems complete, more complete than Philip's at the end of *Where Angels Fear to Tread*. And yet he moves forward, not to freedom and self-reliance, but to "self-sacrifice" and "self-mutilation." When he recognizes Stephen as "a hero" fighting against social injustice, fighting, too, against the "Wilbrahams and Pembrokes who try to rule our world," he feels that it is "worth while to sacrifice everything for such a man." But when he discovers that Stephen has broken his promise not to drink, his whole moral world collapses. His trust in the earth becomes implicated in his broken faith in Stephen.

> "May God receive me and pardon me for trusting the earth."
> "But, Mr Elliot, what have you done that's wrong?"
> "Gone bankrupt, Leighton, for the second time. Pretended again that people were real. May God have mercy on me!"
> (chapter 34).

And it is in the spirit of defeat that "wearily" he does "a man's duty" and pushes Stephen to safety off the railway-line, saving his brother at the cost of his own life.

How extraordinary all this is. What it seems to suggest is that Forster was unable to imagine any future for a liberated Rickie in an Edwardian novel, or indeed in Edwardian society. He therefore huddles together a series of spiritual crises to make his death appear convincing and necessary. The ending also suggests the victory of self-disgust over self-renewal, or at least the author's disgust with the refined squeamish side of his nature that lacked the courage to accept the coarse animality of Stephen. Rickie has been drawn towards two men, the intellectual Stewart Ansell and the physical Stephen Wonham. He cannot accept either, or reconcile such contrasting responses to life within himself, and so must die. In *Maurice*, written a few years later, but not published in his lifetime, Forster was able to deal more frankly with the theme of brotherhood and love between men: the ideal of "comradeship and ecstasy." In *The Longest Journey,* he is driven into using a number of artistic subterfuges to mask his real theme. This enables him to explore areas of experience that interested him but not to carry out the exploration to its logical conclusion. Rickie, in the novel, at first vows never to marry because of his inherited deformity. But he does marry, and not only fathers a child, who is even lamer than himself, but feels guilt-stricken for his offence against the child, his wife, and himself. It requires little ingenuity to substitute homosexuality for inherited deformity. And the question whether a man will accept his illegitimate brother, given the strong taboos against frank acceptance of illegitimacy in the Edwardian middle class, may be another subterfuge for asking the question, will a man accept a form of sexuality that is forbidden by society. Moreover Agnes feels "menaced by the abnormal," overtly by Rickie's deformity and Stephen's illegitimacy, but subconsciously by male comradeship (chapters 1, 14, and 15). Since the publication of *Maurice* in 1971 and the posthumous homosexual short stories in 1972, the meaning behind these artistic subterfuges becomes more apparent. But this new way of reading the novel, although it may illuminate much that has always seemed obscure, still does little to clarify the confusion of themes and symbols within the novel.

Two rather different views have been taken of this confusion. Lionel Trilling, one of Forster's most perceptive critics, sees it as a failure to master technique, the kind of failure that one expects to find in an early but ambitious novel. John Harvey, on the other hand, sees it as an expression of a confused and inadequate vision of life.

> *The Longest Journey,* then, despite—or perhaps because of—its local successes is a failure as a whole. The disparate elements of which it is composed are never brought together into any kind of unity; at best they lie uneasily side by side; more often they actively quarrel with each other.

There is undoubtedly confusion, not simply rich ambiguity. And it is confusion of vision as well as of technique. But the final impression of the novel is more unified than patient analysis would lead one to expect. Although we cannot say what Forster said of Ibsen, "Everything rings true and echoes far because it is in the exact place which its surroundings require," we can say that the great imaginative scenes in the novel cohere in the memory more firmly than Harvey suggests. The vision of Agnes's and Gerald's kiss, the parallel scenes in the Cambridge Dell and in the Cadbury Rings, the ride across Salisbury Plain after which Rickie takes "the world at second hand," Ansell's dramatic irruption at Sawston school, the paper boat "burning as if it would burn for ever," Rickie's death and finally the pastoral coda: all these come together in the memory as an affirmation of the rightness of a life lived close to the rhythms of nature, a life passionate and instinctive. And Demeter, the earth goddess, who transcends sex, says Forster in "Cnidus," binds together the two generations: she presides over Mrs Elliot's experience of instinctive love for Robert, her farmer lover, and over Rickie's and Stephen's experience of the earth and their mother. *The Longest Journey* is something more interesting than a splendid failure or a flawed masterpiece. It is a novel that challenges most of our settled critical categories and is a landmark in Forster's fictional development.

ALAN WILDE

Injunctions and Disjunctions

"I used to admire Forster's work much more than I do now," Angus
Wilson announced recently in an interview, adding: "Forster has receded
from me as a figure." The comments apparently address different aspects of
the Forsterian heritage, although, because of the particularly strong inherence
of Forster's characteristic tone not only in the essays but in the fiction, it
would be too simple to designate these as the writings and the man. Nevertheless, some such distinction is implied, and, accepting it for the moment,
one recognizes that the second remark, conjuring up by way of contrast
memories of Isherwood's "antiheroic hero," is in many ways the more dev-
astating of the two. No doubt it is a fortuitous circumstance that Wilson's
key word is one employed by Lionel Trilling over a quarter of a century ago:
"He [Forster] is not merely a writer, he is a figure"; but the echo, like one
from the Marabar Caves, is no less unsettling for being coincidental, and no
less telling. For Trilling, Forster represented a particular kind of figure: one
who "acts out in public the role of the private man"; and the description,
which is in some ways as penetrating as it is representative of its times,
suggests Forster's status, so congenial to Trilling and other earlier critics (I
include myself), as—along with the not altogether different D. H. Lawrence—the principal moralist of his age. "As for his other traits," writes
P. N. Furbank, Forster's biographer, "I think the most characteristic was his
passion for moralising. He was moralising busily when he was twenty; and

From *Horizons of Assent: Modernism, Postmodernism, and the Ironic Imagination.*
© 1981 by The Johns Hopkins University Press.

he continued, without intermission, for the next seventy years. He plainly regarded it as the business of life; one was on earth to improve oneself and to improve others, and the path to this was moral generalisations." In the light of these observations, Wilson's reaction takes on more than individual significance, becomes, in fact, symptomatic of a larger change of attitude, which has its roots in a revaluation not only of Forster but of modernism as well.

To speak of a revaluation and, by implication, of a devaluation of Forster is, I recognize, to invite a good many objections and a good deal of contrary evidence; and I'm more than willing to admit that there has been no perceptible slackening of academic interest in him or in his works. Indeed, given the critical activity surrounding both in recent years—the eleven volumes that have so far appeared of the late Oliver Stallybrass's Abinger Edition, Furbank's illuminating biography, and Frederick P. W. McDowell's compendious and intelligent bibliography of secondary writings, not to mention the steady outpouring of books, essays, and conference papers—given all this, it might plausibly be argued that we are in the midst of a Forster boom. But whether, to return to Wilson's remark one last time, Forster and the values associated with him retain outside the academy the vitality and influence they once possessed is another and more complex matter; and it's perhaps more to the point I'm making to note that Forster is not for contemporary *writers* the presence he so obviously was for the young men of the thirties and even for novelists and poets of later decades. The voice that appeared at one time, and not so long ago, to speak with such quiet authority, the more persuasive for its hesitant and tentative discriminations, seems to have grown fainter or (to call upon Renata Adler's narrator again: "There they all are, however, the great dead men with their injunctions. Make it new. Only connect") to have hardened into a tone designed for fussy, hectoring, and objectionable pronouncements.

Adler's reference to *Howards End* makes clear what I've already intimated, that Forster's "injunctions" are as much a property of the fiction as they were, according to Furbank, a feature of the man. In other words, the "figure" and the novels are after all—or seem to be—inextricable, and it is reasonable to assume that disenchantment with the one will, as in Wilson's case, entail a rejection of the other. But to accept this formulation is very likely to simplify both terms of the equation and, with it, the nature of modernism. That Forster *is* a modernist, as Adler's placing of him among "the great dead men" implies, needs perhaps to be stressed. The moralizing strain of the work notwithstanding and notwithstanding various of his critical positions—the deprecation of too great a concern with point of view;

the preference for the looser structural device of rhythm over the tighter organizational principle of pattern; and the talk of writers who bounce their readers and of novels that open out—Forster is fundamentally at one with his contemporaries in his formal concerns, in his allegiance to an aesthetic of art for art's sake, and in his sometimes unwitting pursuit of resolution and closure. Furthermore, and to turn the matter around, we are surely in a position now to recognize just how pervasive—if less overtly so than in Forster's writing—the moral impulse of modernism was, even in writers like Joyce and Woolf: to what a large degree form enacts in these works, even as it disguises, moral statement. It may well be, then, that what appears old-fashioned about Forster's fiction today derives not from the ubiquitous "moral generalisations" and their vehicle, his intrusive narrators, but from the too exacting translation of the need for order into inadequately realized or overly insistent redemptive characters and symbols (Stephen Wonham, Mr. Emerson, Mrs. Wilcox, Pan, the egregious hay of *Howards End*) and into shapes that belie and at times coerce the tensions of the works they enclose.

To recognize these tensions is, I'm suggesting, to learn to read Forster differently—can one do otherwise after the publication of the posthumous fiction, particularly the homosexual stories of *The Life to Come*? And it is just possible that in forgoing some of our assumptions about the novels' and stories' aesthetic coherence we will discover heretofore unrecognized levels of complexity, which make of the books, if less perfect and autonomous creations, at any rate a more authentic record of Forster's (and modernism's) struggles. No doubt there is an apparent danger in this enterprise of sacrificing literature on the altar of psychology; and I may be accused of making a silk purse *into* a sow's ear—worse, of proclaiming the sow's superiority. My concern, however, is not with the origins of Forster's contradictory impulses as they are to be discovered in the events of his life but with their manifestation, their inscription, in the very fabric and texture of his fiction: a concern, in short, not with the man behind but with the figure *in* the works, who, more and more with the passage of time, appears to act out, in defiance of those works' implied claim to finality (and of Trilling's neat summary) a variety of different and incompatible roles.

None of the fictions is free of these contradictions, not even the minor and major triumphs, *Where Angels Fear to Tread* and *A Passage to India,* that frame Forster's career as a novelist; and the rest, I'm tempted to assert, retain their interest in direct proportion to the irresolutions they manage (barely) to contain, the tensions they (inadvertently) define. *A Room with a View* remains a charming and genial fairytale, provided one is willing to ignore the problems raised by the presence of George Emerson, just as *Howards End,* so long as one chooses to focus on Margaret Schlegel, represents a memorable attempt to register the difficulties inherent in the effort to achieve satisfactory personal relations. But the resonance, the fascination of these books has its source elsewhere: precisely in those characters—George with his everlasting Why, Helen Schlegel with her never fully explored intimations of the abyss—who threaten to negate the ostensible tendencies and destinations the novels too facilely proclaim. As for *The Longest Journey* and *Maurice,* the books that meant most to Forster himself, they are, or so it seems to me, almost unreadable today—unless, that is, one opts to view them, even more than the other fiction, as battlegrounds of contending values and aspirations. The metaphor is commonplace but accurate: from first to last, the fiction reveals an internecine warfare, in which Forster's moral stance is increasingly undermined and finally subverted (if never, in either case, completely), first by an awareness and then, in part, by an acceptance of life's and the self's profound disunities.

Seen in other and, for my purposes, more relevant terms, Forster's career portrays the progression and interrelations of the century's different ironic modes, as mediate gives way to disjunctive and disjunctive to suspensive irony. This is again to make things too neat, of course, and in several ways. To the degree that Forster's irony is satiric, irony and morality coalesce, but, except in some of the earlier stories, the moral imperatives never issue forth unshadowed by forces that threaten to disrupt the hegemony of a corrective and stabilizing consciousness. It follows that in most of Forster's fiction Adler's "injunctions" are less the expression of a serenity so assured as to impose itself on others in the form of a minatory *sagesse* than they are the reflexive response to an intuition of disjunctions only partly and unwillingly acknowledged by Forster as determining factors of his more urgent vision. Furthermore, as we become familiar with that urgency, we come to recognize as well that Forster's irony generates the compensations not only of an integrating morality but of a more anarchic, freewheeling desire; and if the former contribute to the novels' visible structure and immediately audible voice, the latter, hidden or at least disguised, constitute the subtexts of the fiction: the dimension of what cannot, even in the posthumous *Maurice,* be said directly—at least not until, in some of the final stories, desire is liberated at last, revealing itself not as anything so simple as the homosexuality that covertly informs a number of the earlier novels but as the release from a whole range of constraints that consciousness, usually with marginal success, dictates throughout the fiction.

The amorality or, more properly, the new morality of these stories (oddly, in this last phase of his career, morality and irony, both reconstituted, more or less come together again for Forster) is not, however, a feature of all the work in *The Life to Come*; and one ought not to be surprised, in the light of what has been said, to discover even at the end a vacillation between different forms or dreams of self-realization. In fact, the vacillations, the tensions, the contradictions are, as I read it, the very meaning of Forster's life's work, which lies not in its unstable resolutions but in the intensity of its desperate search; and, in turning now to a more specific examination of some of the novels and stories, I want—not as a fashionable exercise in deconstruction but by way of recovering, salvaging, what seems to me the essential Forsterian spirit—to focus on this inconstant constant that manifests itself, variously, in the contention of consciousness and desire, in the shifting moral impulses the works reveal, and, above all, to come to the controlling perspective of the sections that follow, in the persistent intensities of Forsterian irony (even when most seemingly comic and assured) and of the anironic countervisions it calls into existence.

COSMOS, CHAOS, AND CONTINGENCY

The moral Forster is nowhere more in evidence in than *Where Angels Fear to Tread*, which, in its mediate irony, is among the most coherently satirical of his works. Written with an exuberance that even the most sanguine of the later novels lack (perhaps one ought to make an exception of the still earlier conceived *A Room with a View*), *Where Angels Fear to Tread* testifies to Forster's faith, as he later recalled it, that a "new age had begun" and to Leonard Woolf's that society "should [and would in the future] be free, rational, civilized, pursuing truth and beauty." Clearly, there existed in the early years of the century a group, whatever its size, sharing common standards and aspirations and furnishing that community of belief upon which satire depends. Whether Forster's first novel conforms completely to Woolf's revolutionary fervor or indeed to his own optimism is another matter; and it may be best at this point to state again that, however congenial to him throughout his career, satire proved a confining and often inadequate vehicle for his fundamental sense of life's complexity. Nevertheless, although it ultimately exposes the limits of what he was able to do with the form, *Where Angels Fear to Tread* obviously intends to be, and in some respects at least approximates the condition of, a satiric novel—holding up to ridicule as it does, through its controlled and witty verbal strategies, the triviality, complacency, and dishonesty of the lives exposed in its pages and, more importantly, presenting as the basis for its attacks a comprehensible and coherent world, embodied in the symbolically central figure of Gino Carella.

Gino and his city give a definite shape to the universe of *Where Angels Fear to Tread,* encompassing, as Philip sees it, everything between heaven and hell or between "the sun or the clouds above him, and the tides below." The novel's world may be mysterious and terrible, but it is ultimately limited and contained: an extrapolation (in Pierre Francastel's terms) from a "cube scénographique au centre duquel se déplace l'homme-acteur," "l'image d'une Nature distincte de l'homme, mais à la mesure de l'homme et de ses réactions." Though he is seen by Caroline at one point as "greater than right or wrong," almost a transcendent force, Gino is very much of *this* world, conceived "à la mesure de l'homme," extending but also defining its boundaries.

In other words, Gino is the image of nature in the novel, and despite his occasional brutality (or because of it) a symbol of cosmos, of order. But his order is not Sawston's, and his function is not only to articulate the human limits of *Where Angels Fear to Tread* but to give its world a sense of dimension, to ratify its concern with views, which are as central to this as to Forster's other Italian novel. "Astride the parapet, with one foot in the loggia and the other dangling into the view," Gino exists, without being aware of it, in spatial and moral depth. He is part of the view, at one with, perhaps identical with, the phenomenal world and the world of value into which he merges. As contrasted with the superficial, morally conventional life of Sawston, Monteriano embraces, stretches, unifies (most notably at the opera), absorbing and accepting the melodramatic moments that are part of the texture of its life.

I've suggested already that in *Where Angels Fear to Tread* irony functions largely as a rhetorical weapon in the armory of satire. But the novel reveals as well another kind of irony: the perception of disparities or incongruities inherent in the very nature of existence and consequently resistent to the corrective thrust of satire. Furthermore, this other, disjunctive irony can be seen as the response to as well as the perception of a discontinuous and fragmented world, a world lacking order and coherence and, finally, meaning, as meaning is increasingly located not objectively in the cosmos but subjectively in the eye of the beholder. Longing to cross the gulfs and abysses that scar the landscape of modernist literature, the ironist (Francastel's "l'homme-acteur") is trapped in the dubious safety of distance and uninvolvement.

Gino stands outside this kind of irony. As the vehicle of Forster's satiric vision, he makes clear that the aim of the satire in the novel is to break down barriers, to achieve through a sort of transparency or harmonizing unity a coherence that will make more radical ironies impossible. But Gino is less a solution than an ideal. Like his opposite number, Harriet Herriton, who has no view, no ability to see in depth, Gino is, for very different reasons, irrelevant to the whole problem of disjunctive irony. Absorbed in depth, as she is excluded from it, he has only a limited bearing on the problems raised by Philip, Caroline, and the narrator. Thus, though he continues to mediate Forster's satiric vision to the end of the novel, he comes to seem increasingly less effective as he is juxtaposed with these figures, who, standing on the periphery of the view, can recognize but cannot come to terms with the depth it is Gino's function to express.

Possibly unintended, these more recalcitrant ironies become apparent as soon as one moves to the more general level of moral inquiry on which much of the novel is conducted. So, in the principal normative statement of *Where Angels Fear to Tread,* the narrator contrasts "a sense of beauty and a sense of humour" with "human love and love of truth," a suspiciously resounding collocation of what C. S. Lewis once called "the great abstract nouns of the classical English moralists." Indeed, these abstractions, called upon to carry more conceptual freight than they can easily bear, produce in the reader a sense of slightly blurred vision, and one is hard put to specify the values they are meant to designate. Granted that Philip does in fact transcend the unpleasantness of his early laughter and the crudity of his youthful art-worship, still, more fundamentally, the trajectory of his short career reveals some puzzling insights into Forster's hypothetical ideal. That Philip's instruments in attaining truth are in fact an ingrained irony and what I've elsewhere called "the aesthetic view of life" (that is, variants of what he presumably leaves behind), may be put down to Forster's own deliberate irony at the expense of the limited growth of his ironic protagonist. But it is more difficult to rationalize one's perception that love and truth are not, as Forster's formulation of the ideal suggests, coordinate but disjunctive.

Truth may be granted to Philip, if the word is meant to suggest his increase in self-knowledge and his ability, as the book ends, to "see round" the whole situation "standing at an immense distance." But the abortiveness of his love for Caroline seems, in the final analysis, less the result of circumstance or even of character than of Forster's failure to realize the implications of that love—or, indeed, of Caroline's for Gino. It is difficult to overlook a sense of distaste for sexuality, evident in Philip's thoughts and in Caroline's hysteria, more difficult still to avoid the conclusion that Forster has constructed a fable of impossibility: the offer of love *or* truth—but not both.

What is at issue then is not simply the awareness of "the complexity of life," which Philip and Caroline share, but, more ambiguously, Forster's own notion of human relationships.

Early in the novel, the narrator describes, as a central feature of Italian life, "that true Socialism which is based not on equality of income or character, but on the equality of manners." The passage goes on to envisage the possibility of a relationship as close as David's and Jonathan's, because free from "feminine criticism and feminine insight and feminine prejudice." My point is not, to return to Caroline for a moment, simply that her love is frustrated by her exclusion from this world of masculine camaraderie (as Lilia's to a large degree is), any more than it seems to me adequate to explain away her retreat in terms of the mores of 1905. The problem hinges, surely, on the word "manners," which suggests first and inevitably the drawing-rooms of Sawston. The manners of Italy are very different of course: in the open-air world of the piazza, "in the democracy of the *caffè*," rooms and walls are dissolved, the domesticities of Sawston overturned, transparency and union achieved in "the brotherhood of man." But is the ideal proposed here any less artificial than the decorums of Sawston? "He will spit and swear, and you will drop your h's," the narrator comments, presenting, it would seem, a rather paltry end-product of socialism, democracy, and the brotherhood of man. It appears that we have been offered not a transcendence of but merely an opposition to Sawston, an inversion of its values; and, as a corollary, too feeble a structure to support the weight of the novel's satire.

In fact, it makes a good deal more sense to read the passage as a comment not on brotherhood but on sexuality, specifically homosexuality, and more concretely still, on a particular kind of homosexual relation. "He achieved physical sex very late," Furbank writes of Forster, "and found it easier with people outside his own social class." Seen in these terms, everything in the passage falls into place: David and Jonathan, the destructive "feminine insight," and not least the (Italian) spitting and swearing and the more verbal, passive *h*-dropping of that "you" (Philip, Forster, or the English reader?) who deliberately, artificially remakes his manners to achieve (I am quoting Furbank again) "a kind of private magic . . . an almsot unattainable blessing, for which another person was merely a pretext." What hope for Caroline, then, in a book where the unacknowledged truth is sex and in which sex is finally seen as antithetical to love?

I want to make clear my major point here, which is *not* that Caroline as a woman can find no fulfillment in the homosexual world of the piazza. Indeed this observation seems to me trivial as compared with what is implied by the opposition of character and manners. "Equality of manners" is the end-product of a reductive process, a stripping away of all that individualizes two sexual partners, a minimal, anonymous unity achieved by the suppression of complexity. But Caroline cannot forgo her complexity to join with Gino any more than she can retain it and love the disconsolate Philip; for if "equality of character" implies the possibility (and no more) of love, it also entails self-consciousness, division, and an irony more subversive than any implied by Forster's intended satire. If it is too simple to substitute sex for truth in Forster's formula, then truth needs perhaps to be seen as the incompatibility between love and sex: an ironic intuition of disconnection that shadows almost all of Forster's fiction.

There is, I'm aware, a danger of making too much of the passage I've been commenting on. And yet it seems to me that the total effect of the novel, as articulated in its various techniques, substantiates my reading of it. The predominance of air, light, and view notwithstanding, *Where Angels Fear to Tread* is a sad and chilly book, a novel whose tensions are held in check but not resolved. The sadness, no doubt, is intentional: a conscious and normative irony directed at the protagonists of the story, who have learned much but accomplished little. The lack of warmth and the sense of irresolution are another matter. Forster's signature is partly stylistic, partly narrative, and each of his techniques is in effect double. So the essentially paratactic style is at odds with the predilection for rhetorical figures and occasional high-sounding words and, too, with the addiction to inverted sentence order. The effect of this overlay of slightly old-fashioned elements on a predominantly simple syntax is to create a sense of a voice both fastidious and mannered, a combination which, for all the apparent intimacy of that voice, helps to keep the reader and the characters as well at a distance. Philip, we are told, "always adopted a dry satirical manner when he was puzzled," and the description suits Forster's tone too, if one allows for occasional modulations into enthusiasm and sentimentality.

As for Forster's notorious melodrama, the appearance of violent moments in the context of the book as a whole suggests, paradoxically, a quality of containment. The incidents themselves threaten to explode Forster's world, but the violence of imagination is constantly checked by the coolness of the treatment, by the disconcerting flatness with which even the most emotional incidents are described. The distance from the events (like that from the characters) makes for an understated power in the novel, but it also confirms, through its tonal and stylistic checks, Forster's resemblance to Philip. Viewing his fictional world aesthetically and (to use the word with all of its modernist resonance) ironically, Forster creates more light than warmth; and there is some question as to whether the novel itself manages to express the "human love" its author apparently desires.

The problem of "love of truth" is more complex still. The sexual question apart, it is clear from the start that the very search for truth is compromised by the blurred perspective Forster adopts in his pursuit of it. The stable foundations of satire contrast with the subjective, shifting ground on which disjunctive irony rests. And to acknowledge the transformation of the one into the other (or the uneasy balance between them) is to recognize that an apparently ordered world is about to give way: the objective standard of a solid, essentially unchanging world is threatened by the ambiguous, personal vision of a world in flux. In short, irony, unmoored from satire, becomes autonomous—a vision of the universe held together only in the troubled consciousness of the individual observer. Nevertheless, what is finally important about *Where Angels Fear to Tread* in Forster's career is that, at this stage, these two perspectives are able, however tenuously, however fragilely, to coexist, providing at least an aesthetic coherence Forster was not always able to achieve in his succeeding novels. My aim here, however, is not to pursue all of the byways in the development of Forster's irony. The high road leads to *A Passage to India,* where both the nature of the observation and the sense of control undergo a definitive change. In the metaphysical universe of Forster's final novel, modernist irony, absolute at last, is the dominant vision.

In *A Passage to India,* the humanized conception of a three-dimensional, orderly universe gives way to something vastly larger and less comprehensible. Space and time as well are defined no longer "à la mesure de l'homme" but in terms of infinity and eternity. And if the narrator comments at one point that "vastness [is] the only quality that accommodates them to mankind," it is because man has tried to make over even these ultimate abstractions into analogues of "Heaven, Hell, Annihilation—one or other of those large things, that huge scenic background of stars, fires, blue or black air." But for Forster and for Mrs. Moore, who "in the twilight of the double vision" after the caves, "can neither ignore nor respect Infinity," there is behind the blue or black air only emptiness, silence, and indifference. Distances in Forster's final novel are incomparably greater than in *Where Angels Fear to Tread*; depth has become a bottomless abyss. Beyond the arches and vaults of the book, there is "that further distance . . . last freed itself from blue." Over and over, among the negatives that thread the novel together, the eye seeks rest in a perspective that offers no point of convergence but only "an impartiality exceeding all." With the dissolution of Forster's earlier cosmos, nothing any longer contains—except "the echoing walls," which drive the characters back into the uneasy worlds of their own consciousnesses.

Fielding's momentary belief "that we exist not in ourselves, but in terms of each other's minds" may stand as a symbol for how the self responds to the de-anthropomorphizing of the universe. From the first chapter, where the views of Chandrapore form and reform with changes of perspective, the relativism of human perception asserts itself. In the land of the hundred Indias, truth is splintered; the pretension to it, the subject of the narrator's bitterest scorn. And the conception of love as rape and (in Mrs. Moore's disillusioned thoughts) as "centuries of carnal embracement" completes, notwithstanding the more hopeful relations of the novel, the reduction of "human love and love of truth" almost to the point of travesty. Forster's outlook has become, in short, ironic in a way that *Where Angels Fear to Tread* only begins to suggest. Which is to say that *A Passage to India* articulates a vision of life in which everything disappoints or deceives; in which appearances are equivocal and the possibility of a reality behind them at best a question; in which all things are subject to interpretation, depending upon how, where, and in what mood they are perceived; in which, at the extreme, meaning, no longer supported by value, is dissolved "into a single mess" and even the extraordinary is reduced to nothing.

The word "nothing" echoes through the novel, undermining, like the winds and airs in the middle section of *To the Lighthouse*, all pretension to human structure. But ... I've called irony absolute in *A Passage to India* not primarily because of its despairing vision, which is common to all disjunctive irony, but because of its form. Central to Forster's novel is the unresolvable dilemma—not the disparity between right and wrong or real and pretended on which satire thrives, but the discordant and equal poise of opposites. So in Forster's meditation on unity, carried on through the description of the two well-meaning missionaries, the irony is only superficially at the expense of Mr. Sorley, who "admitted that the mercy of God, being infinite, may well embrace all mammals." More fundamental and more unsettling is the awareness that inclusion and exclusion are alike impossible. It is, as I have suggested in my book on Forster, between these poles that the drama of *A Passage to India* takes place: the factitiousness of any attempt to impose order on the one hand and, on the other, the recognition of the unbounded as the chaotic. "In our Father's house are many mansions," but "We must exclude someone from our gathering, or we shall be left with nothing."

Nothing again; and inevitably one comes to the caves: "Nothing, noth-

ing attaches to them"; "Nothing is inside them . . . if mankind grew curious
and excavated, nothing, nothing would be added to the sum of good or evil."
The use of the caves to symbolize the infinite and eternal is in itself ironic.
The small, discrete, claustrophobic enclosures are made to represent their
apparent opposite, the limitless, formless, agoraphobic universe both because
men "desire that . . . infinity have a form" and because, as in the Kawa Dol,
which is at the same time something and nothing, the extremity of opposition
is identity. In the caves, immeasurable space and immeasurable time are
flattened out in Mrs. Moore's horrified awareness that "everything exists,
nothing has value."

With this sentence, we come to the heart of Forster's irony, as it manifests itself in his final novel. In the disconnection between existence and
value; in the failure of simultaneity to entail relation; in the disappearance
of the dimension that value and relation imply, there is a collapse of the
book's various metaphorical "bridges" and a confirmation of its pervasive
"gulfs." And there is a collapse too of that depth and of those views that
shape the cosmos of *Where Angels Fear to Tread*. "Visions are supposed to
entail profundity, but—," the narrator adds, "The abyss also may be petty."
The repeated emphasis on smallness, when what is at issue are the incon-
ceivable reaches of the universe, has to do with the final reduction of meaning
to a neutral coexistence in chaos. The amorphous and the illimitable come
together when "the horror of the universe and its smallness are both visible
at the same time." We are, in short, in a world of surfaces, where appearances, unresonant and reflexive, signify no meanings beyond themselves and
where life, nonprogressive in its linear disconnection, "went on as usual but
had no consequences."

The reduction of the metaphysical to the temporal and spatial dimensions of the caves parallels the transposition, accomplished through the mediation of consciousness, of the metaphysical into the psychological. Like the
Anglo-Indians retreating from the implacable sun, the self, confronted with
the silence of Forster's infinite spaces, folds in on itself. Viewed subjectively—
and how else to view it when everything is "infected with illusion"?—the
universe dwindles into Mrs. Moore's cynicism and Fielding's solipsism. If
microcosm and macrocosm retain, conceptually and aesthetically, a metaphorical correspondence, effectively, self and world are disjoined. As J. Hillis
Miller puts it: "When God and the creation become objects of consciousness,
man becomes a nihilist. Nihilism is the nothingness of consciousness when
consciousness becomes the foundation of everything." In the shadow of the
caves, the lesson of the Marabar is internalized, and causality gives way, with

signification, to the terrified vision of simple contiguity: "Pathos, piety, courage—they exist, but are identical, and so is filth."

The perception of life as mere surface is a prefiguration of *The Life to Come* in the same way that the personal relationships of Forster's first novel look forward to those of his last. I'll return more fully to the question of depth and surface later on; but to a degree it bears on the human level of *A Passage to India* as well. The two paradigms of relating, mooted in *Where Angels Fear to Tread,* are here both clarified (to a degree) and polarized. Fielding and Adela, we are told, "spoke the same language, and held the same opinions, and the variety of age and sex did not divide them"; and of Ronny and Adela, the narrator similarly comments: "Experiences, not character, divided them." As defined by Adela's relations with the two men, "equality of character" comes to suggest an essentially static conception of character: predicated on the acceptance of the self; grounded on the belief in the possibility of rational understanding; and threatened both by the eruption of unacknowledged emotions and, more simply, by the conjunction of love and sex. Forster's strategy is to show that those who assume the stability of the ego are precisely those threatened by the depths of their own personalities. The intention, however, is not simply to expose the incompleteness of reason (Adela's imperious need to *know*) but, more profoundly, to test conventional notions of psychological depth (as he tests those of metaphysical depth in the caves) in order to reject them.

The point needs further explanation, involving as it does still another paradox. The relationships that dramatize "equality of manners" (Aziz's with Mrs. Moore, with Ralph, and with Fielding) are precisely those that seem, in their acceptance of mystery, instinct, and intuition, to arise from and to thrive on depth. But Aziz's friendships are not an answer to Adela's inability to touch bottom; they suggest, rather, a revolt against psychology, character, and the ego. Based not on being and knowing but on acting and doing, they are a pushing away from conventional psychological depth toward a new kind of human surface, as yet only partly realized in *A Passage to India*. In any case, one begins to see that Forster repeatedly constructs his ideal fictional relationships (the earlier stories and novels, particularly, as we shall see, *Maurice*, provide examples too) in terms of some initial abrasiveness—race, religion, class, age, nationality—which, overcome, yields what is, in essence, not the acceptance of the self but a creation of a new and desired self.

To a degree at least, the characters themselves consciously share Forster's belief. Aziz thinks of Fielding and Mrs. Moore: "He loved them even better

than the Hamidullahs because he had surmounted obstacles to meet them."
And in his last ride with Fielding, he turns aside his friend's attempt at
personal conversation and begins deliberately, almost artificially, the political
argument that leads to the assertion of friendship with which they part. The
novel's ending is a reminder, however, that the achievement of "equality of
manners" depends not only on the transcendence of old patterns of relationship and the transformation of the self but still more on a conception of the
universe in which the self can find its fulfillment. Where there is existence
but no value and where, as Lawrence implied of Forster, there remains the
desire to act on a belief no longer believed in, love, friendship, and sex alike
are futile.

It will be objected at this point, rightly, that I have arrived at the end
of the novel without more than a glance at its third, Hindu section. So much
has been written on the issue of "whether *A Passage to India* reveals a
pessimistic or optimistic view of the universe," that I am reluctant to stir
the pot once again. Something, however, needs to be said about the relation
of "Temple" to the question of irony. Frederick McDowell has written that
the Indian essays in *Albergo Empedocle and Other Writings* "weight the
balance . . . in favor of anti-rationalist, pantheistic, mystical, religious, and
quasi-Hinduistic interpretations of the novel." And he notes, correctly I
think, that the essays counteract Forster's remarks in *The Hill of Devi*. I am
more willing than I once was to admit that the *desire* for what Hinduism
represents throbs through the novel as the most perfect consummation of
that transformation of the self I've already referred to. And no doubt my
concentration on the caves has obscured the change in mood (signaled by
the reappearance of views) that part 3 represents.

Still and all, even before we arrive at "Temple," we are back on the
horns of a dilemma no less potent than, indeed related to, the inclusion-
exclusion paradox of part 1. If Mrs. Moore's perceptions as she travels back
across India and Fielding's as he returns to Venice represent a reassertion of
phenomenal reality independent of the transfiguring self, a return to depth;
then Godbole and his Hinduism, already anticipated in Fielding's conversation with Aziz, are a denial of it. Forster's assertion that the Hindu festival
represents the same thing as the scene in the cave "turned inside out" seems
to me to suggest not a disavowal but an alternate view of the meaning of the
Marabar: a shift of perspective, which equivocally suspends questions of true
and false. Throughout the novel, possibilities are mooted, but desire is not
realization; and it is no easier for the reader to fix Forster's meaning than it
is for Godbole to prolong his vision.

If I seem by now, in my attempt to question the legitimacy of reading

"Temple" as a plunge into oneness, to be questioning as well my reading of "Caves," it is what I intend. The lesson of the criticism of the last fifteen years or so seems to me to be that, thematically considered, *A Passage to India* can be made to yield totally opposed and equally valid interpretations and that on this level no argument is ever likely to be accepted as final. I wrote some years ago, in a mildly existentialist reading of the novel, that, at its close, *A Passage to India* directs the reader back to life. It appears to me now that, more powerful than any suggestion of thematic open-endedness is the effect, described in the last chapter, of formal closure. In short, it is neither in the explication of its discursive content nor in the exegesis of isolated symbols that the key to the novel is to be found but in an examination of its pervasive and controlling technique.

Beginning with the opening sentence of the novel, in which, subtly but firmly, syntax establishes a dizzyingly ironic focus for the reader, Forster's strategy emerges. If Forster's cosmology undergoes a radical change between his first and last novel, the comparison of technique suggests an intensification rather than an alteration of basic approach. To put this another way, the collapse of Forster's earlier world seems to have called forth not a corresponding transformation in aesthetic form but, by way of compensation it would seem, a firmer sense of control. The result, predictably, is an enormous tension in the novel, manifest first of all in the style, whose still essentially paratactic structure supports and holds in check a texture that, in the density of its images and symbols, of its diction generally, is so much richer and fuller than that of the first novel and, too, so much more restrained. With the first view of Chandrapore, the urbane and cultivated voice of the narrator establishes his distance from the scene, the reductive tone expressing, along with the distance, a certain distaste. Matching the abundant stylistic qualifications—the careful *excepts, rathers,* and *thoughs*—the tone, for all its apparent casualness, is ultimately self-conscious, academic, fussy, almost precious in its attempt to produce "the coin that buys the exact truth [which] has not yet been minted."

And so it is throughout the book. His tone verging at times on cynicism, the narrator continues to play down what is positive, to question what is taken for granted, to qualify what is whole. Laying out his narrative as a series of tableaux, discrete and contained despite the violence of the action they describe, he is the embodiment of artistic control surveying an incomprehensible world. Nothing within *A Passage to India* but *A Passage to India* itself is Forster's "self-contained harmony," which gives "us the illusion of perspicacity and of power." Thus it is that, as one comes to "Temple," the ubiquitous irony of the novel plays over Hinduism, as over everything else, enforcing and at the same time questioning its own paradoxes. Forster's description, very near the end of the novel (and anticipating its "No, not yet," "No, not there"), of the "emblems of passage" expresses perfectly the attitude of aesthetic poise: "a passage not easy, not now, not here, not to be apprehended except when it is unattainable." Like this fragment, the book as a whole achieves a stasis of equivocation: the accumulated negatives playing off against the imagination of desire. Suspended between the equally valid polarities of "nothing" and "extraordinary," *A Passage to India* is not so much open-ended as forever ironic in its simultaneous and equal assent to the contradictory possibilities man can entertain. If the fictional world of *Where Angels Fear to Tread* is chilly, *A Passage to India* is (like Virginia Woolf's *The Waves*) frozen, its "wintry surface" directing us, finally, back to itself through the extraordinary perfection of its art.

When Sir Richard Conway, surveying the remainder of his dull, country weekend, thinks to himself: "The visit, like the view, threatened monotony," he gives perfect expression to Forster's sense of ordinary existence in *The Life to Come*. Not the metaphysical terror of the caves but the monotony of "normal" life serves as the background of these stories, and their heroes, unlike Mrs. Moore or Fielding, who react by a movement inward, accept that monotony as an inevitable part of life's texture, while actively accommodating themselves to what are now seen (in a dramatic reversal of Forster's attitude in his last novel) as the intermittent pleasures of life's surface. At least, most of them do. Of the stories I am concerned with (those which, according to the dates offered in Oliver Stallybrass's admirable edition, were composed at about the same time as or later than *A Passage to India*), three deal with love. Significantly, "The Life to Come," "Dr. Woolacott," and "The Other Boat," which I'll examine in greater detail later on, are closer in feeling and strategy to Forster's earlier work. More ambitious and morally more ambiguous than the other five stories, they are also more obviously sentimental, sometimes, as in the opening of "The Life to Come," embarrassingly so. And in the first two at least, the attempt to render love leads to a style that is poetic by intention, yet curiously flat, thin, and conventional.

More striking is that fact that each of these stories ends with death. And although it is possible, given their orthodox psychology, to regard the endings as inevitable effects of causes specified in the stories, it is difficult to avoid the sense that what is being revealed more clearly still is a psychological pattern in Forster. If *Maurice* is predicated on a happy ending, these stories express the more typical lure of failure in matters of homosexual love. Or, rather, not homosexuality as such but, as I've suggested, the conflation of love and sex. To combine the two is, in Forster's imaginative world, to invite, indeed to ensure disaster. To the last, as "The Other Boat" makes clear, Forster was unable to envisage the stability of complete human relationships in a universe of temporal and psychological change. What his imagination sought and intermittently found was a nondynamic world, freed from the impersonal determinations of causality as from the more subtle connections of love. It is, in part, the world to which the endings of many of the earlier fantasies (and of "Dr. Woolacott") unsatisfactorily point; it is also the world of the remaining five stories: "other kingdom" brought down to earth.

The deliberarte avoidance of love in this second group has as its corollary the acceptance of sex as sex and for the moment. What Forster is after is described perfectly in "Arthur Snatchfold" as "the smaller pleasures of life," a one-time affair conducted "with a precision impossible for lovers." "Equality of character" gives way totally in *The Life to Come* to a series of unequal confrontations; and now that physical contact is out in the open, the abrasiveness I spoke of earlier is still more apparent. Indeed, the looser, freer structures of most of the sexual stories create, for the first time, a fictional world congruent with the asymmetric relationships they celebrate—one in which the new allegiance to surface is revealingly defined by means of the curious psychological discontinuity that marks their heroes. Even in "The Other Boat," Lionel, in the midst of his affair, forgets "any depths through which he might have passed." In the sexual stories this habit of mind is endemic: characters forget the men to whom they have been attracted, with whom they have had an affair, indeed by whom they have been raped—thereby ignoring or refusing the depth implied by memory and created by continuity of feeling. In all these stories, depth—spatial, temporal, and psychological—is inessential, inimical, or impossible: a force operating against the disequality of character that is now more than ever a positive good, a barrier not to be minimized or ignored but to be pleasurably overcome.

But the relationships achieved make for an "equality of manners" that needs to be further defined with reference to Forster himself. Furbank's comment: "He valued sex for its power to release his own capacities for tenderness and devotion, but he never expected an *equal* sexual relationship" indicates that equality is, in fact and paradoxically, inequality: a peculiarly limited, discrete moment, in which connecting becomes coupling and love, of course, sex. It is in the contact alone that the participants are leveled—equal in their enjoyment of their unequal pleasures. And so it is in the stories.

Freed from sentiment, if not from sentimentality, they represent a movement from Forster's familiar "as if " to a very different "as it is": self joining with world in an unresonant acceptance of amoral pleasure.

It is part of the donnée of *The Life to Come* that pleasure remains the object of general disapproval, and so Forster continues to attack his old enemy Mrs. Grundy and her relations, who, in the chronological progression of the stories, go down to increasingly violent defeat. Each of the stories has its villain; all are the object of Forster's sometimes unpleasant satire, the corollary to the single-minded assertion of his ideal relationship. Where sex is refused or scorned or rejected, there is, in all eight of the stories, an eruption of violence and vengeance, darkened at times, as in the curious nastiness of "The Classical Annex," by the shadow of sado-masochistic impulses. But Forster's antipathies are more wide-ranging still. The cruelty directed at Hilda in "The Obelisk" derives presumably from Forster's rejection of her rhetoric of salvation, which, whether or not it was so intended, comes across as an inversion and parody of almost identical language in *Where Angels Fear to Tread*. Philip's attitude is clearly no more acceptable by now than his sister's. The search for romance and the mating of character, like the transformation of sex into idealized love, define the attitudes of those who cannot accept the smaller pleasures of life.

The passage of time obviously made imaginative assent to his sexual ideal more of a possibility for Forster. In "Arthur Snatchfold," the first of the group, Forster seems unable as yet to conceive of pleasure triumphant and unpunished, and the story in fact registers a defeat for the smaller pleasures. In the second story, the obelisk that symbolizes them may, in its fallen state, undermine the sense of phallic potency—though one would hardly judge so from the activities of its two sailors. But there is, in any case, no question about the other three stories, which are in every sense tumescent. Forster's rising joy is, however, no guarantee of the reader's sympathy. Unless one accepts the criteria that determine Forster's approval (and which so markedly exclude large areas of human needs and desires), it is hard to accept the repulsive Ernest of "The Obelisk" or the sadistic gladiator of "The Classical Annex" or even Mirko, Forster's generally attractive *porte-parole* in "What Does It Matter?" who includes among the things that do matter "baiting the Jews." All three are presumably meant to be "natural," but from Gino and Stephen Wonham onward, naturalness is more than a little suspect in Forster's writings: a Nietzschean temptation unrelieved, as it is in Gide, by a consistent moral alertness. And it is at the least curious that Forster can accept, if not approve, Mirko's statement.

Still, it is easy enough to see what Forster is after. "What Does It

Matter?" is subtitled "A Morality," and, along with Sir Richard and the
Roman Marcian, Mirko is the most genial expression of Forster's ethic: the
need for diversity and tolerance, especially in sexual matters. The Pottibak-
ians, "do[ing] as they like" inhabit Forster's utopia of activity and participation and acceptance. And so too does Marcian, after the destruction of
the basilica and its *virgo victrix* in "The Torque." The movement of the
story's final pages is, by way of the animals, who "clucked and copulated as
usual," away from Christianity and ascetic morality toward a "natural,"
sexual life, in which where he is is enough for Marcian. "There was nothing
to exorcize," the Bishop unhappily discovers, "and Marcian became gay and
happy as well as energetic, and no longer yearned nostalgically for the hills."
Despite its misplaced touch of fantasy at the end, "The Torque" attains to
Forster's final vision of the here and now. Marcian, with his take-it-as-it-
comes philosophy, is, along with Mirko, a natural inhabitant of a world
"equally dispossessed of good and evil" and thus immune to conventional
ethical categories.

Taken together, the sexual stories in *The Life to Come* define the final
stage of irony in Forster's work: an acceptance of contingency that is perhaps
best illustrated, by its absence, in the figure of Count Waghaghren, the villain
of "What Does It Matter?" and a man "unaccustomed to incidents without
consequence." Obliquely, the description hints at the suspensiveness of Forster's irony and at the priapic ethos of the sexual tales. For Forster's late
figures are, to repeat, men unconcerned with consequences; and the stories
explore and celebrate, precisely, a world without causality, sequence, or
depth. The results of this change of attitude, apparently so striking, need to
be recognized and understood. In the movement from cosmos to chaos and,
further, from the melancholy awareness to the feverish acceptance of surface;
from redemptive moments to desperate snatches of pleasure; from "the
power to love and the desire for truth" of "Albergo Empedocle" (and *Where
Angels Fear to Tread*) to the truth of that discordant sexuality heretofore at
least partly concealed in Forster's fiction, what has most strikingly disap-
peared is the all-embracing ideal of connection set forth in *Howards End*.
Along with the asymmetry of relationships comes, or seems to come, the
acceptance of randomness and multiplicity as the very definition and condition of life and its satisfactions; and, in the light of Forster's earlier work,
the acceptance is as radical as it is surprising. In *The Life to Come*, Forster
goes beyond not only *A Passage to India* but the prewar fiction of his chief
disciple, Christopher Isherwood. *The Berlin Stories* take place, as it were,
"in the cave": cosmos is gone, chaos is unthinkable; one tries (uncomfort-
ably) to live in time and space. But the overriding concern of Isherwood's

novels with disconnection and discontinuity implies the ability still to imagine the theoretical possibility of wholeness and unity as an ideal.

Forster's is a further step: not merely from logical sequence to simple succession but from surface conceived of as the limited and limiting prison of the self to the perception of it as the open ground of the self's sporadic but total fulfillment—an area something like what Wylie Sypher describes as "a visual field, which is quite unlike the visual world we 'know' . . . [and which] cannot be perceived all at once." In other words, we have moved into a world where, although everything continues to exist by contiguity alone, that state of affairs is now for the first time accepted and indeed welcomed. Looking back at the prewar years, W. H. Auden described the need for the writers of his generation to adopt irony as a style of writing and, it is implied, of living:

> And where should we find shelter
> For joy or mere content
> When little was left standing
> But the suburb of dissent?

The Life to Come positions itself quite differently: situated neither between heaven and hell, nor in the shadow of infinity, nor yet "in the cave," it exists, by intention at least, firmly in the midst of the suburb of *assent*.

To invoke the notion of assent at this point is to trespass on the problem of the anironic, a subject I want to explore in connection with Forster further along in this chapter; but there is no easy way of separating into discrete bundles the complementary visions of acceptance and assent: the ironic and anironic impulses that together define Forster's ultimate response (or, since my concern for the moment is still with the sexual stories, one aspect of it) to his world. The fact is that just as Forster's acceptance of contingency leaves behind, or seems to leave behind, mediate and disjunctive irony altogether, so it provides the basis for the anironic counterpart of suspensive irony, namely, the desire for unmediated experience, for direct participation in the world. And indeed, despite the continuation of satiric impulses, Forster is essentially the celebrator, not the critic, of the world he fictionalizes in his final stories. Furthermore, the total collapse of Forster's characteristic distance from his subject matter is, far more than in the love stories (though without their rhetorical infelicities) an assent to a unity achieved through "equality of manners" and "the smaller pleasures of life."

But as one begins to examine more closely the nature of these pleasures, something odd and unsettling emerges, which calls into doubt, as it does in the case of those later and lesser writers Forster adumbrates in *The Life to*

Come, both the thoroughgoingness of his acceptance and the vitality of his assent. To begin with the latter: as one surveys the opposite ends of Forster's career, taking as terminal points the stories in *The Celestial Omnibus* and those in *The Life to Come* that I've been discussing, it becomes clear that if the early ones express the need for love (compare again too the "human love" of *Where Angels Fear to Tread*) and the later ones for sex, still what is central to both is the idea: the *idea* of love, the *idea* of sexuality—Maîtresses de l'âme, Idées." And as the early stories subdue Pan, their tutelary and informing presence, into an urgency made conformable to the demands of consciousness, so the later, priapic tales, for all their often attractive exuberance, remain equally and curiously theoretical: blueprints of desire, amusing schemata of passion, which, because of their abstractness, qualify, in their comparatively decorous way, as at least quasi-pornographic.

Forster's assent is, then, something less than it seems at first glance: not genuine participation but, again, the *idea* of participation. But that is not all. Like the early stories, the later ones achieve their ends through a process of exclusion or substitution. Which is to say that Forster's suspensiveness is less genuine, less comprehensive than it appears; that a world of insupportable density and facticity has been replaced by a more manageable, because more abstract, version of it. Consequently, Forster's response to the dilemma of *A Passage to India* is less a transfiguration than an evasion of his earlier problem: the awareness that "everything exists, nothing has value" is not so much overcome and faced as it is neutralized by the foregrounding of occasional intensities at the expense of the random, incoherent world they imply. What purports to be a movement toward inclusion is in fact the extreme of exclusion: a spurious unity superimposed on a still fragmented world, whose fragmentation is only partly acknowledged. In short, the inadequacy of the sexual stories is twofold. On the one hand, Forster's earthly paradise speaks of assent, of passion, vigor, and sexuality, but the thinness of the dream belies its reality—if not the longing for it. On the other hand, and more importantly, the naturalization of Eden, which is what, in the context of Forster's career, the sexual tales represent, refuses at the last to recognize or to accept fully the background against which the new Eden is made to arise: the contingent world that is in fact its source and meaning. The resolute and deliberate affirmation of a small part of life's possibilities may be stoic or tragic—even and especially the origin of a limited joy. But to act, while celebrating local and discrete pleasures, as if the whole had been embraced and all its parts connected is a delusion and an illusion: the ground equally of pathos and, for the reader aware of the discrepancy between intention and result, of an irony of an altogether conventional kind.

The Life to Come bears most immediately on Forster's own earlier work, and it has already called forth reinterpretations and revaluations of it; but it has other implications as well, which become apparent when one views it in a larger context. The growing insistence in recent years that art is definitively rejecting depth involves not only an animus against ultimate realities and Newtonianly-ordered world views but a reassertion of the relationship between the self and the phenomenal world. "Il est clair, dès à présent," Francastel writes, celebrating the end of Renaissance space, "que le nouvel espace sera un espace construit davantage en fonction de nos comportements que de notre réflexion."

But the movement from *Sein* to *Dasein,* "the return to the surface," has assumed at least two radically different alternative forms. On the one hand, there are those writers who, beginning with an awareness of modernist irony, move beyond or transform it. In the writing of Merleau-Ponty, for example, with its repeated invocations of "horizons" or its notion of co-presence, there is implied, as in *Between the Acts,* a dynamic interaction of consciousness and world leading to a new kind of creation. The world suggested may be predicated on surface, but it is neither fragmented nor static nor flat—as Forster's so conspicuously is.

The Life to Come, on the other hand, predicts not phenomenological art and thought but figures such as Warhol and Robbe-Grillet, certain of the photo-realists, and, in general, those contemporary writers, both French and American, given to the celebration of reflexivity. As in the works of these novelists and artists, Forster presents a surface that is opaque and unresonant; and like the painters in particular, he points to the problem involved in the discrepancy between intention and response. Obviously less neutral than they, he resembles them, by way of his subject matter, in his manifest but not fully realized abandonment of the Arnoldian responsibility for seeing life steadily and whole. From "the smaller pleasures of life" to Campbell's soup cans the psychological and aesthetic leap is not that great; nor is it from Forster's ultimately drab assent to a comment made by one recent painter: "I'm not saying that what I picture is good or bad. It's up to the viewer to make his own response." Whether deliberately or not, the burden of commitment and subjectivity has been shifted to the reader or viewer— along with the recognition that in these cases the artist's uncertain acceptance of his content *is* the irony.

A less ambiguous but finally more evasive approach to the question of intention is to be found in the critical writings of Robbe-Grillet. The business of the novelist, he writes, is to record distances "and to insist further on the fact that these are *only distances* (and not divisions)." The implications of this statement are enormous. If there are no divisions, then all of the anguish of modernist literature is meaningless. Indeed, to see separation as disturbing is to assume that there is such a thing as depth or interiority or transcendence. But there is, in fact, only surface: "The world is neither significant nor absurd. It *is,* quite simply." The attitude is, again, one of acceptance, but the acceptance is achieved not, as in the case of Merleau-Ponty or the later Virginia Woolf, by a restructuring of the relations between self and world but by a semantic sleight-of-hand, whereby the ominous "division" becomes the neutral "distance."

Forster's strategy is the same: redefinition becomes the solution to the problem—in his case, the problem of connecting. The final irony of Forster's suspensive irony is, however, that in *The Life to Come* he does achieve a connection of sorts. But it is a connection by reduction: the joining of self and world at the expense of consciousness. Man is not incarnated in his body; he *is* body, his sexual self, finally an object, a thing. At the last, it is a sad, pinched, meager vision of life that *The Life to Come* expresses. "Give pain, give pleasure an outer body," a character thinks in *The Years,* "and by increasing the surface diminish them." The words suggest the impulse behind Forster's final stories, written one feels, not simply, as he acknowledged, "to excite [him]self " but for personal salvation. They may well have served their purpose, but the diminishing of pain is, inevitably, the circumscribing of pleasure as well.

DESIRE AND CONSCIOUSNESS

From the start, Forster's familiar ideal of permanent connection—which provides the not altogether solid basis for his belief in "personal relations"— is more or less openly subverted by an attraction to the pleasures of passing contact. Generally, connection is made to triumph. Only in *The Longest Journey* among the early books is a protest lodged, not without ambiguity, against "the code of modern morals," with its slogans of "Eternal union, eternal ownership"; and even in that novel "Romantic love" is acknowledged to be greater than Stephen Wonham's more prosaically independent notions about marriage. Still, Forster's occasional tributes to the discrete and discontinuous relationship, however much qualified, act (or should act) as potential threats to the reader's perception of his moral design, which, in the novels from *Where Angels Fear to Tread* to *Maurice* (1914), depends upon the possibility of integration. Divided against themselves, Forster's characters are invited to overcome *through* consciousness their consciousness of isolation in a disordered and incoherent world. Encouraged to "live in fragments

no longer" (*Howards End*), they are asked to undergo a process of transformation by adding to or absorbing into themselves the primitivist values
of the novels' symbolic figures and landscapes. Becoming is the goal of these
characters; choice the instrument Forster offers them; and their ambience,
"the sense of space, which is the basis of all earthly beauty" (*Howards End*).

In a world so conceived, there is, so far as personal relations are concerned, room for failure certainly but not for successes that abort the psychological depths and temporal continuities implied by the attainment of
"connecting." And yet both Forster and his characters entertain the notion
of just such final and depersonalized encounters. So Philip Herriton, in a
manuscript passage excised from *Where Angels Fear to Tread,* addresses
(with no irony intended either by him or by Forster) the "dear friends of
mine whom I have made in Italy! cabmen, waiters, sacristans, shop assistants,
soldiers . . ." and ends, after his perfervid praise of these chance, passing
acquaintances: "oh thank goodness, I shall never see one of you again!"
What is at issue (and there are connections to be made between this passage
and Philip's subsexual relationship with Gino) is an immediacy of gratification to which the discriminations of consciousness are antithetical and for
which the fact of essential personal disequality is prerequisite. Margaret Wilcox's praise of "eternal differences" is a civilized response to the difficulties
of human interaction, the tolerance of a consciousness secure in its own
individuality; Philip's unequal friendships are, rather, a welcoming of anonymity, an escape from the disintegrated self in the interplay of frictional
surfaces.

More revealing still are the remarks Forster makes in his own voice (or
in his narrator's) in *The Longest Journey*: "Love, say orderly people, can be
fallen into by two methods: (1) through the desires, (2) through the imagination. And if the orderly people are English, they add that (1) is the inferior
method, and characteristic of the South. It is inferior. Yet those who pursue
it at all events know what they want; they are not puzzling to themselves or
ludicrous to others; they do not take the wings of the morning and fly into
the uttermost parts of the sea before walking to the registry office." Two
rather large assumptions enclose Forster's analysis, namely, that both of the
"methods" he describes are properly called love and that both will inevitably
eventuate in marriage. The second may be merely a concession to Edwardian
proprieties; the first appears, in a fundamental way, to place Forster himself
among the orderly people he mildly ironizes. The fact is that Forster's early
novels display both a devotion to discriminations and a certain reluctance
or inability to pursue the implications of the abstractions that make the
discriminations possible. It is easy enough to understand in the context of

the novel what is meant by the contrast of the desires and the imagination; it is less easy to see why, since Rickie's method of falling in love inevitably invites disaster, the other is acknowledged as inferior.

The answer lies in a redefinition of Forster's terms. Forster's love is in fact desire; desire, sexuality; and imagination, love—or at least a form of it. Further, if imagination suggests the distortion of consciousness, desire implies its absence; and Forster at this point is no more able to accept unmediated desire (that is, sexuality) than he is able to imagine the successful combination of sex and love. Or at any rate to present it convincingly. Presumably Mrs. Elliot and her lover Robert are meant to suggest the ideal, but Forster's treatment of their relationship—a sketchy, discursive interpolation into the main body of the narrative—demonstrates how theoretical the ideal in fact is. Forster's early novels are filled with "moments" that resonate with sexual feeling or that displace sexuality with violence and death, but the major relationships of these books belie the idea of passion, subordinating it (where it is not rendered impossible) to "the comradeship, not passionate, that is our highest gift as a nation."

Paradoxes begin to emerge. Love is integrative for Forster, sex partial and temporary. Yet sexuality achieves for its brief moment a unity of desire for which connecting strives in vain. The assertion of consciousness, exigent in its demands for the total and enduring, produces the meager Lucy and George of *A Room with a View,* the devitalized Margaret and Henry Wilcox of *Howards End,* but nowhere the intensity of feeling of Helen Schlegel, for example, who is "led to that abandonment of personality that is a possible prelude to love." It is worth quoting at length the passage in which Forster comments on the incident of Helen's kiss, since nowhere else in his work is there so great a tension between the Edwardian moralist and the "amoralist" who emerges in *The Life to Come*:

> But the poetry of that kiss, the wonder of it, the magic that there was in life for hours after it—who can describe that? It is so easy for an Englishman to sneer at these chance collisions of human beings. . . . It is so easy to talk of "passing emotion," and to forget how vivid the emotion was ere it passed. Our impulse to sneer, to forget, is at root a good one. We recognize that emotion is not enough, and that men and women are personalities capable of sustained relations, not mere opportunities for an electrical discharge. Yet we rate the impulse too highly. We do not admit that by collisions of this trivial sort the doors of heaven may be shaken open.
>
> (*Howards End*)

Imagination or desire, to revert to Forster's terms for a moment? Both, obviously. The Paul who kisses Helen is no more "real" than the Agnes with whom Rickie falls in love. The object of the emotion has once again been misapprehended. But the emotion itself, the passage insists, is authentic. Desire and imagination coalesce; and that is precisely the point, or the beginning of it. Not only Forster's vocabulary but his problem needs to be reshaped. In the final analysis, what is central is neither the method of falling in love nor the reality of the object; it is instead the radical subjectivity of desire, revealed in the conflicting attempts of consciousness either to fulfill itself in "sustained relations" or to obliterate itself in the apocalyptic moment of "passing emotion."

But that is to simplify the problem. Forster's comment, in its carefully balanced, modulated progression, means to do full justice to "chance collisions" like Helen's, but only up to a point. As moral statement, its intention is not to ratify an equality of opposites but to assert the ultimate superiority of Margaret's efforts to connect. Rhetorically, however, the passage (which I have quoted only in part) tells another story. Its brief, normative defense dissolves into the two longer, fuller, and more lyrical tributes to poetry and magic by which it is surrounded and engulfed. And so with the novel as a whole: the manifest ideal of integration, buttressed by all of Forster's symbols and "harvest predictions," convinces less than the sisterly affection of Margaret and Helen on the one hand and Helen's sexual collisions on the other. In short, if, as I have suggested, the early novels in general demonstrate— though they are far from acknowledging—the incompatibility of love and sex, the series starting with *A Room with a View* and ending with *Maurice* are something more: a determined, conscious effort to strike a balance (the "proportion" of *Howards End*) between irreconcilables, thereby generating from the discordant vocabulary of prose and passion (to use Margaret's words) a logical syntax of desire.

There is, of course, some imbalance between the contrasted elements that subtend Forster's arc of desire. Margaret's "very good kind of prose," as she describes her feeling for Henry, is less vivid than Helen's electrical discharges, but it is more congruent with the novel's thrust toward an all-embracing harmony. As in *A Room with a View,* where Lucy seeks "equality beside the man she loved," so in *Howards End,* love and comradeship effectively take precedence over the sexuality that is theoretically part of the final amalgam. But in *Arctic Summer* (1911–12), as far as one can judge from the fragmentary nature of the book, and certainly in *Maurice,* the balance shifts toward the activation and realization of passion. Integration remains the objective, but the priority of the physical threatens to skew the ideal, to dissolve the complexity of becoming in the indivisible finality of passing emotion. *Maurice* does not quite do that, but its allegiance to connecting is precariously maintained. It, and not *Howards End,* as we can now see, is the last stage of Forster's early work: the final defense and also the implicit defeat of consciousness as the redeemer of a fragmented world.

The presumptive flight of Maurice Hall and Alex Scudder to the greenwood defines both the goal and the limits of Forster's novel. In Alec, or rather in the relationship with him, Maurice's "part brutal, part ideal" boyhood dreams resolve the familiar divisions of the earlier books. Initially the realization of Maurice's first dream of "a nondescript whose existence he resented," Alec is eventually meant to suggest the "friend" of the second dream as well. Yet for the reader he remains more persuasively the vital antagonist: if the comrade, then the *sexual* comrade of the greenwood. That is so because the greenwood itself remains so oddly vague. There is little in *Maurice,* not much more in the appended terminal note, to suggest its contours, although it is, as the note makes clear, the symbolic space toward which the whole of the novel moves. Inevitably one is reminded again of the early tales, in which characters repeatedly manage to leave their drab, confining situations for one or the other of Forster's "other kingdoms": those ecstatic and static enclaves beyond change and beyond choice, which are so congenial to his imagination. In them, one finds the clue to *Maurice,* for like "other kingdom," the greenwood is, even more than concept masquerading as symbol, a space of fictional absence; and it is the irony of Forster's most overtly sexual novel that it fails at the last quite literally to embody its abstract ideal.

But that is to get ahead of Forster's story. As Maurice's dark, confused "secret life" externalizes itself first in love for Clive Durham and then in sexuality, the novel recapitulates the shifting configurations of desire throughout Forster's prewar fiction. Clive, theoretical, platonic, is the aestheticizing heir of Forster's earliest protagonists, and the love he imposes on Maurice expresses perfectly both a recurrent Forsterian ideal and the limitations that preclude or diminish a variety of relationships elsewhere in the novels. It would no doubt be foolish to overlook the fact that Maurice and Clive are homosexual, but it would be a more egregious error still not to recognize that the problems inherent in Forster's treatment of homosexuality are only a specific instance of how his imagination responds to the conception of personal relations throughout his career. The value of *Maurice* lies in the opportunity it provided Forster to deal directly and openly with his

own desire; but there is no reason to believe that he regarded the psychological dynamics of homosexual and heterosexual love as different in kind—
or indeed to assume that they are. The analogues to Maurice and Clive are
to be found not in the quasi-sexual feelings of Philip for Gino or Rickie for
Stephen or in Mr. Beebe's watery release, but in that quite different and more
sober group of relations—Caroline and Philip, Rickie and Agnes, Martin
and Venetia, Ronnie and Adela—which assume, in Clive's words, that "it's
character, not passion, that is the real bond."

Clive's formula may be regarded as a rationalization after the fact of
his discovery that he is no longer homosexual (earlier his ideal had been
"love passionate but temperate"); but the contrast, as we have seen, is one
Forster himself—his personal sense of division possibly reinforced by Cambridge mentors and Bloomsbury friends—makes in effect from the time of
his first novel onward. Although the later, private stories move increasingly
toward the celebration of passion for its own sake, Forster's public declara-
tions carry on even more deliberately the defense of character, which is to
say, the stable self. So, in "What I Believe" he writes: "Psychology has split
and shattered the idea of a 'Person,' and has shown that there is something
incalculable in each of us, which may at any moment rise to the surface and
destroy our normal balance. . . . [but] For the purpose of living one has to
assume that the personality is solid, and the 'self' is an entity, and to ignore
all contrary evidence."

The solidity of character, the congruence of depth and surface, is in turn
the basis for Forster's defense of personal relationships, most notably in
Howards End and in the essay I've just quoted from. Of course, the Philips
and Carolines and the others whose relationships founder or fade do little
to sustain Forster's belief. And yet the love of Clive and Maurice, the paradigm of all the relations based on character, is such as to have led Noel
Annan to argue that "Forster does not deprecate or diminish this platonic
affair. For him it is as valid and as real as consummated love." In the context
of the novel as a whole, this is surely a misreading, but it is also testimony
to Forster's empathetic imagination. By now biographical reasons have become available to explain Forster's attitude (Annan speculates that he "had
never had a sexual affair until he was in his forties," that is, 1919 at the
earliest), but the published works offer sufficient evidence. The fictional de-
lineation of "personalities capable of sustained relations"—the stable self
defining itself through continuity in time—is meant as concrete proof that
connecting is possible: the sign of that ordered, coherent world Forster longed
for, even in the face of contrary evidence, throughout his life.

The words used to describe the love Maurice and Clive achieve—"consistent," "permanent," "affectionate," "sensible," "calm"—suggest the moderating deliberateness of consciousness. But they imply something more. "They themselves became equal," Forster writes of the two men; and it is, precisely, "equality of character" that defines the shape of their relationship. Not that they are in any obvious sense alike. The point is rather that their assumptions (more accurately, Clive's, which are accepted by the "humble and inexperienced and adoring" Maurice) are the same. Together they inhabit Margaret Wilcox's tolerant, rational, complex world of "eternal differences," in which Maurice, acknowledging his homosexuality, discarding his superficial religion, is able to grow without abandoning his outwardly "normal" life or the class structure he and Clive share. In short, Clive invites Maurice into a world without change, which, ironically, his own change destroys.

Clive's defection, however, important though it may be to Forster's plot, is not the central issue. His sympathy with the relationship notwithstanding, the price it exacts is one Forster is no longer able or willing to pay. It may be that for Maurice "the idealism and the brutality that ran through boyhood had joined at last, and twined into love"; but it is idealism that is in fact the keynote of their love, and idealism, as Forster now partly recognizes, is the disease of consciousness. Looking back from Clive to his many predecessors, one can see that character in Forster is not fate but a guard against it: an index to that inexorable demand for order and stability (Forster's as well as Clive's), which tempers passion with comradeship and transforms the integrating consciousness into self-conscious distance and restraint.

"Passion and the instincts," Lawrence's Birkin tells Hermione Roddice, "—you want them hard enough, but through your head, in your consciousness"; and the analysis of modernism's characteristic debility suits still better the fundamentally ascetic Clive. It is against the imperialism of the head that Forster launches his counterideal of total sexual union, and, as he does so, equability gives way significantly to violence. Though there are precedents in his earlier work, Forster nowhere else (until the stories of *The Life to Come*) delineates so strikingly as in Maurice's growing feeling for Alex Scudder the contours of a relationship generated out of antagonism. Maurice's feeling of cruelty as he first sees Alec; the altercation with him over the tip; the two suggestive scenes of his inadvertently "colliding" with the gamekeeper; and finally the blackmail episode, with its anger and threats—all make for an intensity of opposition that disrupts the continuities of consciousness and disintegrates the stable self.

To what end becomes apparent in the aftermath of the hostile encounter in the British Museum when the two men spend the night together. "Only a struggle twists sentimentality and lust together into love," Forster writes, and the redefinition of love, heretofore a twining of idealism and brutality, provides the necessary clue. The reductive weakening of the first term and the specific intensification of the second indicate that love is now sexuality and sexuality something altogether different, and in every way, from the earlier platonic love. For the stress throughout the second relationship on physical and mental struggle leads not only to the body's fulfillment but to a new psychic equilibrium. So, in the midst of the surface hostility of their encounter in the Museum, Maurice announces: "my name's Scudder"; and as Alec leaves him, presumably for the last time, he thinks: "In a way they were one person."

Oneness (or fusion) is for Forster a far more radical state than integration, comparable in its movement toward unity of some sort but otherwise virtually opposed: the substitution, one might say, of an irreducible finality for the hovering tentativeness of complexity. More fully articulated in *Maurice* than in the earlier novels, it reveals itself in retrospect as a potentiality of Forster's thought from the beginning. Like Philip Herriton, Maurice and Alec find in the anonymity of surface the body's answer to the too exigent mind. Oneness, then, is the reward of activity: the violence, lust, antagonism, and "reaction" that contrast with Clive's Olympian theorizing. Its foundation, not surprisingly, lies in a total dissimilarity of character: the antithetical materials from which struggle fashions an indivisible, if temporary, whole. Maurice's identification proceeds directly from his sense of "some infuriating inequality" that is generated between them, and it symbolizes both his and Forster's rejection of equality of character as the basis for relationships— and indeed the rejection of character itself.

For the passage from disequality to oneness assumes the possibility that "personality [can] melt and be subtly reformed." That Maurice's conscious wish at this point is to become heterosexual is irrelevant or ironic. What matters is that the concept of re-forming is central to *Maurice* and that it implies not simply amendment or growth but the making over of character into something altogether different and new. The change Maurice undergoes is both personal and social—involving on the one hand the full acceptance of his homosexuality and of himself as a physical being: "flesh educating the spirit . . . and developing the sluggish heart and the slack mind against their will"; and on the other, his growing challenge to the idea of class. The appropriation to himself of Alec's name takes place, fittingly, in the presence of Mr. Ducie, the first of the novel's representatives of society and authority and marks the climax of both his social and his personal transformation.

But in some ways the reorientation of Maurice's ideas about class is the more difficult and more basic step, so largely is his sense of himself defined in terms of his social identity. His progress from priggishness to guilt brings him at last to the recognition that "if the will can overleap class, civilization as we have made it will go to pieces." And when he is willing to accept that possibility, he is able to admit that Alec "too was embedded in class" and to reject the entire system. As he now sees, coming to terms with his homosexuality parallels, indeed depends upon, a willingness to move beyond notions of class altogether. The "crack in the floor" that is Forster's recurrent symbol for society's artificial and destructive divisions (and for the homosexual "fault" it sees in his hero's psychic landscape) is Maurice's final barrier; and as he overleaps it, he discards the factitious order of civilization for the more kinetic, abrasive world of sexuality, dissolving Clive's self-conscious *idea* of love in the darker intensity of "primitive abandonment."

But Forster wants something more from his hero (after Alec's apparent departure for the Argentine) than the chastened recognition that "love was an emotion through which you occasionally enjoyed yourself." Though most reviewers have agreed with Lytton Strachey (as quoted by Forster in his terminal note) "that the relationship of the two rested upon curiosity and lust and would only last six weeks," Forster is not yet ready to accept consciously and fully (as he will later in his career) the disjunction between sex and love. Connection still remains the ideal, the need for integration returns, and Forster chooses at the last to have things both ways. The final chapters of the novel are a deliberate and determined effort to surround the intermittencies of sexual satisfaction with the continuity of comradely affection. "A happy ending was imperative," Forster wrote in 1960, ". . . I was determined that in fiction anyway two men should fall in love and remain in it for the ever and ever that fiction allows." By comparison, the final scenes of *A Room with a View* and, still more, of *Howards End* are, despite the inclusive symbols of water and hay, equivocal in their effect. *Maurice* ends "without twilight or compromise"—that is, with the promise of absolute salvation in the unrealized and unresonant spaces of the greenwood.

Beneath the mild belligerence of Forster's defense of his ending there can be heard a more plaintive note: a tacit admission of the gap between the disorders and disappointments of life and the order of which art is capable. But Forster's art is at odds with itself. The exiguous symbol of the greenwood affirms his desire but in its aesthetic emptiness belies the object of that desire. Which is to say that connection is theoretically attained but in fact betrayed. The vacillation between the ideals of integration and oneness—variously, and at times confusingly, conceived as "the actual and the ideal" or comradeship and sexuality or love and truth—occurs everywhere in the prewar fiction; and though in *Maurice* Forster gestures again toward integration, he does so ambiguously—or in a way different from what he intends. Unable to forgo the possibility of reconciliation and equally unable to actualize it in the world Maurice and Alec inhabit, he circumvents it finally by opting (in Yeats's words) for "That quarter where all thought is done." In short, the attempt to restore consciousness by joining the values of Maurice's first relationship with those of his second reveals instead the need to transcend it—to achieve in oneness an absolute freedom from contingency. "Love and Truth—" Forster writes in *Howards End,* "their warfare seems eternal. Perhaps the whole visible world rests on it, and if they were one, life itself, like the spirits when Prospero was reconciled to his brother, might vanish into air, into thin air." The comment is striking in its relevance to *Maurice.* The novel's dilemma is overcome only through the illusive linking of contrary ideals in a hypostatic kingdom of imagination, where, to quote Yeats again, "intellect no longer knows / *Is* from the *Ought,* or *Knower* from the *Known*— / That is to say, ascends to Heaven." For Helen Schlegel, a chance collision shakes open the doors of heaven; the attempt to provide Maurice and Alec with a sustained relation bolts the doors firmly behind them. In the sanctuary of depth offered by the greenwood, the more human vision of equality and integration gives way not to an equally human sexuality but to an eternal moment of fusion, as consciousness melts into fantasy; and Forster's heroes flee, improbably joined, into thin air.

Throughout his career, Forster's various formulations of the ideal relate directly to the changing nature of his irony, in fact depend upon it. So the notion of connecting, for example, correlates, reactively, with the mediate, satiric irony of his earliest writing; or to put it another way, the prewar novels define worlds whose deviations from a presupposed norm are apparently remediable. Theoretically at least, it is possible for Philip to learn the lessons of Gino and Italy, for Rickie to acknowledge the reality that is Stephen; and Lucy does in fact accept the Emersonian gospel and passes from darkness into light. By the same token, the drift from the normative certainties of satire toward a more radical vision of the inherent and unresolvable complexities of life—the disjunctive irony of Forster's second phase—entails the compensating desire for an escape into oneness: the need to transcend rather than to encompass and integrate the discontinuities of life. In brief, and as I've already intimated, the ironic determines the anironic in all of Forster's fiction. It seems to me worth repeating that if irony is best viewed as a mode of perceiving the world and if that perception involves in one way or another a fundamental sense of disunity, then it is hardly surprising that ironists generally, if not inevitably, react to the lapses, discontinuities, or randomness that confronts them by positing, in the face of an unsatisfactory world, redemptive or at least consoling visions of unity. In this respect, the anironic is distinct from but also dependent upon and, finally, in the broadest sense, part of the response initiated by the ironic imagination. As noted, the anironic, inevitably and necessarily, undergoes transformation as irony itself is transformed, and nowhere more clearly than in the fiction that spans Forster's long life. Set beside the ideals of other modernist writers—Yeats's "unity of being," Eliot's "still point," Lawrence's "star-balance," Woolf's ecstatic moments, or Auden's "affirming flame"—Forster's are in some ways more extreme but, closer to the point, they are more various, since Forster, moving as he does through different forms of irony, facing always new and unstable horizons, enacts more spaciously than most of his contemporaries (in this respect at least) the characteristic dialectic of recovery and fall that the anironic and ironic impel.

More raggedly, however, than the preceding paragraph indicates. Disjunctive irony, we've seen, is adumbrated even in the earliest of the novels (though it is only in *A Passage to India* that it becomes, in assuming its most extreme shape, absolute); and, as I have tried to show, there are uneasily contained contradictions between the first two of Forster's anironic ideals in all of the fiction through *Maurice*. What is clear is that the disintegrative vision of the caves in *A Passage to India*, asserting what is only implicit in the prewar work, establishes unmistakably and unconditionally the second stage of Forster's irony and leads to the equally extreme and apparently unqualified vision of oneness in the novel's third section. I don't intend here to argue again Forster's final position in *A Passage to India*. For present purposes, the final adjustment of meaning between caves and temple is less to the point than what is implied by Forster's opposition of the two. Consciousness is, if not annihilated in the cave, then effectively reduced to the status of witness—witness to the chaos of disconnection it can no longer hope to control. And in the novel's next and final section even Godbole fails when he is "seduced" by "logic and conscious effort." His success, on the other hand, derives from his ability to impel Mrs. Moore "by his spiritual force to that place where completeness can be found." Thus the anironic counterideal of part 3 can only be formulated as the subduing of ordinary consciousness to that completeness Godbole temporarily and with difficulty achieves—a state in which, while it lasts, both the nothingness of the caves and the ineffectual human awareness of it give way to "a spiritual unity in which all races and species and sex shall one day be merged."

An extreme position, certainly, particularly congenial to those critics who read the novel as Forster's endorsement of Eastern religion. But in the light of his later (and hardly mystical) fiction, it is important to judge just how extreme. In fact, the "loss of the self" (as the once popular phrase had it) toward which Hinduism looks is only superficially a loss and more fundamentally the discovery or recovery of another, more authentic self. In this sense, the attitude dramatized in *A Passage to India* is by no means as radical in its implications for the idea of consciousness and the concept of the self as that which underlies the homosexual stories of *The Life to Come* (As in the previous section of this [essay], I am concerned only with the last eight stories of the volume, though my focus here is on the three remaining "love stories," which I have so far only briefly glanced at.), where, in Forster's third and final period, there is a cutting loose from all essentialist beliefs in an ultimate, absolute reality—even the negative reality symbolized in the caves.

The existential bias of *The Life to Come* is, as one would expect, most apparent in the five "sexual stories" which, putting aside the earlier ideals of connection and permanence or of transcendent unity, attempt to reclaim the phenomenal world for and through unmediated desire. With randomness ostensibly accepted, even welcomed, as the condition of immediate gratification, irony is transformed again; and in taking as their desiderata "the smaller pleasures of life," the stories place at their center a self—if one can still use that word for what has been reduced to a sort of behavioral tropism—that is the vehicle solely for sexual satisfaction. In one sense, these exclusively sexual stories mark too the culmination of the anironic impulse in Forster: the celebration of Maurice without the greenwood, and even without Alec; the apotheosis of Helen's chance collisions, unencumbered by the demand for either integration or completeness. There is more to it than that, however, as becomes apparent when one turns to the remaining homosexual stories of *The Life to Come,* in which, probably because, as in the novels, sexuality is once again associated with love, the interplay of ironic and anironic is more complex. Of the three, "The Life to Come" (1922) and "Dr. Woolacott" (1927) precede the "sexual stories" and suggest that Forster had not yet completely abandoned his primitivism or, in the second, his need for total union. By contrast, "The Other Boat" (1957–58), the last and finest story in the volume, unambiguously confirms the values implied in the sexual stories. In a sense, then, the "love stories" retrace the three stages of the anironic in Forster. But at the same time, in what they reveal, if not in what they intend, the stories are sufficiently alike to constitute an identifiable, if evolving, group, in which sexual repression plays havoc with all three protagonists and provides the key to what Forster is about. Obviously, repression is meant to indicate the reasons for the sudden and overwhelming attractions in the stories and to mitigate their improbabilities: Lionel March, for one, finds that "sex had entirely receded—only to come charging back like a bull." But more importantly and paradoxically, the rejection of sexuality *creates* consciousness and forms those hidden depths, which in turn give rise to introspection and guilt and constitute the traditionally divided self. Inevitably, the men so affected return to the conformities of society, yielding to the pressures they have internalized, or, following the true direction of these stories, die.

It becomes apparent that the "stable" self of *Howards End* and the books that precede it is, as compared with the empty, static self of the sexual stories, at best a complex equilibrium of contending forces. The love stories, with their uneasily shifting perspectives, stand somewhere between the two, and the earlier of them are still equivocally poised between the attractions of depth and surface. So "The Life to Come" begins, as it were, in the greenwood and manages to reverse the progession of *Maurice* quite literally with a vengeance. Ostensibly concerned with Paul Pinmay, the story chronicles the missionary's fall from sexual grace with a crudely satirical irony reminiscent of Forster's Egyptian books. But the details of his decline are less important than its initial cause, the guilt that overcomes him as he realizes: "Sooner or later, God calls every deed to the light."

Conscience and consciousness, God and light, are then the repressive enemies of Paul's unexpected and ecstatic encounter with the native chief Vithobai in "the depths of the woods." But Forster's imagination, as well as God, militates against depth—or, rather, betrays through stylistic incompetence and an excess of violence its disbelief in what it means to affirm. In the most fundamental sense, it is not the thwarting of love by Paul and the Christianity he embodies but Forster's own covert assumptions that make the conjunction of love and sex more than ever impossible and lead to Vithobai's unforeseen triumph. For it is Vithobai who is the more authentic ideational center of "The Life to Come"; and his belief that "it is deeds, deeds that count" is ultimately Forster's too, in this and in all of the other homosexual stories. Not yet fully acknowledged here, it is nonetheless dramatized at the story's climax. Attracted for an instant by Paul's promise of "Real and true love!"—that is, a prolongation of their initial union (as he understands it) into eternity—the dying man suddenly rejects the offer and, stabbing the missionary, experiences "the most exquisite [moment] he had ever known. For love was conquered at last."

What is at stake in Vithobai's conquest is as much the manner as the fact of it; and the additional chapter Forster projected, in which Paul becomes Vithobai's sexual slave in the afterlife, reveals even more clearly the inner

logic of the story's movement from sentimentality toward disequality, re-
venge, and sadistic cruelty. "If the reverse side of accidie is violence," John
Fraser has recently written, "this is partly because violence is felt to promise
not merely a titillating but a radical relief from accidie." In other words,
what determines the action of "The Life to Come" is a reaction not to the
failure of Forster's unlikely dream of union but to a growing disbelief in the
value of existence itself. Ahead lie the caves of *A Passage to India,* with their
destructive negations; and, anticipating Mrs. Moore, Vithobai comes before
his death to a querulous perception of the chaos of values. The irony at this
point, so much more corrosive than that directed at the perversion of Christian *caritas,* suggests that "The Life to Come" is Forster's attempt to stave
off the vision of the caves in a frenzy of violence. But if the story looks
toward the caves, it looks beyond them as well. Directed against the notion
of an afterlife, "The Life to Come" nonetheless projects one, as if to com-
pensate for the impossibility of love. And in its static eternity, a distorted
image of the original greenwood, it adumbrates the world that, after *A Passage to India,* Forster reconstitutes in his sexual stories—the surface world
of unrepentant pleasure.

But not without a final and revealing attempt to salvage the more comprehensive values of his earlier work. "Dr. Woolacott," a slight story whose
confusions may be mistaken for complexity, resembles "The Life to Come"
in its conflation of love and sex but presumably moves in the opposite direction: roughly, from Clesant's initial repression to his fulfillment in both
sex and love. Like "The Life to Come" again, "Dr. Woolacott" is both
sentimental and violent, though the violence is now largely psychological and,
like the sentimentality, partly, if not successfully, masked by fantasy. Dramatizing Clesant's internal struggle by externalizing the more vital half of it
in his handsome farmhand lover works reasonably well, though the young
interloper is somewhat overburdened by symbolic meanings. The real problem, both ethical and semantic, begins with the story's all too obtrusive
message: "What's life after twenty-five? Impotent, blind, paralytic. What's
life before it unless you're fit?" The opposition implied by these questions—
prolonged, tepid, self-conscious existence versus a short, intense burst of
passionate living—is sufficiently familiar to any reader of Forster; but in the
special context of "Dr. Woolacott" the shrill insistence on those things, and
those things alone, that make sexuality possible provides a facile and disturbing estimate of life as a whole. Furthermore, the culmination of Clesant's
desire, as he accepts the nameless farmhand's invitation to accompany him
to the grave, where "we shall be together for ever and ever," defies satisfactory translation. Forster's fantasy implies not simply that death is preferable

to invalidism or to a socially acceptable but sexually barren life but that death *is* life: the achievement hereafter of that fullness of union Dr. Woolacott and society deny.

This is to be literalist about fantasy, no doubt, but since the afterlife has no substantive meaning for Forster, there is no other way to read his metaphor for dynamic living than as an emblem of stasis, no other way to view the unity of desire than as the total blankness of death. And yet the story is, whatever its contradictions, in its own way instructive. The finality of death that "Dr. Woolacott" exposes is the inevitable complement of the presuppositions that underlie the stories written after it; which is to say that the stress on a particular kind of fulfillment here and now creates, in the absence of that fulfillment, no possible alternative but death. Oliver Stallybrass reports that "The Life to Come" "embodied what Forster described as 'a great deal of sorrow and passion that I have myself experienced' and came, with 'Dr Woolacott,' 'more from my heart than anything else I have been able to turn [out].'" One can see why. The two stories are a turning point for Forster; after them, the recognition that love leads inevitably to death is finally accepted. The hero of Forster's first sexual story, "Arthur Snatchfold," recognizes "that little things can turn into great ones, and he did not want greatness." And no more does Forster. Henceforth, however reductively he celebrates it, the phenomenal world is the locus of his concern.

For this reason, "The Other Boat," though tragic in tone, is akin in spirit to the sexual stories that precede it. What these, in their allegiance to surface assume, "The Other Boat" makes explicit: not, as in "Dr. Woolacott" and "The Life to Come," the impossibility, but instead the *destructiveness* of love and of the psychological depths it entails. Given this intention, Forster's choice of Lionel March as his hero is at first sight unlikely—or would be, were it not for the precedent of Maurice. But Lionel, though as average, dim, and conventional as the other, achieves almost in one step the goal toward which Maurice develops so painfully and slowly. Partly, no doubt, because Lionel's "prejudices were tribal rather than personal," but also because Forster supplies him, some four decades later, with different sorts of expectations and needs. Writing to T. E. Lawrence in 1929, Forster commented on "how over-rated and over-written [love] is, and how the relation one would like between people is a mixture of friendliness and lust." The description accords admirably with the feelings Lionel instinctively brings to the relationship in which he finds himself involved.

In fact, though connected with society and automatically responsive to its codes, Lionel is, far more than Cocoa, his half-caste seducer and lover, capable of the smaller pleasures of life. "Nordic warrior," "half Ganymede, half Goth," "a Viking at a Byzantine court," he is cousin to the soldiers, sailors, gladiators, and barbarians of the sexual stories. It is Lionel, I've noted, who forgets "any depths through which he might have passed" and who tells himself: "Enjoy yourself while you can." So long as he gives himself to his relationship, Lionel incarnates Forster's ideal form of desire, in which emotion adds a grace to the urgency of lust—or, as Lionel himself thinks of it: "luxury, gaiety, kindness, unusualness, and delicacy that did not exclude brutal pleasure."

Lionel's thoughts of his mother as "blind-eyed in the midst of the enormous web she had spun" identifies her with the sense of fate that overhangs the story. But fate is only the outward sign of an inner necessity, and Mrs. March is more importantly a potential within Lionel himself: consciousness waiting to reassert the social conformities and sexual antipathies of the tribe against his homosexual affair. Furthermore, the apparent polarization of Mrs. March and Cocoa into the story's principal antagonists simplifies, even distorts, the situation. Unlikely as the conjunction is, the two are, from the beginning of the story, symbolically identified, and so they are throughout, with good reason. Cocoa, however exotic and bizarre, is in fact closer to the Englishwoman than to her son in his ways of thinking. The web in which he and his lover are "caught"—to use the story's key word—by the fatality of Mrs. March, parallels directly the "net" in which Cocoa himself seeks to entrap Lionel. Anxious, planning, and plotting, Cocoa is "the deep one," unable in his self-conscious awareness to accept the moment without fear or anxiety or to make do with less than the "ever and ever" of "Dr. Woolacott." If, then, Mrs. March is the ultimate, Cocoa is the proximate cause of the disaster. And everything that happens in the final, melodramatic pages of the story, from Lionel's recovery by convention to the murder and suicide, is set in motion by the force of Cocoa's too exacting love. In this way, "The Other Boat" confirms a connection that is shirked in the earlier love stories. On the other side of the grave, there is perverse fulfillment in "The Life to Come," a unity of sorts in "Dr. Woolacott"; but in "The Other Boat" there is only silence—the unequivocal finality of death, which follows implacably from the assertion of love.

That is not quite all, however. Early in "The Other Boat" Cocoa complains about his long wait for his lover, saying, "I thought I should die." And Lionel's answer, "So you will," if it looks forward prophetically to the ending, suggests more immediately the sexual act that follows at this point and also the traditional association of sex with death, which in some ways underlies the sexual stories from "Arthur Snatchfold" to "The Torque." For the love-death of "The Other Boat" is not the opposite but the analogue and mirror of that state of intense but intermittent response which, in the world of Forster's sexual stories, is the condition of the smaller pleasures. Or, to phrase more simply this seemingly bizarre conclusion, the anironic complement to *both* groups of tales is, effectively, the same. In *Howards End,* Helen Schlegel insists that "Death destroys a man; the idea of Death saves him." But Helen's conceptualization, her appeal to consciousness, is precisely what Forster rejects in *The Life to Come.* Not the idea of death but the death of the idea now saves; and Helen's statement of "the vague yet convincing plea that the Invisible lodges against the Visible" has no place in the surface world of Forster's final stories, where the anironic, whether conceived in terms of sex or love, points inexorably in the same direction: toward death or the death of consciousness, the physical or psychological obliteration of the self.

The Life to Come is, then, taken as a whole, a set of variations on a theme. Although, as compared with much recent fiction, the book remains formally conventional (this is relatively true even of the more loosely organized sexual stories), its vision is not. The point has some general importance, since it runs counter to the notion of a sharp break between modernism and postmodernism. It bears repeating that Forster and a significant number of his contemporaries as well come increasingly in the course of their careers to recognize (or to sense) the impasse to which their assumptions have brought them and are led to search out alternate ways of responding. The crisis point, therefore, needs to be located not after, but, more properly, before the war—in Lawrence's rethinking of "the old, stable *ego* of the character," in *Finnegans Wake,* in *Between the Acts,* in the ambiguous allegiances of late modernism, and, however much smaller its literary merit, in *The Life to Come.* If modernism represents, among other things, the imposition of the mind's structure on the external world, then Forster's stories are no longer modernist. Wylie Sypher's notion of "methexis" is relevant here. "The distance between life and art," he writes, "is no longer fixed or definable even as minimal. . . . There is participation as well as observation." And again: "The immediate occasion is sufficient unto itself. . . . If the significance is on the surface, then the need for depth explanation has gone, and the contingent, the everyday happening, is more authentic than the ultimate or absolute." The self-confessed auto-eroticism of Forster's stories falls in its minor, narcissistic way precisely within this ethic of participation, although (and it should be said that Sypher is not discussing Forster) it hardly validates its interest or importance.

The excitement of Philip's anonymous contacts and of Helen's chance collisions translates, when these come to dominate Forster's fiction, into a way of life that is dispiritingly minimal and aleatory—like a good deal of the current art that goes by those names. Not that an allegiance to the phenomenal or to the suspensive necessarily implies a thinning out of either self or world. But in Forster's stories exactly that happens (explaining, perhaps, why Forster found himself unable any longer to deal with the more extended form of the novel). The dissolution of the self—not, as for the structuralists, in a web of language but in the peremptoriness of desire— leaves the self just as effectively a fiction. Hovering and havering in the world to which they have been abandoned, Forster's attenuated heroes are prescient of Beckett and the Surfictionists, and of the chaotic or baffling spaces of the *nouveau roman*. For all their violence, there is something exhausted about Forster's final stories. One has come a long way from the conceptual moments of the earlier fiction, which, however discrete in form, are intended to provide and enforce the opportunity for reflection and change. In the resolutely limited, sexual world of *The Life to Come*, moments exist for their own sake or for the sake of the minimal, limited activity generated by them. What Sypher, following Nietzsche, refers to as the "pathos of distance" gives way to a more pathetic capitulation to simple, disordered sensation.

Forster's stories, particularly after "The Life to Come" and "Dr. Woolacott," are a refusal of compromise in fantasy and a rejection of *Howards End*'s belief in the possible connection of life's antinomies. The injunctions of that novel give way at last, in the enervated suspensiveness of Forster's final work, not simply to the disjunctions that are in fact a feature of his work from the beginning but to something that is both more random and, oddly, more restricted as well. And if the stories become as a result more honest, at any rate less equivocal, still their values are sadly diminished, even reversed, in the process. No longer intent on the disappearance of the visible world, Forster abandons too the attempt to reconcile love and truth. Materializing the greenwood, so to speak, he creates a world in which the unexamined life is the only one worth living. Lionel March's murder of Cocoa in a final, sexual act is described as "part of a curve that had long been declining, and had nothing to do with death." Fate, then, presumably, or, more accurately, inner necessity; but tending no less surely toward the literal or psychological extremity of death. If so, the curve is, mutatis mutandis, Forster's too, fictionally elaborated throughout his career in a movement from Philip's ill-understood desires to their realization in the impoverished relationships of *The Life to Come*. Like Lionel's, a barren climax; but also Forster's dubious passage to the contemporary scene.

BARBARA ROSECRANCE

Howards End

It is time to reinterpret *Howards End,* that strange, ambitious, uneven work, which seems to mark a final affirmation of Forster's humanism and the end of his youth. Forster's fourth novel in six years and his last major piece of fiction before the appearance of *A Passage to India* fourteen years later, *Howards End* is in important respects unique. Alone among the novels it grapples head-on with the claims of the "outer" world, confronting problems of economics and social class in a society transformed by industrial growth and shadowed by approaching war. The fantasy world of *A Room with a View* yields in *Howards End* to the realities of power, money, and class as they impinge on the values of self-realization and personal relations; Forster's critique of industrialism suggests the failures alike of the business mind and the liberalism of upper-middle-class intellectuals.

The religious impulse that in all the earlier novels takes the form of a search for individual fulfillment is here directed to the social arena: the "unseen" is to be sought in right relations of the "seen." The exhortation to "connect" encapsulates an ideal of proportion and compromise that will reconcile the "inner" values of imagination, sensitivity, and personal relations with the "outer" energies of power, practicality, and action. Concurrently with its social application of spiritual values, *Howards End* is the novel most explicitly devoted to the ideal of personal relations. Forster chooses, as his approved missionary of connection, a sensitive and articulate woman, a decision that appears to have freed him from the ambivalence he showed to

From *Forster's Narrative Vision.* © 1982 by Cornell University Press.

earlier male heroes, for he gives Margaret Schlegel almost absolute moral authority. She and Henry Wilcox, the energetic imperialist whom she marries, are terms in the hypothesis that the action tests: can the values of personal relations and connection be made to operate within the context of social reality?

As in *The Longest Journey,* the central issue becomes the question of England's inheritance, envisioned in the values of rural tradition. But England's salvation, which the earlier novel seemed to promise, has become a lost cause. The encroaching city is a dominant menace: in the dwindling countryside Howards End itself is a brave survival. In *The Longest Journey* a shepherd moved to London to embark on inexorable decline. *Howards End* presents that decline in the career of Leonard Bast, a dispossessed yeoman whose urban poverty allows him to reach the life of neither body nor spirit.

Victimized both by industrial capitalism and by the well-meaning intellectual class that is one of its beneficiaries, the petit-bourgeois Leonard is lost, doomed to the failure of his impulse to knowledge, condemned to early death by severance from his rural heritage. Howards End and its shadowy guardian, the first Mrs. Wilcox, symbolize this heritage: bequest of the farm to Margaret is intended to signify the alliance of rural virtue with the humanistic ideal. After vicissitudes, the novel ends with Schlegels and Wilcoxes living in harmony at Howards End, where Margaret presides as regent for the infant heir, who synthesizes earth and intellect and embodies what hope remains for England's survival. The diverse characters who dramatize these ideas function in a plot that must be admired for the degree to which we accept its outrageous premises and far-fetched events: the marriage of Margaret and Henry, the mating of Helen and Leonard Bast, Helen's pregnancy, Leonard's death, and the shattering and reformulation of alignments and inheritance.

Finally, the multiple themes and the action that exists to further them are interpreted by a uniquely intrusive narrative voice. The narrator of *Howards End* retains the familiar techniques of his predecessors. But *Howards End* presents more than an acceleration of earlier modes. For we encounter in this novel the most intensely personal of all Forster's narrators, of all his fictional voices the most self-conscious and dramatic. Critics have never adequately addressed the issues raised by this voice and its alterations as these define and reveal the relations in *Howards End* between Forster's narrative technique and his changing world view. They have instead focused on the novel's engagement with social issues and have accepted as Forster's intention the purpose stated in his epigraph, "only connect." Trilling, whose engaging but limited study of Forster has once again been reissued, regarded *Howards*

End as "Forster's masterpiece," praising its "maturity and responsibility" and contemplating with approval its timely concern with England's fate. Wilfred Stone regards the novel as "a test of the ability of Bloomsbury liberalism to survive a marriage with the great world." Frederick Crews sees it as the projection of "a reasonable hope for the survival of liberalism."

Most critics express a common awareness of disjunction between Forster's avowed purpose of reconciliation and its accomplishment in the action. Crews sees the problem as an incompatibility between themes: "Despite [Forster's] effort to give the Wilcoxes their due, the real point of *Howards End* is the familiar individualistic one." Alan Wilde formulates the issue as a "defective articulation of the symbolic and realistic levels." In this view, plot, symbolism, and motif project Forster's longing for purpose and direction in life as it should be; the psychological dramatization of Margaret and Helen Schlegel's search for meaning comes closer to his vision of life as it is. This split also appears in discrepancies between ideology and dramatization in the portrayals of Henry and Ruth Wilcox. Critics additionally have expressed dissatisfaction with the novel's resolution because, despite the plot's assertion of connection accomplished, the ending seems rather a victory for the Schlegels than a reconciliation between values.

However accurate, such readings are incomplete. Although they recognize that *Howards End* is more complex than its predecessors, they omit an important dimension of the novel's meaning. Critics have rightly noted the strain and failures of Forster's asserted synthesis but have wrongly regarded as causes what are really symptoms of a more fundamental difficulty. Nor do such readings explain the unusual narrator of *Howards End*. Finally, *Howards End* has been seen largely as the climax of Forster's aims in the earlier novels, dramatically separate in content and implication from its successor, *A Passage to India*. Thus, for Trilling, *Howards End* is Forster's greatest work because "it develops to their full the themes and attitudes of the early books and throws back upon them a new and enhancing light." Wilde is explicit about the schism: "The gulf that separates *A Passage to India* from Forster's earlier novels is far more profound than that which exists between any two others of his books." Time and history define the gulf: the Great War appears to most critics an unbridgeable chasm between Georgian meliorism and modern alienation.

Important differences in content and technique do separate the prewar novels and *A Passage to India*. But we may more accurately assess *Howards End* if we recognize the degree to which it already formulates the attitudes and conceptions of the final novel. The substantial passage of time between the two books enabled Forster to structure and refine his issue: his experiences in India in 1912–13 and 1921 gave him the context for its embodiment in fiction. But the essential subject of *A Passage to India* is already present in *Howards End* as a growing sense of existential impasse, as the linguistic and thematic expression of negation. The essence of this view pervades the novel, as does a concurrent impulse toward a transcendent unity. Surely these are the ingredients that come together in the brilliantly coherent images of *A Passage to India,* in which Forster has taken the logical next and last step.

To understand the centrality in *Howards End* of preliminary versions of the vision of *A Passage to India* enables us better to locate and explain the unique qualities of this penultimate novel. It also allows us, while recognizing that *Howards End* brings to culmination important themes of the earlier novels, to define it as more than the climax of one phase in Forster's thought and art. Seen rather as part of a continuum in which it closely anticipates its successor, *Howards End* reveals the progression of Forster's thought toward the metaphysic of *A Passage to India.* Finally, comprehending the relation between Forster's expressions of cosmic apprehension in *Howards End* and his strenuous attempts to prove its values enables us to identify the sources of disjunction in the novel and to understand their consequence in the narrative voice.

The conscious intent of *Howards End* is to resolve conflict and affirm possibility. Yet throughout the novel Forster undercuts his attempts at an optimistic synthesis by repeatedly projecting chaos. The real source of problems in *Howards End* is neither imbalance between "inner" and "outer" values nor contradiction between the aims of conciliation and victory, but rather a deeper tension that these difficulties mirror, between Forster's efforts to "prove" his humanistic values and to sustain Western society through reversion to rural virtues, and a countercurrent of disbelief, a deepening pessimism expressed through images and motifs that evoke, in a new and menacing world, a vision of cosmic disorder and loss of meaning. The rhetoric affirms connection, but the undercurrent describes collapse. This tension invades all aspects of the novel. It explains the disjunctions in theme and character; it pervades and determines Forster's narrative voice.

The case for personal relations and the inner life opens with the novel's first episode, as Helen Schlegel becomes briefly enmeshed in a disastrous romance. The retreating Paul Wilcox who, frightened by his impulsive declaration, "had nothing to fall back on," illustrates "panic and emptiness," a phrase later to suggest a more cosmic vacuum. Here it evokes Helen's credo: "I know that personal relations are the real life for ever and ever." "Amen," responds her sister. A Moorean good-in-itself, personal relations form the keystone of the inner life, and Forster verifies the sisters' article of faith through his endorsement of Margaret, who articulates familiar components of the humanistic ideology: "at thirteen she had grasped a dilemma that most people travel through life without perceiving. Her brain darted up and down; it grew pliant and strong. Her conclusion was that any human being lies nearer to the unseen than any organization, and from this she never varied." The inner life thus comprehends a belief in the primacy of the individual and a concern with the metaphysical implications of human action. The concept also includes, as the action will demonstrate, personal integrity, the capacity for introspection, and the ability to "connect."

Seeking to vindicate the Schlegel sisters' avowal, Forster emphasizes the vicissitudes of the important relationship between them. When Margaret has decided, against Helen's advice, to marry Henry, the sisters can still maintain their relationship because, the narrator explains, "there are moments when the inner life actually 'pays,' when years of self-scrutiny, conducted for no ulterior motive, are suddenly of practical use." Margaret lapses temporarily from her own ideal when she participates in the deception of her husband's plan to "hunt" the sister who has mysteriously withdrawn from contact: to reestablish her credentials, "she had first to purge a greater crime than any that Helen could have committed—that want of confidence that is the work of the devil."

Dramatized as faith between Margaret and Helen, the inner values are more than intrinsic goods. Forster generalizes Margaret's perception of the commercialization of Christmas as "the grotesque impact of the unseen on the seen" to locate the inner life in his metaphysic. "But in public who shall express the unseen adequately? It is private life that holds out the mirror to infinity; personal intercourse, and that alone, that ever hints at a personality beyond our daily vision." The inner life is nothing less than the sole emblem of divinity: to affirm its primacy would seem the novel's major intent.

Yet the epigraph "only connect" suggests a competing purpose. As a plea for wholeness, this ideal does operate in personal relations and may apply both to the union of Margaret and Henry and to the reconciliation of extremes within the individual psyche whose absence Henry's schism of passion and prudery demonstrates: "Only connect the prose and the passion, and both will be exalted, and human life will be seen at its highest. Live in fragments no longer. Only connect, and the beast and the monk, robbed of the isolation that is life to either, will die." Forster here restates the desire to bridge human incompleteness that the earlier novels rendered in the attempts of their flawed heroes to find meaning through contact with the qualities they lack. But in *Howards End*, connection transcends the individual, as Forster seeks a social contract between power and sensibility through

the union of the capitalist mind with the imagination of the liberal intelligentsia. In this search he makes a real attempt, albeit within a limited spectrum, to connect imaginative vision with economic reality. The terms imply
a pluralism whose goal is England's survival. A successful rubber merchant,
Henry Wilcox guides the empire. His ventures provide jobs for a growing
class of urban workers like Leonard Bast and guarantee the incomes of
intellectuals like the Schlegels, who seek a moral distribution of economic
gain. Henry's pragmatism has saved Howards End when its surviving yeoman
owners could not, "without fine feelings or deep insight, but he had saved
it"; and "Henry would save the Basts as he had saved Howards End, while
Helen and her friends were discussing the ethics of salvation."

But in the businessman's relation to social equity and national survival,
Forster depicts neither successful connection nor well-meant failure. Critics
have observed the limitations of Henry Wilcox and decried his emasculation
at the novel's end. Forster's inability to give Henry his due reflects more than
his distrust of Henry: it expresses the general despair of human possibility
that undercuts the novel's formulas of hope and its rhetoric of affirmation.

The business mind offers no social synthesis. The employment Henry
Wilcox gives clerks is subject to the vagaries of a system in which they have
no share. The clichés of nineteenth-century liberalism provide Henry's dis-
claimer of responsibility: "it is all in the day's work. It's part of the battle
of life. . . . As civilization moves forward, the shoe is bound to pinch in
places, and it's absurd to pretend that anyone is responsible personally."
Businessmen destroy tradition and violate the natural order. A millionaire
businessman tears down Margaret's London house to build flats. Henry Wilcox owns shares in a lock that shortens the Thames. Wilcox spoliation is
both personal and symbolic: dust from the Wilcox car "had percolated
through the open windows, some had whitened the roses and gooseberries
of the wayside gardens, while a certain proportion had entered the lungs of
the villagers"; "The Great North Road should have been bordered all its
length with glebe. Henry's kind has filched most of it." Finally, despite Henry's service to Howards End, he has barred himself from relation to England:
"the Wilcoxes have no part in the place, nor in any place. It is not their
names that recur in the parish register. It is not their ghosts that sigh among
the alders at evening. They have swept into the valley and swept out of it,
leaving a little dust and a little money behind."

But Wilcoxes are not simply ephemeral. Part of "the civilization of flux,"
they add number without quantity. "A short-frocked edition of Charles also
regards them placidly; a perambulator edition is squeaking; a third edition
is expected shortly. Nature is turning out Wilcoxes in this peaceful abode,

so that they may inherit the earth." Implicated thus in the issue of inheritance, Wilcoxes provide a pernicious apprehension of the future: "the Imperialist is not what he thinks or seems. He is a destroyer. He prepares the way for cosmopolitanism, and though his ambitions may be fulfilled the earth that he inherits will be gray."

Despite Forster's approval, the Schlegels' share in the national synthesis is no greater than Henry's. Margaret and her sister represent the situation of England's liberal intelligentsia in a time of economic expansion and national unease. The Schlegels and their friends comprehend the economic basis of culture. Their realism extends to concern for the consequences of capitalist exploitation and for the economic and intellectual poverty of the new class of urban workers, and they spend much time discussing ways and means of achieving a more equitable distribution of money and culture. But the modern age displaces them as inexorably as it grinds down Leonard Bast. When the Schlegels' home is destroyed to make way for urban flats, it is clear that although money can save them from want, it cannot save them from the rootlessness that Forster portrays as a modern horror. Ineffective in their attempt to help the struggling classes beneath them, the liberal intellectuals present, finally, an image of liberalism's impotence to influence social change and national survival.

It is significant that although Forster exposes the ineffectuality of the liberal dialogue, he never repudiates Margaret's position. In his endorsement of Margaret's insights and didacticism, in his lack of detachment from her manipulations, Forster identifies himself not only with the intelligentsia, but also with the alienation of the outsider and the powerlessness of women. The female predicament transcends intellectual boundaries, for Ruth Wilcox, not an intellectual but a woman, cannot save her declining farm. "Things went on until there were no men." The eclipse of Margaret and Henry by Margaret and Helen offers additional evidence of his allegiance. *Howards End* takes its impetus from the failure of a heterosexual relationship and finds vindication in the success of a single-sex one. While this countering of the "official" ideology enacts the tension between love and friendship familiar from the earlier novels, its significance here lies in Forster's allegiance to characters who are alienated from power. Margaret triumphs over the philistines: "She, who had never expected to conquer anyone, had charged straight through these Wilcoxes and broken up their lives." But although women prevail at Howards End, they have no power in the public arena. Margaret does not reform Henry's politics: she only destroys the vital energy that was his chief attraction. Henry at the end is "pitiably tired," by his own admission, "broken."

The businessman retreats from the world he sought to dominate; the intellectual withdraws from hopeless debate to vanishing rural sanctities. Whatever Forster's "outsider" status contributed to his inability to conceive Wilcoxes as part of a national synthesis, his derivation of the evils of modern society from their philistinism reflects the doubt that undercuts the novel's attempts at social reconciliation. Furthermore, his displacement of focus from the social hypothesis to the privatism of affection between Margaret and Helen presents an alliance with sterility. In their limitation and disjunction, the ideologies both of personal relations and of connection imply a darker view, even though, at the same time, they represent Forster's most strenuous assertion of social possibility and human potentiality.

Amid the apostrophes to individuality and the inner life, the reader of *Howards End* becomes aware that personal relations are no longer very important. Although the values of nature and the past are posed as complementary to the human efforts to achieve harmony, ultimately these efforts are submerged in the larger question of England's fate. Well before her marriage to Henry Wilcox, Margaret begins to move beyond a concern for personal relations. She prophesies that she will end her life caring most for a place; the realization makes her "sad," but by the novel's close, Forster will describe Margaret's remoteness as an approach to metaphysical insight. Like human life, personal relations are ephemeral; the agitations of personality have no effect on the rural serenity in which ultimate value resides. Margaret's attempts to introduce Mrs. Wilcox into her "set" and her aid with Mrs. Wilcox's Christmas shopping are activities inimical to the inarticulate virtues Mrs. Wilcox represents. The party talk is empty, the shopping futile, as Mrs. Wilcox signifies by her rejection of Margaret's choices. Margaret's attempts at connection are no more germane. Her ability to connect seems the moral prerequisite for her guardianship of Howards End, but as intellectual, social conscience, comrade, and artist of the imagination she is ultimately irrelevant. To assume the mantle of the first Mrs. Wilcox, a character conspicuously devoid of creative imagination, Margaret must withdraw. In spite of her dogged affection for Henry, when she begins to acquire the essential vision, "the sense of space, which is the basis of all earthly beauty" and which leads her to contemplate England as a rural sanctity, she must forget "the luggage and the motor-cars, the hurrying men who know so much and connect so little."

Although initially Forster presented personal relations both as intrinsic good and as the sole path to the spiritually absolute, personal intercourse depends on other values. When Mrs. Munt and Charles Wilcox quarrel, Mrs. Wilcox is able to separate the foes because "she worshipped the past. . . .

and let her ancestors help her." In a nomadic civilization, divorced from its past, can love alone sustain personal relations? The experience of the adepts, Margaret and Helen, is instructive. The scene of their climactic reunion is Howards End, within whose farmhouse are the Schlegel possessions, unpacked by the prescient caretaker Miss Avery against Wilcox injunctions. The Schlegel movables have accrued tradition and value by their status as objects from the past and through their reinstatement in the rural context. Significantly, Margaret and Helen come to reconciliation not by talk or effort but through the past, enshrined in the rural sanctity of Howards End:

> Explanations and appeals had failed; they had tried for a common meeting-ground, and had only made each other unhappy. And all the time their salvation was lying round them—the past sanctifying the present; the present, with wild heart-throb, declaring that there would after all be a future.

The rural values not only transcend the claims of personal relations and the inner life: Forster posits the attainment of a universal human harmony through a vital relation to the rural tradition: "In these English farms, if anywhere, one might see life steadily and see it whole, group in one vision its transitoriness and its eternal youth, connect—connect without bitterness until all men are brothers." But the novel's course suggests rather the remoteness of divine unity from earthly efforts. The inheritance theme thus contains its own contradictions: nature is at once an agent of reconciliation and a non-human force which dwarfs human effort and which, threatened by the encroachments of the modern world, is losing potency as its kingdom diminishes. In reference to the ideals of personal relations and connection, the values of nature and tradition are similarly ambivalent, congruent in that they work together toward the possibility of earthly harmony, disjunct in that the ideologies that assert the primacy of personality and individual effort are irrelevant to the natural environment that transcends them. In its transcendence of human concerns, the natural world is linked to a concept of divine unity briefly adumbrated near the end of the novel. Restated, this idea becomes in *A Passage to India* the search for completion.

What opposes the possibility of unity in both novels is the vision of cosmic evil, rendered in *A Passage to India* through the central symbol of the Marabar caves, which in their absence of distinction suggest the negation of meaning and the absence of divinity. In *Howards End*, the suggestions of an antivision, though pervasive, are more diffuse. But their metaphysical function parallels that of the caves, and the pressure they exert similarly impels the search for a countervailing unity that will restore meaning and order to the universe. This unity is still, in *Howards End,* implied as an agnostic Christianity allied to the romantic tradition. God is no longer anthropomorphic, but the divine existence is never in question. Nature remains the means to its apprehension, still an intermediary between man and God. In *A Passage to India,* nature is no longer visible sign or ally of man; the quest, too, has changed. In *Howards End* Forster asks whether, amid the erosion of traditional values and the emergence of new and threatening modes of existence, the Western tradition and its values can endure. In *A Passage to India* he has accepted alienation as the modern condition and asks the ultimate question. Whether *A Passage to India* affirms or denies the existence of God, it is a far more coherent novel than *Howards End* because it confronts the problem of meaning directly. *Howards End* affirms human potentiality and the existence of divinity, but the unacknowledged pressure of its prevision of apocalypse undermines even its qualified optimism.

There is clearly an affinity between the goblin image of Helen's well-known reverie on Beethoven's Fifth Symphony and the vision in the Marabar caves. The goblins are an important motif. But if *Howards End* has a structural equivalent to the caves, it is not the essay on goblins but the scene at Oniton Grange, a Wilcox country house in Wales. When Helen invades Oniton on the occasion of a Wilcox daughter's wedding, with Leonard Bast and his bedraggled wife in tow, it is discovered that Mrs. Bast was once Henry Wilcox's mistress. Like the caves episode, this scene centers on a sexual catastrophe and precipitates crisis. As in the caves episode, the rhythm of confrontation begins with an apparently trivial but significant accident. Forster's brief line anticipating the Oniton scene, "So the wasted day lumbered forward," presents a compressed version of the final novel's prelude of apprehension and ennui.

The initial note of despair sounded in Helen's cry of "panic and emptiness" as her lover retreats, becomes the series of images and associations which render the cosmic apprehension that undercuts the action's strenuous efforts at reconciliation. Much of this imagery reappears in *A Passage to India,* integrated into a purposeful symbology. In *Howards End* Forster is still groping toward its formulation, but the essence of his vision is discernible in a description of King's Cross Station that considerably precedes Helen's goblins. King's Cross suggests "Infinity," its "great arches, colourless, indifferent," are "fit portals for some eternal adventure." This language inaugurates crucial motifs. The arch figures as gateway to a metaphysical journey whose values lie both in its destination and as the means of escape from urban horror: to which, nonetheless says Forster, "Alas! we return." The arch reappears as a fragment of the "rainbow bridge" that is an image of attempted completion; in *A Passage to India,* arches function in a comparable dualism as one of the symbolic paths to religious knowledge and as part of the infinite recession that questions the existence of the divine. "Colourless," "indifferent," and "Infinity" figure centrally in both novels. The motif of indifference in *Howards End* suggests the remoteness of the infinite and the indifference of the universe to man that will become the prevailing condition of *A Passage to India.* With the closely related adjective "colourless," it describes urban life, as the squalid existence of the Basts indicates, "a life where love and hatred had both decayed." To the cosmic indifference of the arch, Forster counterpoints the comic indifference of characters like Mrs. Munt—"To history, to tragedy, to the past, to the future, Mrs. Munt remained equally indifferent"—and Jacky Bast, who is "equally indifferent" to all her husband's moods.

The colorless arches of King's Cross are linked to a pervasive gray identified with modern life and concentrated in the imagery that describes London and its residents. In *A Passage to India,* "colourless" becomes "beyond colour," and describes the Indian sky that recedes to infinity, its perspective reducing the human scale almost to nonexistence. The "colourless and indifferent" arches of *Howards End* also prefigure the indifference of the Indian environment and the culmination of cosmic indifference in the overturn of all distinctions in the Marabar caves.

Beethoven's goblins formulate the experience of meaninglessness. The mode is casual but the message is not. They "merely observed in passing that there was no such thing as splendour or heroism in the world. . . . Panic and emptiness!" To this void Forster opposes hyperbolic fantasies of romantic individualism and sensory imagination: "Gusts of splendour, gods and demigods contending with vast swords, colour and fragrance broadcast on the field of battle, magnificent victory, magnificent death!" But refuting the shallow optimism of "men like the Wilcoxes or President Roosevelt," the goblins return; this time they threaten existence itself:

> It was as if the splendour of life might boil over and waste to steam and froth. In its dissolution one heard the terrible, ominous note, and a goblin, with increased malignity, walked quietly over the universe from end to end. Panic and emptiness! Panic and emptiness! Even the flaming ramparts of the world might fall.

The goblins recede with Beethoven's closing affirmation. But their warning describes a vision that *Howards End* continues to reiterate and whose implications it struggles to avoid.

The portrayal of Mrs. Wilcox also provides an approach to the negative

vision. A sketch for Mrs. Moore of the final novel, Mrs. Wilcox projects a
strange air of dissolution. Her voice "suggested that pictures, concerts, and
people are all of small and equal value. Only once had it quickened—when
speaking of Howards End." Mrs. Wilcox's voice, which "though sweet and
compelling, had little range of expression," includes humanity and its arti-
facts in a suggestion of meaninglessness. Life—the "quickening" in her
voice—remains only in the rural heritage. Conversely, Mrs. Wilcox's indis-
tinctness, however unsuccessful as characterization, is also intended to suggest her transcendence of personality and her approach to a completion that
becomes the ideal of *A Passage to India.*

The associated images of indifference, sameness, colorlessness all delineate a destructive homogeneity that renders life meaningless. London, the
diabolic symbol of modern life, is evoked throughout the novel by references
to the colorless color, gray. Playing thus with ideas of the absence of distinction, Forster moves in *Howards End* toward the distillation of these ideas
in the master-symbol of the Marabar caves. Forster's London, like that of
Dickens, is a city of fog, its atmosphere "clots of gray," its existence a
mounting violation of the natural order:

> month by month the roads smelt more strongly of petrol, and
> were more difficult to cross, and human beings heard each other
> speak with greater difficulty, breathed less of the air, and saw less
> of the sky. Nature withdrew: the leaves were falling by midsum-
> mer; the sun shone through dirt with an admired obscurity.

The "gray tides" of London proclaim the rootlessness that is the city's essence and the inner condition of its inhabitants: "emblematic of their lives,
[they] rose and fell in a continual flux," and Margaret ponders lost continuities: "Everyone moving. Is it worthwhile attempting the past when there
is this continual flux even in the hearts of men?" London, further, is "a tract
of quivering gray, intelligent without purpose and excitable without love,"
its modern conveniences the machinery of diabolic imprisonment. The lift
that takes Mrs. Wilcox up to her London flat is "a vault as of hell, sooty
black, from which soots descended." Described early in the novel as "Sa-
tanic," London becomes, finally, the demoniac opposite of divinity: "The
mask fell off the city, and she saw it for what it really is—a caricature of
infinity."

The absent Helen, who eludes Margaret and her brother, and whose
strange behavior suggests to them mental illness, seen thus is identified with
the city in a vision of horror: "Helen seemed one with grimy trees and the
traffic and the slowly flowing slabs of mud. She had accomplished a hideous

act of renunciation and returned to the One." The metaphysical semantics of *A Passage to India* are extraordinarily similar. The grimy trees have become the indifferent Indian landscape, the traffic is transposed into the dirty city of Chandrapore, and the slowly flowing slabs of mud have become the abased inhabitants of India, described as "mud moving." The "hideous act of renunciation" in which Helen has merged into nothingness becomes Mrs. Moore's collapse of distinctions, which leads to her own renunciation of life.

Gray pervades the existence of the characters. "His was a gray life," says Forster explicitly of Leonard Bast. Leonard swears "in a colourless sort of way." His wife is "descending . . . into the colourless years." Characters of different classes recognize the problem that is their common condition: thus, Leonard and the Schlegel sisters "had agreed that there was something beyond life's daily gray." And Margaret believes that "doing good to humanity was useless; the many-coloured efforts thereto spreading over the vast area like films and resulting in a universal gray."

Aspects of color, the distinctions of individuality oppose the gray. When, late in the novel, Margaret makes a curious last case for the variations of individual personality, she speaks of "differences—eternal differences; planted by God in a single family, so that there may always be colour; sorrow perhaps, but colour in the daily gray." In nature too, color opposes urban gray. At Mrs. Wilcox's funeral an observer notices "the sunset beyond, scarlet and orange." Howards End is edenic in its variegated hues: "There were the greengage trees that Helen had once described, there the tennis lawn, there the hedge that would be glorious with dog-roses in June, but the vision now was of black and palest green. Down by the dell-hole more vivid colours were awakening, and Lent Lilies stood sentinel on its margin, or advanced in battalions over the grass. Tulips were a tray of jewels." Howards End itself is illuminated by "the white radiance that poured in through the windows."

> Unnoticed, the sun occupied his sky, and the shadows of the tree stems, extraordinarily solid, fell like trenches of purple across the frosted lawn. It was a glorious winter morning. Evie's fox terrier, who had passed for white, was only a dirty grey dog now, so intense was the purity that surrounded him. He was discredited, but the blackbirds that he was chasing glowed with Arabian darkness, for all the conventional colouring of life had been altered. Inside, the clock struck ten with a rich and confident note.

The clock is in harmony with the richness that emanates from the sun. Unlike the hostile Indian sun of *A Passage to India,* the natural environment still has relationship to man.

In contrast to the city, with its increasing population and its "architecture of hurry," the country retains the sense of space that Margaret loses when she rides in her husband's motor car. But the drive to London brings another prevision of void: "once more trees, houses, people, animals, hills, merged and heaved into one dirtiness, and she was at Wickham Place." Again Forster suggests a collapse of distinctions in which the elements of life, as seen in Margaret's kaleidescopic view from the car, achieve a negative unity—"one dirtiness." The image recurs in yet another variant as Margaret contemplates past catastrophe and future crisis. Leonard Bast's death has set in motion legal machinery that, made in the Wilcox image, will result in imprisonment for a Wilcox:

> Events succeeded in a logical, yet senseless, train. People lost their humanity, and took values as arbitrary as those in a pack of playing-cards. . . . In this jangle of causes and effects what had become of their true selves? Here Leonard lay dead in the garden, from natural causes; yet life was a deep, deep river, death a blue sky, life was a house, death a wisp of hay, a flower, a tower, life and death were anything and everything, except this ordered insanity, where the king takes the queen, and the ace the king.

This catalogue of chaos includes elements of life, culture, and nature. It not only links such disparate categories as card games, characters, natural phenomena, and logical and phenomenological concepts, but it displaces images from their earlier contexts. Death, for example, is not elsewhere associated with flowers, hay, or the colorful sky of this novel; life is ultimately to reside not primarily in human relationships but in a house. In addition to its suggestion of cosmic negation, this passage, in some of its imagery—after her vision Mrs. Moore withdraws to her deck of "Patience" cards—and in its projection of an "ordered insanity," presages the world of *A Passage to India* at a comparable moment in its action, as Dr. Aziz's trial impends.

The chaos of Howards End resolves into a harmony of asserted reconciliation and coming harvest, but the red rust of London is already visible from the farm: "Howards End, Oniton, the Purbeck Downs, the Oderberge, were all survivals, and the melting-pot was being prepared for them. Logically, they had no right to be alive. One's hope was in the weakness of logic." Prophesying the dissolution of the variegating countryside into urban gray, Forster distills in the image of a melting pot that eradicates color and distinction the essence of his vision of negation.

Hope remains, but its object has shrunk from fulfillment to survival; its mode has changed from active effort to a passive reliance on default by the enemy. That Howards End and the civilization it represents will be the future as well as the past is unlikely: as Margaret admits, "all the signs are against it." The novel ends with Helen's call to plenty: "'The field's cut!' Helen cried excitedly—'the big meadow! We've seen to the very end, and it'll be such a crop of hay as never!'" Temporarily safe in their diminished territory, the Schlegels prepare for siege.

The contradictory impulses of *Howards End* infuse Forster's narrative voice and have important implications for its quality and function. The voice contains the schism that the action also reflects, for throughout the novel the narrator strains to bring his disparate materials into congruence and the competing formulations of his own voice into compatibility. In an accelerating tension between the impassioned rhetoric of the authorial voice and the ambivalence it attempts to suppress lies the explanation of the peculiar narrator of *Howards End*. Ultimately the increasing pressure of the negative vision undercuts the voice that contains it and alters its very nature.

It seems appropriate that *Howards End,* the novel that seeks most directly to locate ultimate value within the context of human relationships, should reveal an intensely personal narrative voice. The narrator's techniques of omniscience and engagement are familiar, but his voice goes further in self-dramatization, in manipulation of the reader, in the frequency and length of intervention than in any other Forster novel. The tendency of the narrator to step out of the action to formulate its larger significance also reaches its height in *Howards End*. No other Forster narrator establishes so personal a hegemony. His use of Margaret is instrumental to his scope, for he enters her generalizing imagination so often that Margaret functions as an extension of his voice. The narrator's omniscience, his relationship with the reader, and his self-dramatization distinguish him from Margaret. Uniquely in this novel, Forster's narrator indicates his gender, as, speculating on the difference between male and female friendships, he notes that "when men like us, it is for our better qualities. . . . but unworthiness stimulates woman." His language defines a variety of roles. As celebrant of England's glory he is a visionary bard, his literary diction means to a precarious decorum. He emphasizes his manipulations and the centrality of his function more than he does the story itself, intervening, for example, to excoriate Wilcox's repudiation of Mrs. Wilcox's will: "the discussion moved toward its close. To follow it is unnecessary. It is rather a moment when the commentator should step forward. Ought the Wilcoxes to have offered their home to Margaret?" The long essay that follows displays the narrator's judicial wisdom. But he can also present himself as a fellow-citizen, permitting the reader a rare glimpse of domestic intimacy as he extrapolates from Henry Wilcox's failure to mention the mews behind Ducie Street when he hopes to sublet his flat: "So does my grocer stigmatize me when I complain of the quality of his sultanas, and he answers in one breath that they are the best sultanas, and how can I expect the best sultanas at that price?"

Through diction and tone, the narrator seeks control of his structure and reader. With deceptive self-effacement he casts himself as the mind behind the action: "one may as well begin with Helen's letters to her sister." As the narrator continues, his grammatical emphases imply reader agreement—"Certainly Margaret was impulsive. She did swing rapidly from one decision to another." He moves toward fuller control of the reader through frequent mediations between reader and characters, in which he often furthers intimacy by direct address. Thus, defending Leonard Bast's reticence about the adventure of his all-night walk, Forster admonishes the reader: "You may laugh at him, you who have slept nights out on the veldt, with your rifle pat beside you and all the atmosphere of adventure pat. And you may also laugh who think adventures silly. But do not be surprised if Leonard is shy whenever he meets you, and if the Schlegels rather than Jacky hear about the dawn." This passage is singular in the degree to which it defines reader as well as character and commenting voice; its hostility to the imagined reader is perhaps Forster's coy attempt to produce sympathy appropriate to his character. But the passage is also noteworthy for its erosion of the boundary between experience and fiction. The rhetorical nature of Forster's narrative technique is not new, but the frequency in *Howards End* of conflations like this is unique in his fiction.

As he intrudes into a comic scene between Margaret's Aunt Juley and Charles Wilcox, the narrator interrupts his narrative to suggest its irrelevance: "Young Wilcox was pouring in petrol, starting his engine, and performing other actions with which this story has no concern." The narrator's qualification, itself an aside, renders the action he excludes parenthetical also. Yet, in a comic anticipation of *A Passage to India,* his very exclusion includes. For his distinction implies the existence of his characters in a realm of reality that is not the story, a world in which the reader may be presumed to function also. More directly, the narrator identifies Margaret with "others who have lived long in a great capitol," a classification that implies her shared reality with potential readers. Like these city-dwellers, Margaret has "strong feelings" about railway stations, emotions that become the narrator's truth: "They are our gates to the glorious and the unknown." From Margaret the narrator moves to the implied reader who coexists with her in the world outside his fiction, with the judgment that "he is a chilly Londoner who does not endow his stations with some personality, and extend to them, however shyly, the emotions of fear and love." The use of direct address intensifies the reader's participation in the narrator's rhetoric. Hoping that Margaret's connection of King's Cross Station with infinity "will not set the reader against her," he intrudes further to insist on Margaret's insight: "If you think this is ridiculous, remember that it is not Margaret who is telling you about it; and let me hasten to add that they were in plenty of time for the train." The assumption of potential conversation between Margaret and the reader merges the double fiction of character and narrator with the reader's world of experience, for it is the narrator who, ostensibly in the character's behalf, confronts the reader. The commentary has become not only a direct conversation but an argument, in which the narrator disarms potential opposition, assumes responsibility for his characters' perceptions, and buttresses his case with apparent considerations of common sense. These techniques are significant because they reveal the intensity of Forster's need in this novel to persuade, and suggest the degree of his extremity.

For despite the narrator's brilliance, his persuasion must ultimately be regarded as unsuccessful. He does not achieve a harmonious integration of ideology and dramatic representation, of content and form. His reflections are often disconnected from the action, so that the novel appears to present an uneven alternation between essay and scene, comment and action. To a degree found in no other Forster novel, the narrator's diction is abstract, metaphorical, hyperbolical; the anxiety and inflation of his tone suggest the desperation of his attempt to harmonize and persuade. The prominence, the intimate tone, the rhetorical techniques of this narrator are evoked by the impossibility of his task. Equal intensity seems to attend each exhortation. Nowhere does he acknowledge incompatibility among contending values. It is as if Forster is trying to bridge the gap between desire and disillusion by the insistence of his presence, to cover his inconsistencies of attitude and the unlikeliness of character and action by the sheer weight of his rhetoric as narrator. Consequently he is eloquent and hysterical, strained, elaborate, evasive, intimate, familiar, powerful, and unconvincing as he attempts to impose on the world of the novel a coherence that action and voice alike belie.

The narrator's rhetoric thus embodies its own limitations, which appear in all the novel's contexts. The portrayal of Mrs. Wilcox, for example, is an attempt to establish the mythic significance of an unsubstantial character. First seen by Helen, Mrs. Wilcox wears a long dress, she "trails," she picks up a piece of hay, she smells flowers, she is tired, she is "steadily unselfish."

The corroborating narrator assures that Mrs. Wilcox is "just as Helen's letter had described her, trailing noiselessly over the lawn, and there was actually a wisp of hay in her hands." But in the absence of dramatic context, Forster asserts a larger significance: "One knew that she worshipped the past, and that the instinctive wisdom the past can alone bestow had descended upon her—that wisdom to which we give the clumsy name of aristocracy." Mrs. Wilcox, described throughout as shadowy, is too shadowy to bear this weight. To the degree that her behavior is recorded, she is rather a caricature of the traditional wife and mother, naïve, submissive, and insular. The preciosity of Margaret's guests at a luncheon she gives for Mrs. Wilcox is balanced by the parochiality of the lady herself. Margaret's brief experience of Mrs. Wilcox doesn't warrant her belief that she and her family "are only fragments of Mrs. Wilcox's mind," and that Mrs. Wilcox "knew everything." Nor does the characterization support the narrator's direct claim that Mrs. Wilcox is "nearer the line that divides daily life from a life that may be of greater importance." Assertion seeks unsuccessfully to bridge the gap between intention and presentation.

Forster's relation to Leonard Bast is at best uneasy, a mixture of compassion and condescension. The significance of Leonard Bast is in his origin, in his pivotal position as cause célèbre for the liberal intellectuals and victim of the capitalists, and in his sentimental apotheosis into England's future. An uncertainty of narrative tone pursues Leonard throughout. Initially Forster demythifies him: "he was inferior to most rich people, there is not a doubt of it. He was not as courteous as the average rich man, nor as intelligent, nor as healthy, nor as lovable." Leonard has a half-baked mind; his conversation is querulous and banal; he is "one of the thousands who have lost the life of the body and failed to reach the life of the spirit." Margaret's assessment contains no hint of irony, although it catches her in violation of her own individualistic credo: "She knew this type very well—the vague aspirations, the mental dishonesty, the familiarity with the outside of books." Leonard's capacity for spontaneity and his questing spirit redress the balance, but even in this Forster undercuts his praise: "Within his cramped little mind dwelt something that was greater than Jeffries' books—the spirit that led Jeffries to write them." When ultimately Forster transfigures Leonard, his invocation does not create heroic significance: "Let Squalor be turned into Tragedy, whose eyes are the stars, and whose hands hold the sunset and the dawn."

In comparable interventions the narrative voice asserts dimensions that the action cannot substantiate, as when Forster tries unsuccessfully to cover Margaret's crisis with sister and husband by a rhetoric of benediction: "For the present let the moon shine brightly and the breezes of the spring blow gently, dying away from the gale of the day, and let the earth, who brings increase, bring peace." The inflation and unease of these assertions is compounded in many of the essaylike passages that stud the novel. Forster's evocation of a rainbow bridge is replete with questionable images:

> she might yet be able to help him to the building of the rainbow bridge that should connect the prose in us with passion. Without it we are meaningless fragments, half monks, half beasts, unconnected arches that have never joined into a man. With it love is born, and alights on the highest curve, glowing against the gray, sober against the fire. Happy the man who sees from either aspect the glory of these outspread wings. The roads of his soul lie clear, and he and his friends shall find easy going.

How is the reader to interpret the implied parallel between prose and passion and monk and beast, the location and meaning of fire, the literal and metaphorical discrepancy of gray, the location and condition of the man "who sees from either aspect" and to incorporate into all this the sudden appearance of roads in the man's soul? One has only to contrast this jumble with the powerful and coherent imagery of arch and echo of *A Passage to India*. Groping in *Howards End* for the way to embody his thought, Forster too often substitutes preachiness for the integrated imagery of a coherent position.

The narrator presides over the survival theme, and most of the passages that celebrate England emanate from his voice. Elegiac and passionate, sentimental and unabashed, they transcend the focus on personality even as they represent a desperate attempt to retain the civilization for which it was a primary value.

> Branksea Island lost its immense foreshores and became a sombre episode of trees. Frome was forced inwards toward Dorchester, Stour against Wimborne, Avon towards Salisbury, and over the immense displacement the sun presided, leading it to triumph ere he sank to rest. England was alive, throbbing through all her estuaries, crying for joy through the mouths of all her gulls, and the north wind, with contrary motion, blew stronger against her rising seas. What did it mean? For what end are her fair complexities, her changes of soil, her sinuous coast? Does she belong to those who have moulded her and made her feared by other lands, or to those who had added nothing to her power, but have

somehow seen her, seen the whole island at once, lying as a jewel in a silver sea, sailing as a ship of souls, with all the brave world's fleet accompanying her towards eternity?

F. R. Leavis cites this passage to note that Forster "lapses into such exaltations quite easily," and he criticizes the vagueness that Forster's use of "somehow" creates in the last sentence. But do we not react more to the inflated diction of "leading it to triumph ere he sank to rest," to the frenetic personifications of "England was alive," "throbbing," and "crying"? Besides the hyperbole, of which one can find in *Howards End* surpassing examples, the passage is noteworthy for revealing Forster's ambivalence of preoccupation and uncertainty of mode. The rhetorical question about England's fate leads not to concern with "the brave world's fleet" but to an expression of conflict between power and the creative imagination. In this it reflects the disjunction between the goals of reconciliation and victory seen in the action and implies the ascendancy of those who see life whole, who have "seen the whole island at once." These, of course, are the Schlegels, and, as the only voice capable of the rhetorical question, the narrator himself. Thus while appearing to transcend the concern with personality, Forster displays the superiority of the mind whose insight includes but discounts "those who have moulded her and made her feared by other lands." Yet Leavis's uneasiness with "somehow" ought to have extended to the literary echoes and secondhand images, which suggest limitation or, as I. A. Richards put it, a "forcing" of the creative imagination. Again to contrast the ungrounded abstraction of this language with the concrete diction and integrated imagery of *A Passage to India* is to envision the distance Forster still has to travel.

The inner tensions that these "forcings" imply may also be seen in direct expressions of ambivalence within the narrative voice. Noteworthy here is the degree to which Forster's apprehension contains something other than concern for the civilization he loves, for underlying the exhortation to human relations is a striking sense of recoil from humanity.

Their house was in Wickham Place, and fairly quiet, for a lofty promontory of buildings separated it from the main thoroughfare. One had the sense of a backwater, or rather of an estuary, whose waters flowed in from the invisible sea, and ebbed into a profound silence while the waves without were still beating. Though the promontory consisted of flats—expensive, with cavernous entrance halls, full of concierges and palms—it fulfilled its purpose, and gained for the older houses opposite a certain measure of peace. These, too, would be swept away in time, and another

promontory would rise upon their site, as humanity piled itself
higher and higher on the precious soil of London.

The narrative voice discriminates between house and city and, more significantly, between human life and nature. Noise, vulgarity, meaningless aggre-
gation cover simultaneously the flats of a burgeoning city and the ephemeral
but continuous flow of humanity they enclose.

This ambivalence may also be seen in Forster's treatment of characters.
It is curious that this most personal narrator should display so little sympathy
for the characters of whom he claims such profound knowledge. But the
intimacy of his rhetoric obscures the indifference or hostility that underlies
his professions of concern. To the gap between Forster's theory and his
practice with Henry Wilcox and his condescension to Leonard Bast we must
add the overt repugnance he feels for Jacky Bast: "A woman entered, of
whom it is simplest to say that she was not respectable. . . . Yes, Jacky was
past her prime, whatever that prime may have been." Even the Schlegels,
though in a more disguised manner, receive a share of this ambivalence.
Helen is passionate and truthful, the only character to act on the doctrine of
personal responsibility that Margaret and the narrator espouse. But Forster's
disapproval of Helen's excesses and his fear of her enticements undercut his
support of her perceptions. On Margaret the narrator renders little judgment,
but whether from unconscious intention or inability to separate himself from
her characteristics, Forster has produced a character whose stridency evokes
a certain recoil. And the narrator's impulse to protect himself from the vulgar
crowd and the less comfortable realities of existence is mirrored in Margaret,
to whom the appearance of Leonard Bast's wife, "Mrs. Lanoline," causes
an anxiety that is not solely concern for the Basts: "She feared, fantastically,
that her own little flock might be moving into turmoil and squalor, into
nearer contact with such episodes as these."

Thus, even as Forster describes with some compassion the consequences
for Leonard Bast of his entrapment in class (Mrs. Lanoline is such a consequence), he draws back from contact with the imperfectly washed. Concerned though he is with social equity and social cost, Forster shrinks from
humanity in the aggregate. His ideology may be seen partly as an expression
of this ambivalence: the individual is nearer to the "unseen" than any organization, humanity as a concept is associated with isms and programs.
The consequences of this position engender what has been described as Forster's critique of liberalism. But although he dramatizes the impotence of the
liberal intelligentsia to solve the problems of modern society, there is little
evidence of Forster's separation from liberal values.

Portrayed as inhabitants of a feminine culture and divorced from power, the intelligentsia are dilettantes. While Forster yearns for masculinity, he can conceive it only as Henry Wilcox, whom he repudiates, or as Leonard Bast, who is so disadvantaged he doesn't signify. With apprehensions about the feminization of culture, expressed in his criticism of Margaret's effeminate brother Tibby and in the sisters' awareness of the need for balance, he nevertheless places his moral weight behind the Schlegels. To women as a group he is less generous. Margaret and Helen's all-female discussion club presents something of a parallel to the Apostolic session of *The Longest Journey*. But the women discuss social questions whereas the men engaged in metaphysical speculation, a Forsterian estimate of their relative capacities, as the narrator's misogynistic comment that "the female mind, though cruelly practical in daily life, cannot bear to hear ideals belittled in conversation" suggests. One should note, however, that both discussion groups are equally ineffectual.

Although Forster treats Leonard Bast more as representative of a class than as an individual, he does not conclude that social or economic action to improve the situation of Leonard Bast is desirable. On the contrary, the members of the debating society avoid the issue by bequeathing their fictional millionaire's legacy within their own class. Margaret wishes to help only the individual, but the very values of integrity and honor that comprise the "inner" ideal nullify this possibility in the novel itself. For when Helen undertakes to realize Margaret's ideal of personal philanthropy, the near-starving Leonard Bast declines her offer. His refusal, "very civil and quiet in tone," aligns him with the gentlemanly standards of Forster's own class. One could wish that Forster had shown here the hardheaded sophistry of his contemporary Shaw, whose Mr. Doolittle is concerned only about his translation to gentility. At any rate, Leonard's "higher" instincts doom him even more effectively than the indifferent machinations of capitalism. Nice guys finish last, as the contrast of his honorable behavior to Jacky with Henry's sexual opportunism also demonstrates. But although Forster dramatizes these ironies, he clings to the old formulations of honor. For him, the only alleviation of the modern condition lies in escape from the encroaching mass and its urban hive.

Forster's authorial voice itself expresses the conflicts that character and action embody. More than in any other novel Forster directs, exhorts, emphasizes, and seeks to harmonize, as the realities he presents become increasingly intractable to his hopes. Attempting for the last time to demonstrate a hopeful synthesis, straining to bring recalcitrant materials into conformity with his ideology, Forster's voice projects an anguish that moves us but does not solve the novel's problems. The narrator's intense rhetoric is a last, desperate exercise of personality, a final attempt to celebrate the creed of individuality through the colorful tonalities of a highly personal voice.

But *Howards End* demonstrates the limits of the personal, and Forster's movement away from the values of individual fulfillment and personal relations engenders the eventual effacement and withdrawal of his narrator. A valedictory persona, the narrator spends himself in a last violent effort to sustain, through his intense relationship with the reader and through characters in whom he no longer believes, his commitment to individual effort and personality. As the action converges upon Howards End, the narrator begins to withdraw. This is not a dramatic movement, but as his presence diminishes, the narrative voice abandons its exhortations and its intimate tone: in the final pages it appears only to validate Margaret's ominous apprehension of the end of rural civilization and to underline briefly the last revelations of plot, as Margaret discovers that Mrs. Wilcox had bequeathed her Howards End long ago. With this withdrawal the novel approaches the mode, the insights, and the austere voice of *A Passage to India*.

The movement of Forster's narrative voice in *Howards End* from the celebration of personality to a near-detachment from worldly concerns, a progression mirrored in the course of his central character, may be seen as the expression of exhaustion and defeat. But it also represents the impulse to a larger unity that has been present, though in less complex forms, from the first novel. A search for human wholeness and for the perception of cosmic unity underlies the efforts and adventures of all Forster's protagonists, except Maurice, whose depiction presents a special case. The novels that precede *Howards End* focus on the metaphysical resonances of individual self-realization, dramatized in Philip's progress to salvation, Rickie's search for the meaning of reality, and Lucy Honeychurch's acceptance of her sexuality. As we have seen, Philip begins as incomplete both in character and vision. The price of Philip's eventual insight, his withdrawal from participation in life, is a paradox whose implications Forster does not explore. But completion remains both as the ideal for the individual and as a metaphysical condition to be perceived in the universe. Thus Forster insists in *Where Angels Fear to Tread* on the coexistence of opposing qualities. In the world some of these are separate from Philip, but they are what, to approach wholeness, he must come to see.

Forster urges Rickie Elliot to engagement with life and reiterates the moral value of Rickie's participation. Forster's equivocal treatment of Rickie undermines his conception of wholeness in *The Longest Journey*. But Rickie's incompleteness is submerged in the greater capacity of his half-brother, Stephen, and the novel suggests a more or less complete world in the alliance of Cambridge and Wiltshire, which forms a symbolic connection of mind and body, the creativity of intellect and the spontaneity of a not-yet-lost primal paradise. Simpler than its predecessors, *A Room with a View* defines wholeness both as happy sexual union and as the spiritual comradeship of man and woman.

The formulation of an ideal of completeness is far more complex in *Howards End,* and all the novel's themes partake of its conception. In *Where Angels Fear to Tread* the suburban ethos was domestic, the issue formulated simply as a clash between convention and instinct, safely played out across the Channel. The contemporary context enters with the Pembrokes of *The Longest Journey,* whose "public" values threaten the life of imagination, and with the first depiction of a technological progress that threatens the values of nature and tradition. In *Howards End* Forster extends his examination of these issues to the whole of society, seeking an application of the humanistic values that will bring the disparate elements of the social order into harmony. Because the novel asserts harmony and presents conflict, because its efforts to vindicate personal relations and social connection collide with each other and with the increasingly dominant theme of inheritance, the movement it describes appears more impasse than development. But for all its strains, *Howards End* gropes toward what becomes in *A Passage to India* the controlling idea of completion. Personal, social, and metaphysical, the attempts to connect in *Howards End* are all expressions of a single impulse to unity, whose avenue of fulfillment alters significantly in the course of the action.

Margaret herself enacts this alteration. That she has been moving toward a new definition of value is suggested quite early. As a result of Mrs. Wilcox's death, Margaret "saw a little more clearly than hitherto what a human being is and to what he may aspire. Truer relationships gleamed. Perhaps the last word would be hope—hope even on this side of the grave." This language, which hints at ultimates, recurs in association with Howards End and its wych-elm, which, in transcending sex, transcend the personal: "to compare either to man, to woman, always dwarfed the vision. Yet they kept within limits of the human. Their message was not of eternity, but of hope on this side of the grave. As she stood in the one, gazing at the other, truer relationship had gleamed."

House and tree project a sense of man's insignificance in time:

> The present flowed by them like a stream. The tree rustled. It had made music before they were born, and would continue after their deaths, but its song was of the moment. The moment had passed.

> The tree rustled again. Their senses were sharpened, and they
> seemed to apprehend life. Life passed. The tree rustled again.

Notable here is the effacement of personality, as the narrative voice sharply
distances the characters. Forster's reiterations emphasize the power, continuity, and creative expression not of man but of nature. The human characters have a moment of perception, "their senses were sharpened and they
seemed to apprehend life," but its transitoriness is immediately asserted in
the short, bold, declaratory two-word sentence, "Life passed." The tree has
the last word. The moment of apprehension is a moment of peace, both
timeless and ephemeral.

> The peace of the country was entering into her. It has no com-
> merce with memory, and little with hope. Least of all is it con-
> cerned with the hopes of the next five minutes. It is the peace of
> the present, which passes understanding. Its murmur came
> "now," and "now" once more as they trod the gravel, and "now"
> as the moonlight fell upon their father's sword. They passed up-
> stairs, kissed, and amidst the endless iterations, fell asleep.

This passage presents a significant anticipation of *A Passage to India*,
in which humanity is dwarfed by the vast Indian landscape and distanced
by the Marabar hills, "older than anything in the world." In the final novel,
nature is no longer redemptive, but there, as here, Forster develops man's
subordination to a timeless and powerful nature and fixes a visionary moment at once permanent and transitory.

Howards End retains the possibility of redemption through nature,
clinging to the romantic tradition and an agnostic Christianity in which,
although no longer anthropomorphic, God still exists. Margaret, although
"not a Christian in the accepted sense," because "she did not believe that
God had ever worked among us as a young artisan," lectures to Helen on
"eternal differences, planted by God in a single family." She believes in
immortality for herself: "An eternal future had always seemed natural to
her." But although, in contrast to the contingency of the final novel, *Howards
End* clings to belief, its conceptions of negation and harmony are closely
analogous to the symbolic chaos of the caves and the precarious harmony of
the Indian Krishna celebration. In a passage quoted earlier, Margaret adumbrated a catalogue of chaos, a "jangle" of arbitrary values and their
negation. Amid this collapse of distinctions that presages the vision of the
caves, motifs associated with Mrs. Wilcox suggest an ultimate harmony:

> Ah, no; there was beauty and adventure behind, such as the man

at her feet had yearned for; there was hope this side of the grave; there were truer relationships beyond the limits that fetter us now. As a prisoner looks up and sees stars beckoning, so she, from the turmoil and horror of those days, caught glimpses of the diviner wheels.

As in *A Passage to India,* turned the other way out, the vision is one of inclusion in God's plan, an affirmation of cosmic unity.

In the novels before *Howards End,* the potential attainment of harmony on earth is not in doubt. Although the equivocal heroes of *Where Angels Fear to Tread* and *The Longest Journey* are permitted only a glimpse of possibility, their fertile comrades, Gino and, more directly, Stephen, are candidates for fulfillment. In the triumph of Lucy Honeychurch, Forster comes closest to the depiction of earthly harmony. But although Lucy's accomplishment mirrors a cosmic wholeness, it is self-contained. Perhaps because there is no discrepancy between earthly possibility and divine unity, the latter is assumed within the terms of Lucy's struggle and victory. There is no significant context beyond her.

But in *Howards End* the search for wholeness becomes implicated in a changing world view, as an intrusion of cosmic evil threatens the entire fabric. Imaged as goblins, gray, city, melting pot, the approach of a disintegrative vision lurks beneath the action, casts in doubt human possibility, and anticipates the apocalyptic symbolism of *A Passage to India.* The pressure of this vision undercuts and nearly effaces worldly hope—in the inner life, in personal and social connection, in a last desperate embrace of nature and the past. Despite the suggestions of divine order, *Howards End* presents more forms of negation than of unity, seen in its recurring imagery of indifference and collapse, in Forster's recoil from the proliferating human scene, in the strained solutions of action, in the shaky optimism of the ending, and finally, in the loss of energy of the narrative voice.

Confronting such negation, the search for meaning acquires new urgency. Forster's insistence and desperation in *Howards End* express his reluctance to admit the insufficiency of the old values, and as we have seen, the problems of the novel arise from Forster's inability to face the issue directly, to confront the implications of his own presentation. His apprehension of cosmic disaster engenders a network of allusion to infinity, eternity, the unseen—a machinery behind the action, invoked throughout the novel by the narrative voice to suggest the discrepancy between human flux and divine stasis. This discrepancy points the way toward a resolution that only the final novel articulates fully. But Margaret's development in *Howards*

End shows the direction. As crisis descends, she accepts the subordination of human effort to the forces beyond it: "No, there was nothing more to be done. They had tried not to go over the precipice, but perhaps the fall was inevitable." But to approach an intuition of ultimate harmony, Margaret must withdraw: "At such moments the soul retires within, to float upon the bosom of a deeper stream, and has communion with the dead, and sees the world's glory not diminished, but different in kind to what she has supposed. She alters her focus until trivial things are blurred."

In her detachment Margaret moves toward the vision and mode of Mrs. Wilcox, in which "daily life appeared blurred." The "trivial things" that Margaret's new insight enables her to blur are the very values she has heretofore been at pains to assert and reconcile. The condition for Margaret's enlarged vision is withdrawal. It is doubtful that Forster intended that the dramatization of this movement should render Margaret as unattractive as she appears. The visible signs of her increased insight are indifference, irritation, and a proprietary concern for Howards End that focuses on matter rather than spirit. But whatever Margaret's deficiencies, her situation is significant because it expresses a dualism inherent from the beginning in Forster's fiction and paves the way for the insights of the final novel.

As she withdraws from worldly effort, Margaret reenacts the paradox seen in Forster's removal of Philip and Rickie from participation in life at the very moment of their real or potential acquisition of crucial insight. But Margaret's situation represents a new development. For her acceptance of limitation is itself an attempt to articulate a new synthesis, to penetrate to a new metaphysic. Paradox remains, in that withdrawal from the values she championed throughout the novel is the condition for Margaret's insight of divine harmony. But *Howards End* has begun the movement, developed fully in *A Passage to India,* beyond the paradox of action to the more complex paradox of implication: Margaret's eventual position hints at the condition of Professor Godbole of the final novel, for whom the abnegation of personality and withdrawal from action are the conditions necessary to the insight of metaphysical unity.

Forster's creation in *Howards End* of a universe that must accommodate evil as well as good suggests that the negative vision must inevitably be included in any assertion of cosmic unity. Although in much of the novel Forster has seemed primarily concerned to test his humanistic philosophy in the social arena, preoccupation with the metaphysical implications of his values underlies the action more thoroughly here than in any earlier novel. *Howards End* still presents the most comprehensive expression of Forster's liberalism. But although we may find irritating the aura of sanctity that surrounds Margaret Schlegel, Forster's message in *Howards End* is that even the saved are not safe. England's decline is not averted, only postponed. Profound and irrational forces threaten the survival alike of individual and society. In *Howards End* Forster fights the implications of the personal and social failures that his novel dramatizes. In *A Passage to India,* he accepts the consequences of human inadequacy and takes as subject the limitation he sought earlier to transcend.

MARTIN PRICE

Forster: Inclusion and Exclusion

One may as well begin with Miss Bartlett's words to Lucy Honeychurch. The scene is Florence, the Pension Bertolini. The ladies have been given rooms that overlook an interior court. Mr. Emerson and his son offer their own rooms in exchange: rooms with a view. Miss Bartlett is offended by the indelicacy of the proposal, but Lucy is less certain how to take it: " 'No, he is not tactful; yet have you noticed that there are people who do things which are most indelicate, and yet at the same time—beautiful?' " " 'Beautiful?' said Miss Bartlett, puzzled at the word. 'Are not beauty and delicacy the same?' "

Miss Bartlett's delicacy is the tiresome self-assertion of a threadbare ego. She uses gratitude as reproach, self-denial as accusation. That she does this unconsciously makes her invulnerable to criticism; that she thinks she acts for the sake of others forces the others to preserve guilty and resentful silence. Miss Bartlett is a fine portrait of the tyranny of the underdog; she has only to allude with delicacy to her dependence on others' wealth to free herself of any reproach of selfishness.

We find Miss Bartlett taking her inevitable place in that crucial scene where, walking out on a natural terrace to admire a magnificent view, Lucy Honeychurch comes unexpectedly upon George Emerson.

> For a moment he contemplated her as one who had fallen out of heaven. He saw radiant joy in her face, he saw the flowers beat

From *Forms of Life: Character and Moral Imagination in the Novel.* © 1983 by Yale University. Yale University Press, 1983.

135

against her dress in blue waves. The bushes above them closed.
He stepped quickly forward and kissed her.

Before she could speak, almost before she could feel, a voice
called: "Lucy! Lucy! Lucy!" The silence of life had been broken
by Miss Bartlett, who stood brown against the view.

Such a discovery releases all of Miss Bartlett's powers. She works "like
a great artist," presenting to Lucy "the complete picture of a cheerless,
loveless world in which the young rush to destruction until they learn better."
In contrast, George's father, Mr. Emerson, is the celebrant of the open, the
naked, and the sincere. "The Garden of Eden," he declares in the manner
of Blake, "which you place in the past, is really yet to come. We shall enter
it when we no longer despise our bodies." His wardrobe bears the inscription, "Mistrust all enterprises that require new clothes." But when three
young men bathe in a pond, their clothes lie in bundles on the bank and
proclaim in a voice like Miss Bartlett's, "We are what matters. Without us
shall no enterprise begin. To us shall all flesh turn in the end." Miss Bartlett,
one might say, seems a creature composed entirely of scarves and buttons.

And yet at the close of the novel, when George Emerson and Lucy are
married and have returned to Florence, they brood over Miss Bartlett's role.
It was she who arranged for Lucy to meet George's father, to be shaken by
him out of cant, waste, and muddle. For Mr. Emerson "robbed the body of
its taint, the world's taunts of their sting" and taught Lucy "the holiness of
direct desire." Could Miss Bartlett have meant this to happen? George offers
his surmise:

> "That from the very first moment we met, she hoped, far down
> in her mind, that we should be like this—of course, very far
> down. That she fought us on the surface, and yet she hoped. I
> can't explain her any other way . . . she is not frozen, Lucy, she
> is not withered up all through. She tore us apart twice, but . . .
> that evening she was given one more chance to make us happy.
> We can never make friends with her or thank her. But I do believe
> that, far down in her heart, far below all speech and behaviour,
> she is glad."

What are we to make of Miss Bartlett? Is she one character or two? Is the
final revelation too ingenious, too surprising, too romancelike? Has a flat
character suddenly become round at the wave of the novelist's wand? The
final treatment of Miss Bartlett is a stroke of wit, much like the gratuitous

confirmation of a truth otherwise demonstrated, as when a sacred pun confirms the plain truths of revelation.

For *A Room with a View* is a novel about repression, muddle, and bad faith; to allow Miss Bartlett her view at some level of unconscious passion—"far down in her heart"—is to celebrate the holiness of the heart's affections and to permit those affections to perform one of their miracles, acting beneath Miss Bartlett's consciousness but making her their instrument. A neat resolution, even a brilliant one, but one that tends to undermine Forster's own categories of flat and round characters.

I should prefer to define those categories in different terms. The repetitive character, in Forster as much as in Dickens, is often powerfully obsessive. He has found a way of meeting all situations, and it may require outrageous energy to preserve this response as well as to shut out all the complexities it avoids. One may see this monotonous and costly expense of energy at work or one may see the vestige of that energy in the husk of a person, a self withered into a type, emotions trivialized into rigid manners, a character who is—in Forster's terms—all clothes. As the sociologist Peter Berger has put it: "Society gives us names to shield us from nothingness. It builds a world for us to live in and thus protects us from the chaos which surrounds us on all sides. It provides us with a language and with meanings that make this world believeable. And it supplies a steady chorus of voices that confirm our belief and still our dormant doubts. . . . [Society] is a conspiracy to bring about inauthentic existence."

The central theme in Forster's earlier novels is the eruption of reality, its bursting through structures that have been built to disguise or conceal it. In *Aspects of the Novel* Forster writes of the tension between the vision of "life in time" and that of "life by values." The violence that runs through his novels—he spoke [in an interview with P. N. Furbank and F. J. H. Haskell, published in *Writers at Work: The* Paris Review *Interviews,* edited by Malcolm Cowley] of the scene in Marabar Caves as "a good substitute for violence"—is a way of dramatizing the insufficiency of life in time, without which of course there can be no life by values either. Sequentiality and logic must be shattered by coincidence or inconsequence, by sudden deaths and improbable meetings. At such moments life in time gives way to romance. In *Howards End* Forster writes about the common "tragedy of preparedness," the sad waste of "staggering through life fully armed." "Life," he goes on, "is indeed dangerous, but not in the way morality would have us believe. It is indeed unmanageable, but the essence of it is not a battle. It is unmanageable because it is a romance, and its essence is romantic beauty." *Romantic beauty* sounds soft and Edwardian. What Forster's romance serves to admit, however, is nothing less than reality. In contrast to it is the specious order of life in time: "Actual life is full of false clues and sign-posts that lead nowhere. With infinite effort we nerve ourselves for a crisis that never comes." There is no better way of describing the overpreparedness of the flat characters, always ready for an imaginary crisis in the armature of a rigid posture.

Reality is, of course, a slippery term. Our ontology is a commitment to what we have chosen to regard as real and what as derivative. Forster's emphasis upon sincerity, self-awareness, and personal relationships becomes a way of dismissing those long stretches of life when we feel little or feel what we are told to feel or, worst of all, try to feel what we have persuaded ourselves we should feel. The unreal has almost inevitably a social setting, for, while Forster is no rebel against the idea of society, he remains a connoisseur of its inauthenticity. He learned from Jane Austen, he tells us, "the possibilities of domestic humour," but he adds, "I was more ambitious than she was, of course; I tried to hitch it on to other things." The chief of those other things, I would propose, is the idea of reality.

In his comments on a fragmentary novel, *Arctic Summer,* Forster draws a distinction between the heroic man who is at home in reality and the more commonplace one who belongs to society:

> I think I know about March. He is first and foremost heroic, no thought of self when the blood is up, he can pounce and act rightly, he is generous, idealistic, loyal. When his blood is not up, when conditions are unfavourable, he is apt to be dazed, trite and sour—the hero straying into the modern world which does not want him and which he does not understand. . . .
>
> How should such a character be presented? Impressionistically— that is to say he should come and go, and not be documented, in contrast to the Whitbys and Borlases [other characters in the novel], who can't be documented too much. . . . The only way to present this hero was to root him as little as possible in society, and to let him come and go unexplained. T. E. Lawrence, whom I did not then know, offers a hint.

Related to this contrast is the one Forster draws in his essay, "Anonymity: An Inquiry":

> Just as words have two functions—information and creation—so each human mind has two personalities, one on the surface, one

deeper down. The upper personality has a name. It is called S. T. Coleridge, or William Shakespeare, or Mrs. Humphry Ward. It is conscious and alert, it does things like dining out, answering letters, etc., and it differs vividly and amusingly from other personalities. The lower personality is a very queer affair. In many ways it is a perfect fool, but without it there is no literature, because unless a man dips a bucket down into it occasionally he cannot produce first-class work. There is something general about it. Although it is inside S. T. Coleridge, it cannot be labelled with his name. It has something in common with all other deeper personalities, and the mystic will assert that the common quality is God, and that here, in the obscure recesses of our being, we near the gates of the Divine.

Forster's contrast between the time-bound and social, on the one hand, and the heroic and impersonal, on the other, is one way of separating the less real from the more, and it governs both the structure of the novels and the conception of character. For the characters are, so to speak, people of the book: whatever their source in Forster's experience, "the original material," as he tells us, "soon disappears, and a character who belongs to the book and nowhere else emerges." The novelist can make his characters more fully "explicable" than actual people—"we get from this a reality of kind we never get in daily life"—but he also exercises the "right to intermittent knowledge": he may enter characters' minds at will but refuse to enter as well, he may show us limited aspects of his characters and even different aspects of each. Forster's conception of character is flexible. One may say that his characters are only people enough to be characters. They are created by a system of notation and reference which permits varying degrees of closeness and varying levels of consciousness, and everywhere we find the filter of free indirect discourse, of characters' thoughts reported in the novelist's words and inevitably shaped in the process, sometimes dryly undercut or gently dislocated from inherent plausibility toward ironic incongruity.

In A Passage to India we enter frequently into Fielding's mind, more occasionally but significantly into Mrs. Moore's, only once into Professor Godbole's and then at a moment when he is meditating. We never see into Godbole's upper personality, in short, and it is the dehumanizing force of Mrs. Moore's vision more than her normal sensibility that concerns us. Each character is real in a somewhat different dimension of its being.

Critics have often remarked that there is no dominant character in this novel, and there is certainly none untouched by weakness or ineffectuality.

The slightness of the characters is due not to their imprecision but to the powerful design which contains them. The presence of India is both ground and theme. It serves to provide setting but it embodies, in its own brilliant metaphors, the central themes that shape the characters as well. They are not figures *in* a landscape but figures *of* a landscape. Forster was afraid at one point that "the characters are not sufficiently interesting for the atmosphere. This tempts me to emphasize the atmosphere, and so to produce a meditation rather than a drama."

D. J. Enright speaks of India—"too big, too diverse, too elusive, to possess what we call 'character' "—as a "vast amorphous Anti-Character," against which human characters "dwindle in the direction of types or even caricatures." I should not see India as a rival force, an Anti-Character, but as a common predicament. There "is scarcely anything in that tormented land," Forster wrote in 1922, "which fills up the gulf between the illimitable and the inane, and society suffers in consequence. What isn't piety is apt to be indecency; what isn't metaphysics is intrigue." The common predicament of Forster's characters is the problem of interpretation. "How can the mind take hold of such a country?" India is in part a country of the mind, or rather a country that creates anxiety by its resistance to the mind's utmost efforts. "Perhaps life is a mystery, not a muddle; they could not tell. Perhaps the hundred Indias which fuss and squabble so tiresomely are one, and the universe they mirror is one. They had not the apparatus for judging." And each kind of apparatus creates its own version of reality. What gives this novel its peculiar form is that the enigmatic resistance India offers to interpretation is stated and restated at each level. As in earlier novels a few phrases gain resonance through repetition, but here their effect is different. If "panic and emptiness" or "telegrams and anger" are clear Wilcox leitmotifs in *Howards End,* the effect of such repetition in *A Passage to India* is less to clarify and consolidate than to unsettle and perplex. Chandrapore, we are told at the outset, is "edged rather than washed by the Ganges," and "the Ganges happens not to be holy here." Later, when Godbole sings to Krishna, "Come, come, come," he explains that in the song the god refuses to come; then he insensibly alters that to "neglects to come." Such terms as "happens" and "neglects" catch the note of contingency—the formless and seemingly accidental nature of experience. So later "the countryside was too vast to admit of excellence. In vain did each item in it call out, 'Come, come.' There was not enough god to go round." Here the "Come, come" is no longer Godbole's; it is a universal cry, and it is disappointed again, not by refusal, not by intention, but simply by insufficiency. There is too much body for spirit to inhabit, too much matter for form to shape.

So too there is just enough suggestion of intention to make India's illegibility the more telling. "The sky settles everything—not only climates and seasons but when the earth shall be beautiful. By herself she can do little—only feeble outbursts of flowers. But when the sky chooses, glory can rain into the Chandrapore bazaars or a benediction pass from horizon to horizon. The sky can do this because it is so strong and so enormous." We have the sense of power but of uncertain purpose, of the arbitrary made all the more striking by its irresistible force. So, Godbole's song invites but resists comprehension. "At times there seemed rhythm, at times there was the illusion of a Western melody. But the ear, baffled repeatedly, soon lost any clue, and wandered in a maze of noises, none harsh or unpleasant, none intelligible. . . . The sounds continued and ceased after a few moments as casually as they had begun—apparently half through a bar, and upon the subdominant." The song, one might say, does not end; it straggles into silence.

India is full of sounds, but there is not enough meaning to make them a language. Where everything is ambiguous—assertion or expletive? message or noise?—there is no determining what has meaning, much less what the meaning may be. Or, in contrast, the very assumption that there should be meaning may lead one to project it with paranoid intensity. The novel is full of phrases that undergo misadventure, whose intention is lost in their reception. This is inevitable in a climate of political domination, of deference and condescension. Everywhere suspicion and distrust force men into confirming their identity by herding in clubs or compounds. And each group inevitably creates its own language, by whose distinctive grammar it seeks to construe what others say. The consequence is that blurring of words into dissonance, the surrender of sense to sheer echo. Words return with new and mocking meanings, with too many, or with none at all. When Mrs. Moore utters her benediction on the wasp, her voice floated out, we are told, "to swell the night's uneasiness."

We are frequently guided in the process of interpretation, learning how to read remarks before we can misread them or they are misread by others. When Hamidullah's servants shout that dinner is ready, they "meant that they wished it was ready and were so understood, for no one moved." When Aziz visits Hamidullah's wife in purdah, it is "difficult to get away, because until they [that is, the men] had their dinner she would not begin hers, and consequently prolonged her remarks in case they should suppose she was impatient." When Aziz recites poetry, no one demands meaning but only mood; they take "the public view of poetry," "never stopping to analyze," never bored by "words, words." But while we are taught to interpret some messages, we are left to encounter other remarks or events that remain puzzles. Is a thing really a sign or a sound a message, or is it like the snake that seems really to be a mere tree? We are often left uncertain; the novel has its own impassivity.

Perhaps the most fundamental metaphor for this problem is that of incarnation, with its inevitable puzzles as to how spirit and flesh may join, as to how much flesh the spirit can sustain or how little it can inhabit, as to why the spirit requires a spot of filth to make it "cohere" (at the moment of the Despised and Rejected). These questions are like the problem of why the spirit required or chose a stable and manger in an obscure province for the Christian nativity. India as always carries its puzzles beyond Christianity's "acceptable hints of infinity." As Aziz and Fielding take their final ride, "the scenery, though it smiled, fell like a pavestone on any human hope. They cantered past a temple to Hanuman—God so loved the world that he took monkey's flesh upon him—and past a Saivite temple, which invited to lust, but under the semblance of eternity, its obscenities bearing no relation to those of our flesh and blood." The Marabar Caves are the ultimate instance of matter refusing spirit—"They are older than anything in the world . . . flesh of the sun's flesh. . . . Nothing attaches to them." They, too, give the illusion of meaning, in the invitation of the polished surface of their circular chambers. But their form, for all its apparent design, proves the very denial of meaning. There are caves with "nothing inside them: if mankind grew curious and excavated, nothing, nothing would be added to the sum of good or evil."

Within this common predicament of the need to interpret and of its constant frustration, Forster creates characters who bring different kinds of apparatus for judging. Each of them seems a deliberate selection from the whole range of human motives and perceptions. They embody different kinds of reality, and we are constantly teased with the question that is more clearly answered in the earlier novels, whether they embody different degrees of reality, whether one is to be preferred to or exalted above others.

Aziz is the most fully realized character in the book. He provides the narrative matrix, he undergoes the most varied and intense experience, and he includes the greatest range of feeling. We see him as host and guest, as friend and father, in his scientific skill and his erotic fantasies. He occupies that most awkward and anxious place in the structure of Indian society—somewhere between the ancient mysteries of Hinduism and the administrative modernity of the English. As a Moslem he is more a rationalist in his religion than the Hindu, perhaps even more than a Christian like Mrs.

Moore. He is warm, generous, eager to be loved and to show regard; and also prickly, resentful, easily depressed and frightened. Still, in the author's words, "he possessed a soul that could suffer but not stifle, and led a steady life beneath his mutability."

Of all the characters in the novel Aziz is most steadily consumed by anxiety, aware of how he is regarded by others, needing confirmation in his own identity, finding it only momentarily and in part through shutting out what he cannot bear to see. In the party at Fielding's he is made comfortable by his host's casual good will, and he fortunately finds no provocation in the women. "Beauty would have troubled him, for it entails rules of its own, but Mrs. Moore was so old and Miss Quested so plain that he was spared this anxiety." He can at first be "entirely straightforward." But, as the ladies lament the failure of their Indian host to fetch them, he soon swings to identification with the English. "Slack Hindus," he exclaims. "It was as well you did not go to their house, for it would give you a wrong idea of India. Nothing sanitary. I think for my own part they grew ashamed of their house and that is why they did not send." And carried along by his fantasy of identification, in spite of the fact that he has just been describing his own home, he invites everyone to his bungalow. When the literal-minded Miss Quested eagerly asks the address, he is filled with horror and changes the subject. In another moment, he is carried away into a glorious nostalgic dream of Mogul justice. He is sentimental and irresponsible, exhibiting the "tenderness of one incapable of administration."

When Ronny Heaslop comes and, with the obtuseness of an assured administrator, ignores the Indians, Aziz cannot give up the "secure and intimate note of the past hour" and becomes "offensively friendly" and provocative. "He did not mean"—how often that phrase must occur in the novel—"to be impertinent to Mr. Heaslop. . . . He did not mean to be greasily confidential to Miss Quested . . . nor to be loud and jolly towards Professor Godbole." Aziz loses all taste and control.

The unpleasantness Aziz attains is only a symptom of his anxiety. "He isn't a bounder," Fielding protests. "His nerves are on edge, that's all." What makes the scene fascinating is not only the dramatic tension Forster gives it, but the way in which it catches, at a level that is far deeper and more momentous than the merely aesthetic, the lack of proportion and of taste that characterize India. It is not just that Aziz would have spoiled a room that Fielding has the good taste to leave unadorned. More delicate and more moving is the difficulty Aziz has in sustaining an identity, in knowing on what terms he can meet the English. Behind his anxiety lie the social and political enigmas of India; its metaphysical puzzles never trouble him and hardly enter his awareness. Hinduism scarcely provokes his curiosity. And so, in cheerful ignorance, he can lead the others to the Marabar Caves.

For Aziz the deepest religious experience is his communion with Mrs. Moore. It survives and governs his life, a moment somehow taken out of time—purified of its irritation at Mrs. Callendar's snub and its aggressive beginnings—preserved as a vision of disinterested union, a moment of release from a politicized world. Forster said of Mrs. Wilcox that he was "interested in the imaginative effect of someone alive, but in a different way from other characters—living in other lives." This is the case with Mrs. Moore. Not only does she become the goddess Esmiss Esmoor, but she presides over Aziz's generous forgiveness of damage payments from Adela.

In the final section, when her uncanny son Ralph comes to Mau, Aziz is once more shaken by her survival. Aziz has retreated to a native state and removed all the sources of strain he felt in Anglo-India; this has meant giving up the serious practice of medicine as well. The false note is that Aziz has built his new life on the belief that he has been betrayed by Fielding. He is unsettled to learn that Fielding has married Stella Moore rather than Adela Quested. In his treatment of Ralph he adopts some of the cruelty Callendar had shown to the Nawab's grandson. When Ralph exclaims, "Your hands are unkind," Aziz protests that he is causing no pain. Ralph quietly agrees. "But there is cruelty." Ralph's candor is a revival of Mrs. Moore's directness. "You should not treat us like this," Ralph says. "Dr. Aziz, we have done you no harm." At this moment a prisoner is released from the jail nearby as part of the annual Hindu festival. "Mixed and confused, the rumours of salvation entered the Guest House." Aziz is released from his anger, his hands become kind, and he acknowledges Ralph Moore's intuitive power: "Then you are an Oriental." As he says it, Aziz shudders. "Those words—he had said them to Mrs. Moore in the mosque in the beginning of the cycle, from which, after so much suffering, she had got free. Never be friends with the English! Mosque, caves, mosque, caves. And here he was starting again."

At this moment Forster makes Aziz himself acknowledge and accept the pattern of nonlogical repetition, of "life by values" as opposed to "life in time." More than that, Aziz repeats the titles of the two parts of the novel itself, "mosque, caves," and makes their structure the pattern of his own memory. It is a moment at which Aziz seems almost to dissolve into thematic form; it is appropriately at the close of the novel that the principal character comes to an awareness closest to the author's. The shudder is a token of an action whose impulses lie below consciousness; yet Aziz makes the action his own, avows and intends it, and becomes free in the process.

Adela Quested and Cyril Fielding are, in contrast with Aziz, trapped within the limits of liberal, rational intelligence. They are well-meaning, tolerant, open. Adela is high-minded, theoretical, and unconsciously patronizing; but she has courage and conscience. Her crisis is one induced by insincerity. Adela and Ronny are brought together in the ride with the Nawab and Miss Derek by their difference from the others—"to the animal thrill there was now added a coincidence of opinion." It is hardly enough for marriage, as Adela comes to recognize; and her revulsion from the insincerity to which she is committed affects her at the caves. Instead of the vertigo of meaninglessness and the horror of total unity that Mrs. Moore feels, Adela's less imaginative mind demands a literal cause and, in its breakdown, invents one. The worst of her later suffering is the recognition of this self-betrayal. To Fielding, she becomes—under the stress of her suffering—a real person. But for Hamidullah, she does not. Her behavior "rested on cold justice and honesty; she had felt, while she recanted, no passion of love for those she had wronged." Her sacrifice "did not include the heart." But the point of Adela's charge is that her mind—honest and admirable—is out of touch with her feelings, does not know her heart.

Fielding in a comparable way suffers an excess of detachment, an inability to escape his intelligence and to lose himself in feeling. About Aziz he thinks, "'I shall not really be intimate with this fellow,'" and then, "'nor with anyone.' And he had to confess that he really didn't mind." He is content to help people, but he travels light: "Clarity prevented him from experiencing something else." When he talks with Indians, his line of thought does not trouble them, but his words are "too definite and bleak." The most expansive vision of Fielding's humanism is the interlude at the close of the second part of the novel, the assertion of Mediterranean order and form which just precedes the formlessness of the Hindu festival. Venice provides escape from anxiety into assurance. It offers the "harmony between the works of man and the earth that upholds them, the civilization that has escaped muddle, the spirit in a reasonable form, with flesh and blood subsisting." This vision of Italy is different from the overrefined ones of Philip Herriton or Cecil Vyse, but it is different too from the sacramental violence in the Piazza della Signoria or in Monteriano. It becomes, in this novel, an image of ideal incarnation. In the earlier, fragmentary work *Arctic Summer,* Forster gave a vision of Italy to the unheroic man, Whitby:

> The train ran downward into a beauty that admits romance but
> is independent of it. Youth demands colour and blue sky, but
> Martin, turned thirty, longed for Form. Perhaps it is a cold desire,

but it can save a man from cynicism; it is a worker's religion, and Italy is one of its shrines. . . . She, like himself, had abandoned sentiment; she existed apart from associations by the virtues of mass and line: her austere beauty was an image of the millennium towards which all good citizens are cooperating.

That is a somewhat chilling version of the religion of Form, but it serves to suggest the limitations that are at least implicit in Fielding's too. For if these images, like the characters of Adela and Fielding, have human centrality, they also have an austerity that seems more pinched than august, a clarity that may even seem like a defense against reality. The characters sense this themselves: "As though they had seen their own gestures from an immense height—dwarfs talking, shaking hands and assuring each other that they stood on the same footing of insight." There is a "wistfulness," a suspicion of being cut off from a reality their rational clarity cannot quite admit exists.

Mrs. Moore and Professor Godbole are the characters whose status is most equivocal. They lack the human centrality that we associate with rational awareness, with moral responsibility, with form on a limited scale. They are less fully human than the others, and we are teased with the question of whether they are something more.

Mrs. Moore's age sets her apart from most of the characters in the novel. It is presumably not greater than Mrs. Turton's. What matters again is that it creates anxiety: the strain of fatigue and depression induced by a world suddenly grown incomprehensible and a god who has lost much of his credibility. "She found [God] increasingly difficult to avoid as she grew older, and he had been constantly in her thoughts since she entered India, though oddly enough he satisfied her less. She must needs pronounce his name frequently, as the greatest she knew, yet she had never found it less efficacious. Outside the arch there seemed always an arch, beyond the remotest echo a silence."

Mrs. Moore appears to us in only a few aspects. She has no elaborately documented history; large areas of concern do not touch her. We see her first in the mosque with Aziz; her generosity and candor dissolve his anger and free his deeper self. As she recalls the episode later, she realizes how easily "it could be worked into quite an unpleasant scene. The doctor had begun by bullying her, he had said Mrs. Callendar was nice, and then— finding the ground safe—had changed; he had alternately whined over his grievances and patronized her, had run a dozen ways in a single sentence, had been unreliable, inquisitive, vain. Yes, it was all true, but how false as a summary of the man; the essential life of him had been slain." This ability to see reality without confusion and outside merely social categories is the most impressive of Mrs. Moore's qualities. We see her first in gestures of inclusion, openness, and extension: ready to accept invitations, to be accepted in turn as a Moslem. None of her later meetings with Aziz is so satisfactory as the meeting in the mosque, but each of them builds upon and confirms that meeting. In fact, most of the feeling one might hope to see in her personal relationships is displaced into the curiously limited and intense relationship with Aziz. And one may see even in that relationship something of a withdrawal from the personal to the impersonal, a turning from the limited and timebound to the cosmic and illimitable. As she herself senses, God enters prematurely into her discussion of most matters, such as imperial policy. "God has put us on the earth in order to be pleasant to each other. God . . . is . . . love." Her son attributes this religious strain to "bad health," and among the ironies is the fact that in some measure he is right.

The scene in the cave presents the dark, ironic side of pantheism; a God without personality, a God who includes wasps as well as men, crocodiles as well as moonlight, is wonderful and terrible like the Ganges, but ultimately impassive, indifferent, a formless smother. "Pathos, piety, courage—they exist, but are identical, and so is filth. Everything exists, nothing has value." Unlike Adela Quested, Mrs. Moore cannot project her sense of violation upon another person. She must live with the metaphysical vision itself. She realizes that she doesn't want to communicate with anyone, "not even with God." She bristles thereafter with resentment and irritation; she refuses to testify at the trial of Aziz, although she has no doubt of his innocence. Gradually the sense of outrage takes the form of self-hatred, a sense of her own evil as well as the evil of others ("Good, happy small people. They do not exist, they were a dream"). We may be reminded of two comparable experiences: one is the sense of universal vileness Anna Karenina feels as she moves toward her suicide, the other is the spectacle of a vast disorder that Marlow finds opened by the grief of Jewel in *Lord Jim*.

It is only at the moment of her departure from India that Forster gives us something like a social history of Mrs. Moore's beliefs. As she withdraws, turned petty and peevish, unable to entertain any "large thought," we are made to see the rather naïve expectations that were the conscious surface of a deeper disquietude. She was attracted by a goal that seemed beautiful and easy—"To be one with the universe! So dignified and simple." Now she senses that the abyss may offer not profundity but pettiness, that the serpent of eternity may be made of maggots. She shelters herself in intense self-pity, and she rejects all consolation lest she lose that shelter. Even so, as she leaves India, its variety and particularity reassert themselves. Asirgarh offers noble bastions and a mosque; they disappear and then return, without meaning, without connection ("What could she connect it with except its own name?") but with stubborn and indestructible life. The universe is dissolving into a number of things, each existing in its own right, none enhanced or eclipsed by absorption into unity, none simply legible as a sign.

Mrs. Moore's beliefs have a history, but Professor Godbole's do not. Of all the principal characters, he remains the most opaque. We are allowed to enter his mind only during the ritual, and the consciousness we then explore is devoted to the exercise of meditation. Earlier, Godbole is always presented as out of phase with the social world about him, abrupt, unpredictable, and impassive as India itself. When we first see him at Fielding's, his discussion of the Marabar Caves seems a thrilling game to Aziz. "On [Aziz] chattered, defeated at every move by an opponent who would not even admit that a move had been made, and further than ever from discovering what, if anything, was extraordinary about the Marabar Caves." But Godbole is so inscrutable that one cannot with confidence ascribe intention to him. Is Aziz justified in believing him an opponent? Are the countermoves merely imaginary?

It is Godbole's prayer that causes him and Fielding to miss the train for the Marabar Caves. When Fielding sees him again, after the arrest of Aziz, Godbole politely hopes that "the expedition was a successful one." Does he not know of its consequences? "Oh, yes. That is all around the College." And he proceeds to question Fielding, who is sick with concern about Aziz, on the matter of an appropriate name for a new school to be founded in Mau. It is too much for Fielding, and he puts the question to Godbole inescapably: "Is Aziz innocent or guilty?" No, not inescapably, for Godbole dances away: " 'Dr. Aziz is a most worthy young man. I have a great regard for him; but I think you are asking me whether the individual can commit good actions or evil actions, and that is rather difficult for us.' He spoke without emotion and in short tripping syllables." The inhuman effect of the voice contributes to the stupefying vision of unity: "Because nothing can be performed in isolation. All perform a good action, when one is performed, and when an evil action is performed, all perform it." Godbole illustrates:

> "I am informed that an evil action was performed in the Mara-
> bar Hills, and that a highly esteemed English lady is now seriously
> ill in consequence. My answer to that is this: that action was
> performed by Dr. Aziz." He stopped and sucked in his thin
> cheeks. "It was performed by you." Now he had an air of daring
> and of coyness. "It was performed by me." He looked shyly down

the sleeve of his own coat. "And by my students. It was even performed by the lady herself. When evil occurs, it expresses the whole of the universe. Similarly when good occurs."

That final anticlimax, the all but simpering gestures, the single-minded reductionism—all of these become near-farcical attributes of the proponent of unity. To borrow words Forster used on an earlier occasion (1921), Godbole exhibits "the same mixture of fatuity and philosophy that ran through the whole festival." He seems to deny the reality of suffering, and at the very least he reduces responsibility to something so diffuse as to become trivial. If one substitutes for the attempted rape of Adela Quested almost any public crime—whether it be assassination, forced labor camps, or something so comparatively pardonable as high crimes and misdemeanors, this doctrine of responsibility becomes appalling. Fielding protests: "You're preaching that evil and good are the same." Godbole's reply must be given in full:

> "Oh no, excuse me once again. Good and evil are different, as their names imply. But, in my own humble opinion, they are both of them aspects of my Lord. He is present in the one, absent in the other, and the difference between presence and absence is great, as great as my feeble mind can grasp. Yet absence implies presence, absence is not non-existence, and we are therefore entitled to repeat, 'Come, come, come, come.'" And in the same breath, as if to cancel any beauty his words might have contained, he added, "But did you have the time to visit any of the interesting Marabar antiquities?"

This passage deserves attention. If "absence is not non-existence," we might seem to approach the idea of intention, of a God who refuses rather than neglects to act. And we might in turn approach the moral vision of worshipping God because he is good rather than because he is God. But, if any of this is hinted, it is immediately lost in ludicrous inconsequence. In his guide to *Alexandria*, Forster presents comparable mysteries of Neoplatonism with as much lucidity as mystery permits: "We are all parts of God, even the stones, though we cannot realise it; and man's goal is to become actually, as he is potentially, divine. . . . The Christian promise is that man shall see God, the Neo-Platonic—like the Indian—that he shall be God." But here we are left with the muddle of religious paradox, moral insensibility, and social nicety. The muddle will be redeemed in the Temple festival, but, while one can see its eventual place in the dialectic of the novel, one must hold on to the element of fatuity in Professor Godbole's vision of unity. For

Godbole remains serene amid all the muddles that so demoralized Mrs. Moore. His mind stretches to embrace all of Krishna's guises, whereas her mind recoiled and her heart congealed with the terror of the undifferentiated and formless. Both have moved beyond moral involvement, Mrs. Moore in her refusal to testify, Godbole in his sudden disappearance.

One may feel that Professor Godbole's elasticity comes from a deficiency of awareness rather than from a mysterious depth. For Mrs. Moore's recoil is far more readily understandable. Dr. Johnson wrote a sentence that has its relevance:

> To love all men is our duty, so far as it includes a general principle of benevolence, and readiness of occasional kindness; but to love all equally is impossible; at least impossible without the extinction of those passions which now produce all our pains and all our pleasures; without the disuse, if not the abolition, of some faculties, and the suppression of all our hopes and fears in apathy and indifference.
>
> (*The Rambler,* no. 99)

Forster had drawn an important contrast in "The Gods of India," a book review that appeared in 1914:

> Religion, in Protestant England, is mainly concerned with conduct. It is an ethical code—a code with a divine sanction, it is true, but applicable to daily life. We are to love our brother, whom we see. We are to hurt no one, by word or deed. We are to be pitiful, pure minded, honest in our business, reliable, tolerant, brave. . . .
>
> The code is so spiritual and lofty, and contains such frequent references to the Unseen, that few of its adherents realize it only expresses half of the religious idea. The other half is expressed in the creed of the Hindus. The Hindu is concerned not with conduct, but with vision. To realize what God is seems more important than to do what God wants. He has a constant sense of the unseen . . . and he feels that this tangible world, with its chatter of right and wrong, subserves the intangible. . . . Hinduism can pull itself to supply the human demand for morality just as Protestantism at a pinch can meet the human desire for the infinite and the incomprehensible, but the effort is in neither case congenial. Left to itself each lapses—the one into mysticism, the other into ethics.

This passage helps to make clear the polarity in Forster's conception of character in *A Passage to India*. It is caught at one extreme in the Anglo-Indians and at the other by Godbole—the one a social and moral uniformity that denies personal vision or undisciplined feeling, the other an openness to all possibilities so complete as to exclude nothing; the one all inauthentic order, the other all transcendence and obliviousness of humanistic claims. The former is the ideology of the efficient administrator, the latter the mystical faith of those who cannot be trammeled or troubled by consistency and order. Aziz can participate to an extent in both of these extremes, but he is at home in neither. India itself I have called their common predicament. Its landscape suggests the threat it offers to those who expect meaning; its political and social life represent that threat in visible, limited, but still insoluble form. The predicament India embodies is not restricted to one time or place.

Mrs. Moore and Godbole are more receptive than others to a world of apparent contingency; but they differ from each other. Mrs. Moore finds her faith stretched to the point of collapse and savage disenchantment, whereas Godbole is never seen (except perhaps at the final moments of the Temple ritual) as in the least troubled by any cost his faith exacts. To the skeptic, the adept may seem like a dupe, and Forster never quite allows us to lose all of our skepticism. Forster writes the novel in the style of a lucid, ironic, liberal intelligence, and the style presents its limits in order to indicate its insufficiency. The ineffable is intimated through incidents that may be symbolic but need not be. They are part of such a welter of farcical incongruity that we can only tentatively accredit their meaningfulness. Nor can we altogether disallow it. They create the vertigo of the uninterpretable.

Godbole, of course, is to provide Aziz with a new post in Mau, and he is to summon up the vision of Mrs. Moore, to love her as God, and to summon God on her behalf. There is no question of his benignity and of the sincerity of his doctrine; but he contributes his "highbrow incoherence" (I borrow the phrase from Natwar Singh) to the total pattern of mystery and muddle, of spirit and flesh, of meaning and misinterpretation. The festival will introduce the grossness of the melting butter running down the forehead, the tatty indecorum of the music and decorations, the jolly disorder of practical jokes, the untidiness of accident—all dimensions of this disparity between matter and spirit. Godbole contributes to that pattern the comic immediacy of a man enmeshed in the matter he aspires to ignore—his pince-nez is caught in his garlands, just as his reaching behind him for his food makes it all the more grotesquely conspicuous. Like Mrs. Moore he is less a person than the other principal characters, and, even more than she, he seems to expose directly, almost without mediation, that deeper self that is at once a perfect fool and the nearest approach to the gates of the Divine.

One might close with a brief glimpse of two minor characters who catch supremely well the puzzles of incarnation which lie at the center of the book. The first is the punkah wallah, the man who pulls the fan in the courtroom. "He had the strength and beauty that sometimes come to flower in Indians of low birth. When that strange race reaches the dust and is condemned as untouchable, then nature remembers the physical perfection that she accomplished elsewhere, and throws out a god." He seems "apart from human destinies, a male fate, a winnower of souls," but in fact he scarcely "knew that he existed and didn't even know that he worked a fan, though he thought he pulled a rope." When the trial has been dismissed and the court abandoned, he remains alone, "the beautiful naked god," still "unaware that anything unusual had occurred."

Near the close of the novel, a model of the village of Gokul—the Hindu Bethlehem as it were—is pushed into the waters by a splendid servitor, "naked, broad-shouldered, thin-waisted—the Indian body again triumphant." As the boats containing Aziz and the English visitors collide, they drift forward "helplessly against the servitor. Who awaited them, his beautiful dark face expressionless." Again, we have the impassivity, the resistance to meaning, as the ritual peters out in mud, straggling crowds, "ragged edges of religion . . . unsatisfactory and undramatic tangles." The theme of the festival, earlier voiced by Mrs. Moore, has been characteristically misspelled—"God si love"—untidy, resisting meaning, but also suggesting obliquely an "if" for an "is." God if love. We create God through our love. Love creates meaning. Two cheers for morality.

The subtlety of the novel lies in its unrelieved tension of flesh and spirit, exclusion and invitation, the social self and the deeper impersonal self. At one extreme are the caricatures caught in the social grid—the Turtons and Burtons. At the other are the characters who slip out of the meshes of social responsibility through despair or obliviousness. We move from the elaborate rituals of Anglo-India to Mau, where the only aspects of life we are shown are ecstasy and negligence. Where does the mind rest? The difficulty with looking at reality directly is that reality will tend to dissolve: "not now, not here, not to be apprehended except when it is unattainable." Transcendence dehumanizes, the deeper self is a source rather than a habitation, we cannot see the unseen. We only glimpse it through paradox, violence, or farce; and each of these contributes something to Forster's conception of character.

RUSTOM BHARUCHA

Forster's Friends

It is a sad photograph that should have faded with time. Perhaps it should not have been taken in the first place. The camera catches the two figures in a blank moment, their faces stiff, their eyes wide and vacant. The men seem to belong together like a married couple, but there is a rift between them. Outwardly, they resemble men of property, utterly respectable: their hair parted neatly on the side, their moustaches trimmed. Yet it is not a club that they belong to but a universe—of oblivion, separation, and death. Almost as a sign, the photographer has left an enormous space above their heads, a nothingness that seeps into the gulf between the men.

Looking at the photograph many years after it was taken, Forster observed that he looked "starry-eyed" in it, "very odd indeed." Significantly, he tore up all the letters that he had written to his mother from Tesserete, Switzerland, where the photograph had been taken. It was a time he would rather forget, reminding him of a relationship that hadn't worked out. As he put it, the holiday in Tesserete was like "a honeymoon slightly off-colour." The man who lost interest in him, preferring to flirt with a waitress, was Syed Ross Masood, Forster's lifelong friend to whom *A Passage to India* was originally dedicated. He is the other figure in the photograph.

Otherness is what initially attracted Forster to Masood. This "oriental" was unlike anyone he had met. In the suburban milieu of Weybridge, where Forster lived with his mother, Masood must have appeared like a sultan from the *Arabian Nights*—an alluring, exotic figure, well over six feet tall, regal

From *Raritan: A Quarterly Review* 5, no. 4 (Spring 1986). © 1986 by *Raritan*.

in style, histrionic in manner, and very handsome. When he got bored with
the Latin Forster attempted to teach him, he would pick up his tutor bodily
and tickle him. When his fellow students at Oxford ragged him about using
scent, he simply "wiped the floor with one of them in a wrestling match."
Masood was everything Forster was not—physically, socially, and cultur-
ally—and it is perhaps for that very reason that Forster came under his spell.
On New Year's Eve, 1910, he confessed his love in his diary:

> Let me keep clear from criticism and scheming. Let me think of
> you and not write. I love you, Syed Masood; love.

These lines illuminate Forster's style of thought. First, the individual
utterance—"I love you, Syed Masood"—then a break, an intake of breath
signified by a semicolon, and then the thought itself—"love." Rooted in a
person, and yet anonymous, detached. On reading the details of Forster's
love for Masood so intimately recorded by P. N. Furbank in his celebrated
biography—an intimacy so natural that Forster himself seems to be speaking
to us—one realizes how much turmoil there was within Forster not only
because Masood did not reciprocate his love, but because their friendship
itself was based on differing conceptions of love, enigmatic, and left unex-
plained. Forster loved Masood and Masood loved Forster, but not in the
same way.

It is too easy to use the dichotomy of East and West to explain the
incompatibility of love between Forster and Masood. For one thing, if Masood was an "oriental," a man of the East, he was also an unqualified wog.
And like all wogs, he was and was not Indian. He was the grandson of Sir
Syed Ahmed Khan, the great Muslim reformer, but he was also the devoted
foster son of Theodore Morrison, the principal of the Muslim Anglo-Oriental
College at Aligarh which resembled Eton in its early years. Masood's sentiments were eastern, but his education was almost entirely western. On the
one hand, he was entranced by Urdu poetry, particularly by the verse of
Ghalib and Hali, but he also played the banjo and read the French symbolists.
He never found time to attend meetings of the India Society at Oxford, but
he was invariably free for a game of tennis. So how "oriental" was Syed
Masood?

It would seem that Masood played with oriental images, fully aware of
their stereotypes. Never embarrassed to indulge in grandiloquence, he once
said: "Ah, that I had lived 250 years ago when the oriental despotisms were
in their prime!" Clearly, he lived before Wittfogel and Said had their say
about orientalism, and at a time when the British could still be tolerated by
educated Indians. Masood enjoyed his role as an "oriental" and frequently

wrote to Forster in the epistolary style of a Scheherazade: "let it be known to thee that thy slave's house was this day brightened by the arrival of an epistle from thee—the source of all his happiness." Even in jest, it is ironic for Masood to speak of himself as the "slave" (and of Forster as his "master"), because it was he who dominated the friendship. In fact, Masood was possessive of all his friends, whose attention he commanded in a vehement way. Not surprisingly, by the time he graduated from Oxford, his only friends were Indian with the exception of Forster and another Englishman. It seems that Masood's English "friends" could no longer accept his despotic view of friendship.

Forster learned to accept it in time. But in the early years, he must have been confused by Masood's protestations of love, particularly when they were yearning and not in the least possessive. For instance, in a letter written to Forster eight months before they went to Tesserete, Masood writes:

> Dearest boy if you knew how much I loved you & how I long to be alone with you. . . . Let us get away from the conventional world & let us wander aimlessly if we can, like two pieces of wood on the ocean & perhaps we will understand life better. . . . I only wish that you & I could live together forever & though that is a selfish wish I feel sorry that it will not come to anything. Did you see the eclipse, how beautiful it was!

What was this? Rhapsodic "oriental" rhetoric or true sentiment? It would seem that Masood had the latter in mind because in a subsequent letter he tells Forster: "you are about the only Englishman in whom I have come across true sentiment & that, too, real sentiment even from the oriental point of view." He then urges Forster to cultivate a faculty that every "true and well bred oriental" possesses—*Tarass*. For Masood, *Tarass* is that capacity to enter the feelings of another and absorb the atmosphere of a place. The oriental senses are always ready "*to receive* & quivering to receive some impression."

If Forster had possessed or had been possessed by *Tarass,* he would have embraced Masood when they once parted company at the Gare du Nord in Paris. He would have understood why Masood was so "extraordinarily sad." When Forster defended his crisp English goodbye by saying that they would be meeting in three days, Masood wailed: "But we're *friends!*" A parting had to be lingered over for Masood, otherwise how could friendship be savored? What was the point of saying goodbye if there was no sentiment attached to it?

Not only are the signs of friendship different for Forster and Masood, but their acceptance of sentiment in relation to love is also at odds. For Masood, sentiment seems to be the grace of love, and in its excess of feeling, it becomes the raison d'être of friendship. It is beautiful in itself and does not have to lead anywhere or prove anything. Like a verse by Ghalib whose sounds hang in the air, waiting to be received and then fading away, it becomes that moment of intimacy which true friends share. In contrast, it would seem that for Forster sentiment is merely an attribute of friendship. In itself there is no guarantee of intimacy. No wonder he felt compelled to clarify his relationship with Masood. When he eventually confessed his love, Masood merely said, "I know," and allowed the moment to pass. For Masood, the intimacy of their friendship lay in the exchange of sentiment itself, not in the physical act of love. Many years later, Forster was to understand this. There is that inexplicable moment in A Passage to India when Aziz quotes Ghalib, and Forster reflects:

> The poem had done no "good" to anyone, but it was a passing reminder, a breath from the divine lips of beauty, a nightingale between two worlds of dust. Less explicit than the call to Krishna, it voiced our loneliness nevertheless, our isolation, *our need for the Friend who never comes yet is not entirely disproved.*

As Masood knew, his friend Forster would find *Tarass* in his art.

It is actually quite amazing that Forster and Masood were able to share as much as they did because the world they belonged to had a very rigid conception of how men should behave with men, and more specifically, how white men should treat black men. Colonialism, one might say, did not approve of intimacy between the rulers and the ruled. Not only did familiarity breed contempt, it also undermined the fundamental premises of authority and separatism that characterized the colonial administrative system. This position is staunchly upheld by Turton, the prototype of the *burra sahib* in A Passage to India, who says, "I have never known anything but disaster result when English people and Indians attempt to be intimate socially. Intercourse—yes. Courtesy—by all means. Intimacy—never, never." The sexual racism of the British is even more conspicuous in McBryde who assumes that "the darker races are physically attracted by the fairer, not vice versa." The intimacy he envisions, of course, is between a man and a woman. What would he have thought—and this is merely a perverse hypothesis on my part—if Aziz had made sexual advances to Fielding (or vice versa)? It is more than likely that this "crime" would have outraged not only his sense of decency and morality, but his very idea of manhood—not only his own sense of being a man, but his absolute faith in the masculine identity of his culture.

An ethos of masculinity developed during the British Raj of India, first in England, and then later, through a process of imitation, within India itself. Whether a man was serving his country at home or abroad, he was required to be "manly"—aggressive, competitive, and in control of his emotions and duties. The Empire had no particular use for women or for the values associated with femininity. Homosexuals were tolerated only insofar as they remained discreet about their activities and functioned within the strict confines of marginal societies like Bloomsbury and Oxbridge. It was among select and "understanding" members of these societies that Forster circulated his homosexual novel *Maurice,* which he knew could not be published "until his death or England's." While Forster was to have a fairly active homosexual life in England, particularly after he returned from India, he was no doubt aware that he belonged to the silent minority, a secret society of the sensitive, whose sexual ambivalence was symptomatic of their innate resistance to the authoritarian and paternalistic rule of their government. Fundamentally, Forster was caught within a system that upheld norms of manhood that contradicted his own.

Even in India he could not entirely escape these established norms, because they had been adopted by Indian men as their only alternative to defeating the British at their own game. In psychoanalytic terms, Indians had begun to "identify with the aggressor." Elaborating on this phenomenon in his brilliant study *The Intimate Enemy,* Ashis Nandy situates the opposition between *purusatva* (the essence of masculinity) with *klibatva* (the essence of hermaphroditism) as the essential conflict in the colonial psychology of Indians. "Femininity-in-masculinity," he claims, "was perceived as the final negation of a man's political identity, a pathology more dangerous than femininity itself." In reaction to this "pathology," there was an upsurge of "manly" sentiments and attitudes, martial acts of defiance, and frequently humiliating attempts to emulate the "tough politics" of the British. In *A Passage to India,* Ronnie speaks derisively of this nascent masculinity among the Indians, which his own government has unconsciously enforced. "They used to cringe," he says, "but the younger generation believe in a show of manly independence. . . . Whether the native swaggers or cringes, there's always something behind every remark, and if nothing else he's trying to increase his *izatt*—in plain Anglo-Saxon, to score."

The kind of "native" who asserted his masculinity was more often than not semi-Westernized. Masood, of course, was so Westernized that "manliness" was second nature to him. There is the famous story of his abrasive encounter with a British officer who ordered him out of a railway compartment. With his legs stretched out, Masood coolly said, "D'you want your head knocked off?" whereupon he and the officer became "excellent friends." The anecdote reveals the kind of tolerance, even camaraderie, that could develop between Indian and English men, particularly if the former imitated the manners of manhood assumed by the latter.

The real antagonists of Indian men were not their sahibs but the memsahibs who formed a minuscule society of their own. Excluded from any kind of meaningful social activity, they increasingly saw themselves, as Nandy puts it, as "the sexual competitors of Indian men with whom their men had established an unconscious homoeroticized bonding." Though this "bonding" is suggestively, though not explicitly, explored in the relationship between Fielding and Aziz, there can be no doubt of Mrs. Turton's racist abhorrence of Indian men. "They ought to crawl from here to the caves on their hands and knees whenever an Englishwoman's in sight, they oughtn't to be spoken to, they ought to be spat at, they ought to be ground into the dust." Significantly, this invective is aimed primarily at the white men in the room, Mrs. Turton's men, whom she considers "weak, weak, weak."

What is so astonishing about A Passage to India is that it resonates with these colonial attitudes and tensions while remaining a novel "set out of time." Forster scrupulously avoids specifying dates, though the imaginative space of the novel suggests an India that has passed through the Swadeshi Andolan and the Partition in Bengal. Now there is a deceptive calm, a scarcely controlled tension that threatens to break out into a national uprising. The novel is set within this tension and maintains a precarious equilibrium. Certainly, when Forster visited India for the first time in 1912, he became fully aware of the resistance to British rule, particularly through his meeting with two radical Muslim leaders, the brothers Shaukat and Mohammed Ali. Joint editors of an anti-imperialist journal, the Comrade, they condemned the British endorsement of Italian rule in Tripoli and supported the pro-Turkish movement among Indian Muslims. It is possible to see traces of this radical fervor in the "manly" Indian characters of A Passage to India, particularly in Aziz after the trial, when he becomes "an Indian at last." But Aziz's resistance to the British is deeply confused not only because he is a Muslim before he is an Indian, but because he doesn't know how to get rid of the British. All he has is rhetoric, emotion, and manliness. His cheers at the end of the novel, "Hurrah for India! Hurrah! Hurrah!" are like the echoes of the Empire mocking him.

> And Aziz in an awful rage danced this way and that, not knowing what to do, and cried: "Down with the English anyhow. That's certain. Clear out, you fellows, double quick, I say. We may hate

one another, but we hate you most. If I don't make you go, Ahmed will, Karim will, if it's fifty or five hundred years we shall get rid of you, yes, we shall drive every blasted Englishman into the sea."

Clearly, the novel was written before Gandhi's advocacy of nonviolence had acquired a national dimension. He needed less than fifty years not to "drive every blasted Englishman into the sea," but to convince them that it was time that they left. He alone knew how to deal with the manliness of the Turtons and the Burtons, not to mention Sir Winston Churchill. With his deceptively childlike and gentle manner, he strategically debunked the ethos of *purusatva* not to capitulate to the British, but to defeat them with another concept of manhood that brought the feminine instincts of man to the surface. As Ashis Nandy so accurately perceives, "Gandhi was clear in his mind that activism and courage could be liberated from aggressiveness and recognized as perfectly compatible with womanhood, particularly maternity." Though this alternative to the Western concept of manhood is something that Aziz has yet to learn, there is a moment in the novel when he does assert his manhood, not in Gandhian terms, but in the deeply personal tone of his author. It occurs when Hamidullah is talking to him man-to-man about "sticking to the profession" and earning the respect of European doctors. Aziz listens to the spiel, then winks and says, "There are many ways of being a man: mine is to express what is deepest in my heart." This is my moment of *Tarass* in the novel.

In *A Passage to India,* Forster attempted to express what was deepest in his heart. The writing of the novel was not easy. It wasn't just the incompatibility between East and West that proved to be an obstacle; Forster had reconciled himself to the fact that "most Indians, like most English people, are shits, and I am not interested whether they sympathize with one another or not." The novel was hard to write for personal rather than political reasons: it followed the death of a friend, another Muslim, Mohammed-ed-Adl.

They had met in Alexandria in 1916 when Forster worked for the Red Cross and Mohammed was employed as a tram conductor. Not only was Mohammed Forster's first true lover, he was also the first man who challenged Forster to cross "a big racial and social gulf." He was Egyptian, a race more despised by the British than the Indians, and he belonged to the working class. He had more reason to be anti-British than Masood, particularly when in 1920, at the height of British colonialism in Egypt, he was sentenced to six months' hard labor in prison on a false charge of attempting to buy firearms. "They shaved the hair they used a filthy basket instead of a towel,

took off my civil clothes and gave me a prisoner's clothes," he wrote inco-
herently to Forster who was "wrecked" by the news. The political forces of
his country had humiliated his friend. There is some reason, I believe, for
Forster to have written the notorious statement many years later in *What I
Believe*: "If I had to choose between betraying my country and betraying
my friend I hope I should have the guts to betray my country."

On returning from his second visit to India in 1922, Forster stopped
over in Port Said to spend a few days with Mohammed, who was dying of
consumption. He arranged for his friend to live in a health resort, bought a
silk shawl for his wife, and made provisions for the family. This extension
of friendship to the family of his friend is typical of Forster's later relationships with men. Mohammed's world mattered to Forster as much as did
Mohammed himself. On returning to England, Forster simply waited for his
friend to die. In his diary, he confided: "I want him to tell me that he is
dead, and so set me free to make an image of him."

Mohammed died within four months, bequeathed a ring to Forster, and
A Passage to India was well under way. If this sounds somewhat ruthless,
an exploitation of life in the pursuit of art, it should be remembered that
Forster also wrote a private "letter" to Mohammed after his death that
contains some of the most poignant autobiographical writing that I have ever
read. Through recollections of dreams and a confrontation of the struggle
involved in making a dead person live, Forster forged his way to an acceptance of his friend's death in the larger context of being alive in the universe.

In the spring of 1923, he went for a walk in Chertsey Meads, wearing
Mohammed's ring, and found that he could no longer remember his friend.
He acknowledged the sad truth of this experience in his diary, and in the
process of recording it, he crystallized his vision of friendship.

> You are dead, Mohammed, and Morgan is alive, and thinks more
> about himself and less of you every word he writes. You called
> out my name at Beebit el Hagar station after we had seen that
> ruined temple. . . . It was dark and I heard an Egyptian shouting
> who had lost his friend: Margan, Margan—you calling me and I
> felt we belonged to each other, you had made me an Egyptian.
> When I call you on the downs now, I cannot make you alive, nor
> can I belong to you because you own nothing. I shall not belong
> to you when I die—only be like you.

There is no otherness in this friendship. The categories of "you" and "me"
are dissolved; Forster can be Egyptian. Or more precisely, he can be made
Egyptian by his friend. Ultimately, these national distinctions are of no con-

sequence because in death, there is nothing to own—neither a name nor a country. Even friends no longer belong to each other: they *are* each other.

This magnanimous view of friendship had evolved over time. Certainly, it would be wrong to assume that Forster had always upheld it or had been guided by it in his attitude to men. During his second trip to India, for instance, we have a document of his relationship with an Indian boy called Kanaya that disturbingly reflects an authoritarian view of friendship based on the principle of ownership. Forster had met "this barber-boy" while serving as the secretary to the Maharaja of Dewas Senior. Unable to control his homosexual instincts ("the heat provoked me sexually") and oppressed by his constant masturbation and vacancy of mind, Forster eventually found comfort in Kanaya, whose services were arranged by none other than the Maharaja himself. While officially an "anti-sodomite" (unlike the Maharaja of Chatrapur whose attachment to boy-actors was well known), the Maharaja of Dewas sympathized with Forster's problem.

> "Why a man and not a woman?" he once asked. "Is not a woman more natural?"
>
> "Not in my case," replied Forster. "I have no feeling for women."
>
> "Oh, but then that alters everything. You are not to blame."

Not only was the Maharaja Forster's active accomplice in his sex life, he even advised Forster to accept homosexual jokes made at his expense and, at all costs, to avoid passivity, "for a rumour of that kind would be bad." In a more tantalizing way, he revealed Forster's age to his courtiers under the dubious assumption that "at forty-two any properly constructed Indian is impotent or nearly so and can dally no more with maiden or boy."

While the Maharaja appears to us, quite literally, as a character—he is whimsical and delightfully absurd in his maneuverings and strategies—one should also keep in mind that he embodies power. As the ruler of the state, he *owns* Kanaya's life. In his manuscript, Forster reveals that Kanaya was "terrified of H. H., whose severity towards his class seemed notorious." And significantly, as His Highness's friend, Forster also assumes an ownership of Kanaya who has, in his words, "the body and soul of a slave." When Kanaya eventually attempts to exploit the relationship by endearing himself to the Maharaja, Forster reacts sharply:

> I hesitated not but boxed his ears. . . . He had been such a goose—had done himself and the rest of us in because he couldn't

hold his tongue. What relationship beyond carnality could one
establish with such people?

The petulance of Forster's tone and his very English dismissal of Kanaya as
a "goose" indicate that he wrote his description of Kanaya to be read by or
to friends in the Bloomsbury Memoir Club. It is for the amusement of these
friends that Kanaya himself becomes a character, a source of entertainment.

Needless to say, one has no idea who Kanaya is apart from what we
learn from Forster. Even his appearance implies ridicule: "Somewhat over-
dressed in too yellow a coat and too blue a turban, he rather suggested the
part and his body was thin and effeminate and smelt of cheap scent." Kanaya
hardly speaks, and when he does, he sounds as real as any slave in the
Arabian Nights talking to his master. We have no way of knowing what he
really felt and thought about being sexually involved with a sahib, because
Forster does not permit him a point of view. It is possible that the value
judgments made by Forster on Kanaya's behalf are a reaction to the "little
racial vengeance" that he received from the local people in Dewas, who
teased the sahib for liking boys. But there is no justification, I think, for the
peremptory tone adopted by Forster in the conclusion of the piece:

> I resumed sexual intercourse with him, but it was now mixed
> with the desire to inflict pain. It didn't hurt him to speak of, but
> it was bad for me, and new in me, my temperament not being
> that way. I've never had that desire with anyone else, before or
> after, and I wasn't trying to punish him—I knew his silly little
> soul was incurable. I just felt he was a slave, without rights, and
> I a despot whom no one could call to account.

Despite the self-criticism which actually hints of selfishness ("it didn't hurt
him, it was bad for me"), this attitude is undeniably despotic. I cannot help
wondering how Kanaya reacted to this change in attitude by Forster. What
happened to Kanaya anyway? And who *was* he in the first place?

I see a very slight and ineffectual Indian beginning to speak, but then,
absurdly, there is an image of Forster's barber-boy "skipping away through
the sunshine holding up a canvas umbrella to protect his complexion."

The inherent problems in representing Kanaya are symptomatic of the
contradictions faced by Flaubert when he represented the Egyptian courtesan
Kuchuk Hanem as the prototype of Oriental womanhood. Kanaya's mis-
representation seems inconsequential in comparison, but it echoes what Edward Said has said about Kuchuk Hanem: "She never spoke of herself, she
never represented her emotions, presence, or history. [Flaubert] spoke for

and represented her." It seems that representation in itself poses an unavoidable paradox: on the one hand, we have reason to be concerned when we believe that something or someone has been misrepresented, and yet, can there be a true representation of anything? What is the truth in a representation? Is it an essence that has been faithfully reproduced in the re-presentation? Or is it, less ambiguously, a point of view that you happen to share with the author?

It is well known that the representation of the Anglo-Indian characters in A Passage to India was strongly criticized by many Anglo-Indian readers as "unfair" and "inhuman." "Your Collector is impossible," wrote a retired Indian civilian of "thirty years' experience" (as opposed to Forster's "year-and-a-half"). "All the fuss about the bridge-party is hopelessly out of date," wrote another. Ultimately, as Forster was to acknowledge with daring candor, "I loathe the Anglo-Indians and should have been more honest to say so." But does the fact that he "loathes" the Anglo-Indians imply that he doesn't *know* them? I think not, but then I speak as an Indian. Turton is not a one-dimensional caricature for me: he represents a particular combination of pomposity and power that was known to exist in colonial India. In fact, we still have Turtons in India today, only now their skin is "coffee-colour" as opposed to "pinko-gray." The *burra sahib* mentality is not obsolete at all: it is a living presence in post-Independence India and can be traced to the behavior of company directors and bureaucrats. In fact, replicas of Turton can be found all over the world, notably in members of Margaret Thatcher's party and in immigration officials at Heathrow Airport.

If I seem to be arguing as an "oriental" here, it is because I know when I like or dislike certain people, not unlike Mrs. Moore and her author. "Sympathy is finite," as Forster once remarked. As for "fair-mindedness," it was to be commended as a "rare achievement" in art, but "how sterile in one's soul." What mattered to Forster most of all as a writer was what he called the *accent* in a work of art. "If I saw more of Anglo-India at work," he explained to a critical reader, "I should of course realize its difficulties and loyalties better and write about it from within. Well and good, but you forget the price to be paid: I should begin to write about Indians from without. My statements about them would be the same, but the accent would have altered." It seems that the "accent" involves a great deal more than a change in emphasis of tone or point of view. In the case of Forster's depiction of the Indian characters in A Passage to India, notably Aziz, it becomes a sympathetic link that an author feels for a particular character that transcends the objectivity of his representation. The author may criticize this character, but fundamentally, he is linked to him rather like a friend.

One could say that Forster wrote *A Passage to India* as an "oriental," which in the context of the book signifies "a friend of the East." This does not mean, of course, that he wrote the book as an Indian. How could he? Like any author, his sympathies were circumscribed by his intellectual milieu, his personal and political commitments, and his sense of history—all of which had been unavoidably shaped by his English upbringing, education, and cultural inheritance. Obviously, the truth to be found in Forster's novel is something that has been shaped by Forster himself. It is not a metaphysical essence of India that has simply been borrowed and absorbed into the book. Therefore, in asking the inevitable (and problematic) question, How true is the book to India? one should keep in mind that the truth represented in the book is itself a representation. In other words, we have to examine it, as Said advises in *Orientalism,* not in relation to "some great original," but more concretely through the book's style, figures of speech, and narrative devices. The very exteriority of a text is what constitutes its truth.

Upholding this critical premise, Said quotes the famous ending of *A Passage to India* (perhaps more famous now after its rendition in David Lean's film) and comments that it is *this style* that "the Orient will always come up against."

> But the horses didn't want it—they swerved apart; the earth didn't want it, sending up rocks through which riders must pass single-file; the temples, the tank, the jail, the palace, the birds, the carrion, the Guest House, that came into view as they issued from the gap and saw Mau beneath: they didn't want it, they said in their hundred voices, "No, not yet," and the sky said, "No, not there."

It is almost as if Forster's language is setting up a barrier which prevents the East and West from coming together. Otherness seems to be affirmed through the rhetoric itself. One is left, in Said's words, with "a sense of the pathetic distance still separating 'us' from an Orient destined to bear its foreignness as a mark of its permanent estrangement from the West."

My problem with this interpretation is that it is much too strategic in its focus and situation in the wider spectrum of Orientalist thought. Yes, there is separation in the final moments of *A Passage to India,* but it is so subtly juxtaposed with intimacy that one might say that Aziz and Fielding have acquired a mutual understanding of each other for the first time—perhaps because of the separation. Let us not forget that before the horses "swerve" apart, the language is steeped in a physical detail that totally contradicts the "distant" style of the conclusion. Aziz is shouting,

"We shall drive every blasted Englishman into the sea, and then"—he rode against him [Fielding] furiously—"and then," he concluded, half kissing him, "you and I shall be friends."

"Why can't we be friends now?" said the other, holding him affectionately. "It's what I want. It's what you want."

The irony that Forster suggests so seductively is that Aziz and Fielding *are* friends at the moment of parting. If history and the universe are bent on separating them, Forster seems to imply that it is "not yet" time for them to be permanently united.

For me, the ending is not "disappointing" as Said claims. If Aziz and Fielding had galloped away into the sunset, it would have been as unconvincing as their gentlemanly handshake in Lean's film. Forster, I believe, is attempting something a great deal more complex than an orientalist vision of irreconcilable differences between East and West. One could say that he is juxtaposing three kinds of friendship: the friendship between friends, between nations, and between friends and (their friends') nations. The struggle between these different kinds of friendship is most richly textured in the final exchange between Aziz and Ralph. As Mrs. Moore's son, Ralph has to be Aziz's friend:

"But you are Heaslop's brother also, and alas, the two nations cannot be friends."

"I know. Not yet."

"Did your mother speak to you about me?"

"Yes." And with a swerve of voice and body that Aziz did not follow he added: "In her letters, in her letters. She loved you."

"Yes, your mother was my best friend in all the world."

Truly, it is in language that the ambivalent truths of books are ultimately conveyed. In the passage quoted above, we find so many of the tussles within Forster's characters—their allegiance to themselves, to their friends, and to their nations—all cohering in an irresolute conflict. It is the words that carry this irresolution through to the end of the novel. It is "not yet" time for the nations to be friends. But more subtly, in Ralph's "*swerve* of voice and body," I sense a movement *toward* Aziz and the very counterpoint of the final separation between Aziz and Fielding when the horses swerved apart. In the separation, I hear an echo of the earlier movement.

Separating and uniting, giving and receiving, the novel moves between these states of being. The possibilities of friendship that lie at the very core of Forster's vision may be questioned, but they are not absolutely denied. As

Ralph instinctively knows, even a stranger can be a friend. He is white and, in a sense, unavoidably related to the Turtons and Burtons (on a racial level) and to Ronnie (through his mother's first marriage), but he can also be an "oriental." And not through manipulative or exploitative means but by feeling something extraordinary about India of which Aziz himself is unaware. Stella also feels "that link outside either participant that is necessary to every relationship"—a link that she discovers after experiencing the Hindu celebration of Krishna. Forster poses here a controversial paradox in making Mrs. Moore's children seem more "oriental" than Aziz through their insight into Hinduism. As a Muslim whose allegiance is to Babur and Alamgir, the poetry of Ghalib, and the spirit of Islam, which is "more than a faith" for him, Aziz seems excluded from India in a significant way. While he is an "oriental" by birth (though he has no "natural affection" for his motherland), Ralph and Stella feel connected to their colony on a spiritual level. Forster may be criticized for mystifying the "link" felt by the Moores, but it is gratifying that he does not uphold the orientalist dichotomy of "them" and "us" in a rigid way.

This does not mean, of course, that all Westerners can be "orientals." Good old Fielding remains committed to his "Mediterranean norm." As for the other Anglo-Indian characters, they are orientalists by profession for the most part and are in India "to do justice and keep the peace." Their necessary commitment to recording, controlling, administering, and defining the Orient in their own terms is what prevents and forbids them from being "oriental." Forster's dislike of these orientalists is what prevents him from celebrating the "marriage" of East and West that Walt Whitman affirmed in his own "Passage to India." Written to memorialize the opening of the Suez Canal in 1869, the poem has nothing in common with the novel but the title. In fact, it seems that Forster has quite deliberately debunked almost every ideal rhetoricized in the poem.

The "doubts to be solv'd" and "blanks to be filled" mentioned in Whitman's poem are neither solved nor filled in the novel. "Old occult Brahma" becomes nothing and "reason's early birth" seems the very antithesis of the "muddles" that Forster's India seems to generate. The "great achievements of the present" which Whitman glorifies are conspicuous by their absence in Forster's world. Technology cannot explain the echoes in the Marabar Caves. Ultimately, what Forster refutes in Whitman's vision of "the marriage of continents, climates, and oceans" is its assumptions of global order and universal brotherhood. The poem reeks of belief, an abstraction odious to Forster. All he really believed in, as he mentioned in a famous essay, was personal relationships. It is not surprising, therefore, that he did not share the grandiose vision of man symbolized in the building of the Suez Canal.

This ambitious project was unanimously heralded as a revolutionary step in uniting the peoples and nations of the world. "Now we will be one" is what Ferdinand de Lesseps must have envisioned. Not inappropriately, his investment company for the project was called the *Compagnie universelle.* "The whole earth" seemed to be involved in the project. On its completion, "this cold, impassive, voiceless earth," in Whitman's words, "would be completely justified." The truth, of course, is that it was the "engineers, architects, and machinists" from the West who "justified" the project. They were the initiators of this vision for the unification of the world. Their missionary zeal is very clearly reflected in a prize-winning poem on the Suez Canal written by Bornier. In the poem, it becomes clear that the Suez Canal has been created not only "pour l'univers," but "pour le Chinois perfide et l'Indien demi-nu." And inevitably, "Pour ceux à qui le Christ est encore inconnu." In such sentiments one realizes the racist dimension underlying global missions and projects.

A Passage to India does not share this global mission. The only oneness that is alluded to in the novel is one that an individual may find on coming to terms with Nothing. But apart from this uncertain tryst with the unknown, there are no solutions provided by Forster for the oneness of the world. Unlike de Lesseps, he would not, in all probability, believe that "le rapprochement de l'occident et de l'orient" could be achieved through building a canal. But perhaps, if a Brahmin schoolteacher with clocks on his socks remembered a wasp once observed by a white "oriental" lady—perhaps it was at such moments that the East and West could enter each other's minds. Now this preoccupation with wasps may seem precious to Forster's critics, but even the severest among them would have to agree that there is nothing orientalist about it.

Minute in detail, it is symptomatic of Forster's distrust of big events—a distrust that challenged the pomp and ceremony of the Raj, its laws and proclamations, its edicts and messages. There is no colonial fervor in Forster to change India, no humanist scheme of progress imposed on a country ridden with problems. Forster accepted India for what it was, and therein lies the extraordinary strength and love of his novel. One can say that India was like so many of his friends. If he saw faults in them, they became part of his love for them. And as in any true friendship, his friends were "his for ever and he theirs for ever: he loved them so much that giving and receiving became one."

Forster's love for India endured and deepened over the years. It did not fade with time. When he finally returned to India in 1945 to attend a conference of writers, he again visited Hyderabad, Masood's home city, and realized "how much of his heart had gone into the place." Now he was a famous writer and Masood was dead. Seeking refuge from all the attention he received as a dignitary, Forster retreated to a hillside one evening and watched the sun set. Later, he revealed that he had been thinking of Egypt. In his memory, Egypt and India had coalesced, and his friends, too, Mohammed and Masood, were one. Forster never wrote about this moment. Perhaps he realized that some accounts of friends can be written only in the heart.

SARA SULERI

The Geography of
A Passage to India

The adventure of twentieth-century narrative in English has engendered an area of studies that, in the act of taking India as its subject, transforms the locality of an historic space into a vast introspective question mark. From *A Passage to India* on, "books about India" have been more accurately books about the representation of India, with each offering variants of the peculiar logic through which a failure of representation becomes transformed into a characteristically Indian failure. In order to examine such acts of represen-tation as a mode of recolonization, I wish to present a reading of a paradig-matic text—Forster's *A Passage to India*—of the subterranean desire to replay, in twentieth-century narrative, the increasingly distant history of nineteenth-century domination. The mode is characterized by the desire to contain the intangibilities of the East within a Western lucidity, but this gesture of appropriation only partially conceals the obsessive fear that India's fictionality inevitably generates in the writing mind of the West. The symbolic violence of this fear underlies the impulse to empty the area out of history, and to represent India as an amorphous state of mind that is only remem-bered in order for it to be forgotten.

From their titles on, narratives on the Indian theme declare their inten-tions to name something so vague as to be nearly unnameable, implying that their subject is disturbingly prone to spill into atmospherics rather than remaining fixed in the place to which it belongs. Something is dislocated, and the fictions proceed to develop on precisely those lines. Typically, the narrator is a cartographer, the only locus of rationality in an area of engulfing unreliability, so that ultimately the narrative mind is the only safe terrain the texts provide. India itself, like a Cheshire cat, functions as a dislocated metaphor for an entity that is notoriously remiss in arriving at the appointed place at the correct time. As a consequence, it becomes a space that imposes its unreality on Western discourse to the point where the narrative has no option but to redouble on itself, to internalize the symbolic landscape of India in order to make it human. Thus geography is subsumed into the more immediate and familiar territory of the liberal imagination, in the act of recolonizing its vagrant subject with the intricacies of a defined sensibility.

Such is the imagination, of course, that legitimizes a text like *A Passage to India* as a humanely liberal parable for imperialism, and allows a reader like Trilling to interpret the novel's depiction of Eastern action as a metaphor for the behaviour of the West. In other words, the only difference of India inheres in the fact that it is symbolic of something the Western mind must learn about itself. The paradigm that Forster establishes is of crucial importance to all subsequent narratives on India, which, with their exquisite caving in upon themselves, embody a response to the difference of India that Forster so effectively literalized. For it is Forster rather than Kipling who initiates the Western narrative of India: a text like *Kim* in fact reinforces the reality of India by seeing it so clearly as the other that the imperial West must know and dominate. *A Passage to India,* on the other hand, represents India as a metaphor of something other than itself, as a certain metaphysical posture that translates into an image of profound unreality. It thus becomes that archetypal novel of modernity that co-opts the space reserved for India in the Western literary imagination, so that all subsequent novels on the Indian theme appear secretly obsessed with the desire to describe exactly what transpired in the Marabar Caves.

"How does one interpret another culture," asks Edward Said, "unless prior circumstances have made that culture available for interpretation in the first place?" [*Covering Islam*]. This question, that of the historic availability of India, is certainly not a problem that preoccupies Forster's protagonists, who are far more interested in decoding that which India tells them about their own interpretability. Thus Forster initiates a narrative mode that is perhaps more fraught with violence than the Orientalist code that Said charts, which is that "imaginative yet drastically polarized geography dividing the world into two unequal parts, the larger, 'different' one called the Orient, the other, also known as 'our' world, called the Occident." Where Forster transgresses even an Orientalist decorum is by implying that India is really not other at all, but merely a mode or passageway to endorse the infinite variety that constitutes a reading of the West. To approach the Indian fictions of the modern West is indeed to confront a secret attack on difference, and to reread the text that is *A Passage to India*. For this fiction most clearly delineates the desire to convert unreadability into unreality, and difference into an image of the writing mind's perception of its own ineffability.

Forster, I hope to demonstrate, constructs a symbolic geography that provides Western narrative with its most compelling and durable image of India, which is, of course, the figure of India as a hollow, or a cave. It is the desire to know the hollow, but to leave defeated, that informs the dainty ironies of Forster's narrative, for the narrative mind can only empty its defeat upon the landscape, and depart from the area exhausted, but a little lighter. Since Forster, this model has been rehearsed repeatedly, but nowhere as effectively as in the ostensibly nonfictional text, V. S. Naipaul's *An Area of Darkness*. Both fictions share in that Western project which represents India as an empty site that is bounded only by an aura of irrationality. In examining the two narratives as a genealogical unit, I will attempt to chart the development of that amorphous idiom which begins in the novel an Englishman writes about India, but finally gains a nonfictional authority in the work of an Indian writer fully prepared to cite himself as a living emblem of India's inauthenticity.

In my reading, *A Passage to India* and *An Area of Darkness* are remarkably predisposed towards complete alignment. They are not only the two best British novels about India, but constitute parallel texts where the question posed by one is answered by the other. What can happen here? asks Forster: Nothing, responds V. S. Naipaul, except history as the act of possible imagination, because there is only me. He thus proceeds to literalize Forster's image of disappointing emptiness by representing himself as the one self-conscious embodiment of India's massive failure to present a cohesive shape. Whereas this failure functions as the atmospherics of *A Passage to India*, in *An Area of Darkness* it becomes as palpable as the excrement that so appalls Naipaul that he must note and describe it each time it comes his way. To the imperial English mind, India can only be represented as a gesture of possible rape; to the postcolonial and equally English mind, India is nothing more than the imbecile act of self-exposure, whose outrage is too literal to allow for even the secrecy of shame.

That the Orient has traditionally been represented as a figure of seduction, duplicity—and, more darkly, rape—is a commonplace that is clearly established by European historical and travel narratives from the seventeenth century on. It takes Forster, however, to carry the rape image to its most finely wrought conclusion. While *A Passage to India* ostensibly centres on an hysteric who believes she has been raped, the course of the narrative suggests that the real outrage lies in the fact that this rude encounter has been withheld from her. India diffuses into emptiness before it completes the seduction it had promised, as though its own formlessness demands that it can be master of only an incomplete performance. Rape becomes, therefore, dangerously synonymous with sexual disappointment: that the novel is traversed by Western travellers invaded by sensations of impotence as long as they remain on Western territory is a crucial index of Forster's obsession with representing India as a figure of both an erotic yet sterile duplicity.

Forster's narrative is found, and founders on, the idiom of a god who neglects to come. In the key scene where the Hindu Godbole sings for the uncomprehending audience of Fielding's Muslim and British guests, he offers the following commentary:

> "It was a religious song. I placed myself in the position of a milkmaiden. I say to Shri Krishna, 'Come! come to me only.' The god refuses to come. I grow humble and say: 'Do not come to me only. Multiply yourself into a hundred Krishnas . . . Come, come, come, come, come, come. He neglects to come.'"

Despite the parodic sentimentality of this version of Hinduism, the passage nonetheless provides Forster with a refrain that he uses to envelop all the inhabitants of India, where the god neglects to come. The structure of the novel images this neglect through its emblematic representation of empty institutions, or buildings that are somewhat wanton in their lack of habitation. *A Passage to India* makes neat architecture of this lack, in that the three sections of the book—"Mosque," "Caves," and "Temple"—function primarily as cavities to contain Western perceptions of that which is missing from the East. The edifices thus constitute shells into which Forster can uncurl echoes of what first appears to be a humane compassion, but what gradually and more threateningly develops into an exquisite nostalgia for betrayal. While the novel attempts to delineate a Hindu "type" as opposed to a Muslim "type" in its portrayal of native characters like Godbole and Aziz, finally the Muslim merely represents a slightly obscene accessibility that is less than authentically Indian, while the Hindu becomes a little too Indian to be true, always teetering on the brink of transfiguration. Both Mosque and Temple, therefore, collaborate and collapse into the emptiness that is the Cave.

How does one traverse a landscape replete with images of Krishna, but where Krishna will not come? Forster's response, of course, is to construct a retreat through a dualistic vocabulary in which India is ultimately reprehensible because it denies the fixity of an object that the narrative subject can pursue and penetrate. Instead, like the self-dissipating echoes in the Marabar Caves, it can only be approached as a sexuality that lacks a cleft, or a single certain entry of understanding. Throughout the novel, Forster manipulates the image of landscape as metaphoric of that possible fulfillment which is continually on the verge of emptying into disappointment. Finally, his only mode to chart the symbolic geography he names India is by means of locating a structure that perfectly resonates with its own absence. Here, he invites his readers to join him in the Marabar Caves.

Forster approaches the Caves with the polite bewilderment of an intelligent tourist guide who wishes to be respectful of an entity that is really not very interesting. The restraint with which the narrative seeks to image the cave's unbeauty is, however, its secret method of attack:

> The caves are readily described. A tunnel eight feet long, five feet high, three feet wide, leads to a circular chamber about twenty feet in diameter. This arrangement occurs again and again throughout the group of hills, and this is all, this is a Marabar Cave. Having seen one such cave, having seen two, having seen three, four, fourteen, twenty-four, the visitor returns to Chandrapore uncertain whether he has had an interesting experience or a dull one or any experience at all. He finds it difficult to discuss the caves, or to keep them apart in his mind. . . . Nothing, nothing attaches to them, and their reputation—for they have one—does not depend upon human speech.

The crevices that are India, in other words, are completely exposed to description, but are offensively impervious to interpretation, like the obscene echo that so torments Forster's female characters. To the Western imagination, the horror of the caves is their lack of metaphoricity and their indifference to experiential time. That they could represent an historical autonomy can only be envisioned as a nightmare, or as a parodic pretension towards meaning. After having named the caves as areas of empty experience, the narrative proceeds to explore the hideous possibility that they may indeed possess strata of significance:

> But elsewhere, deeper in the granite, are there certain chambers that have no entrances? Chambers never unsealed since the arrival of the gods. Local report declares that these exceed in number those that can be visited, as the dead exceed the living—four hundred of them, four thousand or million. Nothing is inside

them, they were sealed up before the creation of pestilence or
treasure; if mankind grew curious and excavated, nothing, nothing would be added to the sum of good or evil.

To entertain such a possibility, however, as Fielding attempts and fails to
entertain Indians and Europeans to tea, merely corroborates the narrative
fear that India is only real in prehistory, or when it arrives after the fact of
history. In relation to the existing authority of Western narrative, India represents the terrifying docility of Cordelia's nothing, and the further obscenity
of that word in the face of power, which knows that nothing can come of
nothing.

It is therefore a matter of some perplexity that most of Forster's readers
still see in *A Passage to India* a dated kindliness towards the "Indian question," or an imperial allegory in which an unattractive European female
falsely accuses an attractive Indian male of rape. In considering Adela
Quested, it is difficult to ignore the complicated defences that cause Forster
to represent her as a cipher almost as arid as the Marabar Caves. For rather
than a woman abused or abusive, Adela essentially plays the part of a conduit
or a passageway for the aborted eroticism between the European Fielding
and the Indian Aziz. That, finally, is the substance of the novel: the narrative
is not brought to rest with the melodramatic rape trial and Adela's recan-
tation, but is impelled into a description of the Indian's ugly failure to apprehend a European sensibility, and the seductive qualities of his continuing
ignorance. Aziz's Muslim accessibility is made impenetrable by such an ignorance, which allows the novel to conclude with the "half-kissing" embrace
of the two men who know that rape is unavailable, "not yet," "not here."
The potential seduction of India is thus perpetuated by the lovely, half-
realized slave boys of Forster's will to power; his revulsion takes the darker
shapes of the caves and the empty nothings of Adela Quested's requesting
womb.

Finally, what prevents the European and the Indian from completing
their embrace is the obliterating presence of the landscape. The European
wants the completion of his desire in the present moment, yet the narrative
gives the last word to the land's great power to deny and disappear:

> But the horses didn't want it—they swerved apart; the earth
> didn't want it . . . the temples, the tank, the jail, the palace, the
> birds, the carrion, the Guest House . . . they didn't want it, they
> said in their hundred voices, "No, not yet," and the sky said,
> "No, not there."

With this concluding sentence, even the difference of India is subsumed into a trope for a vacant and inexplicable rejection. It becomes instead an unimaginable space which cannot be inhabited by the present tense, resisting even the European attempt to coax it into metaphoricity.

Chronology

1879   Edward Morgan Forster born in London on January 1. His father, an architect of Anglo-Irish descent, dies the following year. His mother is descended from the Thornton family, of "Clapham Sect" fame.

1883–93   Forster lives in Hertfordshire at the home that will be the prototype of "Howards End."

1887   Forster's favorite aunt, Marianne Thornton, dies, leaving him a legacy of £8,000.

1893   Forster's family moves to Tonbridge, where he attends Tonbridge School as a day boy.

1897   Enters King's College, Cambridge, where he studies Classics (B.A. 1900) and History (B.A. 1901), (M.A. 1910). Among the teachers that influence Forster: G. Lowes Dickinson, J. M. E. McTaggert, Roger Fry, and Nathaniel Wedd.

1901   Forster travels to Italy and Greece; lives in Italy until 1902, when he moves to Abinger Hammer, Surrey.

1903   Forster's first short story, "Albergo Empedocle," is published in *Temple Bar*. Several of his Cambridge friends, including Dickinson, G. M. Trevelyan, Wedd, and Edward Jenks, found the *Independent Review,* to which he will contribute.

1905   *Where Angels Fear to Tread* published.

1907   *The Longest Journey* published.

1908   *A Room with a View* published.

1910   *Howards End* published.

1911   *The Celestial Omnibus and Other Short Stories* published.

1912–13   Forster takes his first trip to India with Dickinson and R. C. Trevelyan. The visit, lasting from October until March, includes a stay with the Maharajah of Dewas Senior. Begins work on *A Passage to India*.

1914   Essays and reviews for *New Weekly*.

1915–19   Volunteer officer with the Red Cross in Alexandria, Egypt.

1919   Forster becomes literary editor of the *Daily Herald*, a Labour publication.

1921   Returns to India, as private secretary to the Maharajah of Dewas Senior. At the end of his stay he is presented with the Tukyjirao Gold Medal, the highest honor possible for a Westerner.

1922   *Alexandria: A History and a Guide* published.

1923   A collection of essays and sketches, *Pharos and Pharillon*, published.

1924   *A Passage to India* published. All the novels are reissued.

1925   Forster receives the Femina Vie Heureuse and James Tait Black Memorial Prizes for *A Passage to India*.

1927   *Aspects of the Novel*, a lecture series presented at Cambridge during this year, published. Forster elected a Fellow of King's College.

1928   *The Eternal Moment and Other Stories* published.

1934   Forster's first biography, *Goldsworthy Lowes Dickinson*, published. *The Abinger Pageant*, one of several dramatic efforts, is produced at Abinger Hammer. Forster becomes the first president of the National Council for Civil Liberties. He is elected again in 1942 and resigns in 1948.

1936   A collection of essays, *Abinger Harvest: A Miscellany*, published.

1939   *What I Believe* published.

1940   *Nordic Twilight* and *England's Pleasant Land, a Pageant Play* published.

1941 Forster delivers the Rede Lecture on Virginia Woolf.

1943 The first major critical work on Forster is published by Lionel Trilling (*E. M. Forster*), accompanied by the republication of all Forster's novels. This initiates a Forster revival in the United States.

1945 October–December, Forster makes third visit to India, for a conference in Jaipur. After his mother's death, Forster accepts honorary fellowship at King's College, Cambridge, his chief residence for the rest of his life.

1947 At Harvard University symposium on music criticism, gives lecture "The Raison d'Etre of Criticism in the Arts." *Collected Tales* published in the United States.

1948 *Collected Short Stories* published in England.

1949 "Art for Art's Sake" given as lecture at the American Academy of Arts and Letters.

1951 *Two Cheers for Democracy,* a collection of essays, published. Honorary degree from Nottingham University. *Billy Budd,* an opera written in collaboration with Eric Crozier and Benjamin Britten, produced at Covent Garden.

1953 Awarded membership in the Order of Companions of Honor to the Queen by Elizabeth II. *The Hill of Devi,* a memoir of his first two India trips, published.

1956 *Marianne Thornton,* a biography of Forster's aunt, published.

1961 Forster is named Companion of Literature by the Royal Society of Literature.

1969 Forster awarded the Order of Merit.

1970 On June 7, Forster dies at the age of 91.

Contributors

HAROLD BLOOM, Sterling Professor of the Humanities at Yale University, is the author of *The Anxiety of Influence, Poetry and Repression,* and many other volumes of literary criticism. His forthcoming study, *Freud: Transference and Authority,* attempts a full-scale reading of all of Freud's major writings. A MacArthur Prize Fellow, he is general editor of five series of literary criticism published by Chelsea House.

LIONEL TRILLING, University Professor at Columbia University, was one of the most eminent critics in American literary history. His works include *The Liberal Imagination: Essays on Literature and Society, Beyond Culture: Essays on Literature and Learning,* and *Sincerity and Authenticity.*

GEORGE H. THOMSON is Professor of English at the University of Ottawa and is the author of *The Fiction of E. M. Forster.*

JOHN COLMER is Jury Professor of English at the University of Adelaide. He has published on Coleridge, and is author of several books, including *E. M. Forster:* A Passage to India and *Coleridge to* Catch-22: *Images of Society.*

ALAN WILDE is Professor of English at Temple University. He is author of *Christopher Isherwood* and *Art and Order: A Study of E. M. Forster,* as well as various essays on British and American literature.

BARBARA B. ROSECRANCE is Assistant Professor of English at Cornell University and has been an assistant editor of *Partisan Review.* She has written on Forster, early modern British literature, and the poetry and music of the Renaissance.

MARTIN PRICE is Sterling Professor of English at Yale University. His previous books include *Swift's Rhetorical Art: A Study in Structure and*

Meaning, To the Palace of Wisdom: Studies in Order and Energy from Dryden to Blake, and a number of edited volumes on literature of the seventeenth, eighteenth, and nineteenth centuries.

RUSTOM BHARUCHA teaches Dramaturgy and Criticism at the State University of New York at Stony Brook. He is now working on a collection of essays entitled *Double Exposure.*

SARA SULERI is Assistant Professor of English at Yale University and coeditor of *The Yale Journal of Criticism.* She has published on Arnold and V. S. Naipaul.

Bibliography

Allen, Walter. *The English Novel.* New York: Dutton, 1955.

Ault, Peter. "Aspects of E. M. Forster." *Dublin Review* 209 (October 1946): 109–340.

Bedient, Calvin. *Architects of the Self: George Eliot, D. H. Lawrence, and E. M. Forster.* Berkeley and Los Angeles: University of California Press, 1972.

Beer, Gillian. "Negation in *A Passage to India.*" *Essays in Criticism* 30, no. 2 (1980): 151–66.

Beer, J. B. *The Achievement of E. M. Forster.* New York: Barnes & Noble, 1962.

Bell, Quentin. *Bloomsbury.* London: Weidenfeld & Nicolson, 1968.

Ben-Ephraim, Gavriel. "Dying in the Right Place: The Importance of Sophocles' *Oedipus at Colonus* to E. M. Forster's 'The Road from Colonus'." *Hebrew University Studies in Literature* 3, no. 1 (1975): 37–46.

Bodenheimer, Rosemarie. "The Romantic Impasse in *A Passage to India.*" *Criticism* 22, no. 1 (1980): 40–56.

Bolling, Douglass. "The Distanced Heart: Artistry in E. M. Forster's *Maurice.*" *Modern Fiction Studies* 20, no. 2 (1974): 157–67.

Bowen, Elizabeth. "E. M. Forster." In *Collected Impressions,* 119–26. London: Longmans, Green, 1950.

Bowen, Roger. "A Version of Pastoral: E. M. Forster as Country Guardian." *The South Atlantic Quarterly* 75, no. 1 (1976): 36–54.

Bradbury, Malcolm, ed. *E. M. Forster:* A Passage to India. London: Macmillan, 1970.

Brower, Reuben A. *The Field of Light.* New York: Oxford University Press, 1951.

Brown, E. K. *Rhythm in the Novel.* Toronto: University of Toronto Press, 1950.

Burra, Peter. "The Novels of E. M. Forster." *Nineteenth Century and After* 116 (November 1935): 581–94.

Cammarota, Richard S. "Musical Analogy and Internal Design." *English Literature in Transition* 18, no. 1 (1975): 38–46.

Colmer, John. *E. M. Forster: The Personal Voice.* London: Routledge & Kegan Paul, 1975.

Crews, Frederick. *E. M. Forster: The Perils of Humanism.* Princeton: Princeton University Press, 1962.

Daleski, H. M. "Rhythmic and Symbolic Patterns in *A Passage to India.*" *Studies in English Language and Literature* 17, edited by Alice Shalvi and A. A. Mendilow. Jerusalem: Hebrew University, 1966.

Das, G. K. and John Beer, eds. *E. M. Forster: A Human Exploration (Centenary Essays)*. London: Macmillan, 1979.

Dowling, David. *Bloomsbury Aesthetics and the Novels of Forster and Woolf*. London: Macmillan, 1985.

Faulkner, Peter. *Humanism in the English Novel*. London: Elek/Pemberton, 1976.

Finkelstein, Bonnie Blumenthal. "Forster's Women: *A Room with a View*." *English Literature in Transition* 16 (1973): 175–87.

Friend, Robert. "The Quest for Rondure: A Comparison of Two Passages to India." *Hebrew University Studies in Literature* 1, no. 1 (1973): 76–85.

Furbank, P. N. *E. M. Forster: A Life*. 2 vols. London: Secker & Warburg, 1977.

Gardner, Philip. "E. M. Forster and 'The Possession of England.'" *Modern Language Quarterly* 42, no. 2 (1981): 166–83.

——, ed. *E. M. Forster: The Critical Heritage*. London: Routledge & Kegan Paul, 1973.

Gillen, Francis. "*Howards End* and the Neglected Narrator." *Novel* 3, no. 2 (1970): 139–52.

Gillie, Christopher. *A Preface to Forster*. London: Longman Group, 1983.

Gransden, K. W. *E. M. Forster*. Edinburgh: Oliver & Boyd, 1962.

Hardy, Barbara. *The Appropriate Form*. Evanston, Ill.: Northwestern University Press, 1971.

Herz, Judith Scherer, and Robert K. Martin, eds. *E. M. Forster: Centenary Revaluations*. Toronto: University of Toronto Press, 1982.

Hoffman, Frederick J. "*Howards End* and the Bogey of Progress." *Modern Fiction Studies* 7 (1961): 243–57.

Johnstone, J. K. *The Bloomsbury Group: A Study of E. M. Forster, Lytton Strachey, Virginia Woolf, and Their Circle*. New York: Noonday, 1954.

Langbaum, Robert. "A New Look at E. M. Forster." *Southern Review* 4 (1968): 33–49.

Leavis, F. R. "E. M. Forster." *Scrutiny* 7 (1938): 185–202.

Macaulay, Rose. *The Writings of E. M. Forster*. New York: Harcourt, Brace, 1938.

McConkey, James. *The Novels of E. M. Forster*. Ithaca: Cornell University Press, 1957.

McDowell, Frederick P. W. "By and About Forster: A Review Essay." *English Literature in Transition* 15 (1972): 319–31.

——. *E. M. Forster*. Revised edition. Boston: Twayne, 1982.

——. "Forster's Conception of the Critic." *Tennessee Studies in Literature* 10 (1965): 93–100.

——. "'The Mild, Intellectual Light': Idea and Theme in *Howards End*." *PMLA* 74 (1959): 453–63.

Meyers, Jeffrey. "The Politics of *Passage to India*." *Journal of Modern Literature* 1, no. 3 (1971): 329–38.

Natwar-Singh, K., ed. *E. M. Forster: A Tribute*. New York: Harcourt, Brace, & World, 1964.

Page, Norman. *E. M. Forster's Posthumous Fiction*. Victoria, B.C.: University of Victoria, 1977.

Pradhan, S. V. "*A Passage to India*: Realism versus Symbolism, A Marxist Analysis." *Dalhousie Review* 60, no. 2 (1980): 300–17.

Pritchett, V. S. "Mr. Forster's Birthday." *The Living Novel and Later Appreciations.* New York: Random House, 1964.

Richards, I. A. "A Passage to Forster: Reflections on a Novelist." *Forum* 78 (1927): 914–20.

Rosecrance, Barbara. *Forster's Narrative Vision.* Ithaca: Cornell University Press, 1982.

Rutherford, Andrew, ed. *Twentieth-Century Interpretations of* A Passage to India: *A Collection of Critical Essays.* Englewood Cliffs, N.J.: Prentice-Hall, 1970.

Schwarz, Daniel R. "The Originality of E. M. Forster." *Modern Fiction Studies* 29, no. 4 (1983): 623–41.

Shahane, V. A., ed. *Perspectives on E. M. Forster's* A Passage to India: *A Collection of Critical Essays.* New York: Barnes & Noble, 1968.

Shusterman, David. *The Quest for Certitude in E. M. Forster's Fiction.* Bloomington: Indiana University Press, 1965.

Spender, Stephen. "Personal Relations and Public Powers." *The Creative Element: A Study of Vision, Despair, and Orthodoxy Among Some Modern Writers.* London: Hamish Hamilton, 1953.

———. "Forster's Queer Novel." *Partisan Review* 1 (1972): 113–17.

Stallybrass, Oliver, ed. *Aspects of E. M. Forster: Essays and Recollections Written for His Ninetieth Birthday January 1, 1969.* New York: Harcourt, Brace, & World, 1969.

Stone, Wilfred. *The Cave and the Mountain: A Study of E. M. Forster.* Stanford: Stanford University Press, 1966.

———. "'Overleaping Class,' Forster's Problem in Connection." *Modern Language Quarterly* 39, no. 4 (1978): 386–404.

Summers, Claude J. *E. M. Forster.* New York: Frederick Ungar, 1983.

Thomson, George H. *The Fiction of E. M. Forster.* Detroit: Wayne State University Press, 1967.

Thumboo, Edwin. "E. M. Forster's *A Passage to India*: From Caves to Court." *Southern Review* 10, no. 4 (1978): 386–404.

Trilling, Lionel. *E. M. Forster: A Study.* 1944. London: Hogarth Press, 1951.

Turk, Jo M. "The Evolution of E. M. Forster's Narrator." *Studies in the Novel* 5, no. 4 (1973): 428–39.

Warren, Austin. "The Novels of E. M. Forster." In *Rage for Order,* 119–41. Chicago: University of Chicago Press, 1948.

Wilde, Alan. *Art and Order: A Study of E. M. Forster.* New York: New York University Press, 1964.

———. "Depths and Surfaces: Dimensions of Forsterian Irony." *English Literature in Transition* 16, no. 4 (1973): 257–73.

Acknowledgments

"Mind and Will: Forster's Literary Criticism" by Lionel Trilling from *E. M. Forster: A Study* by Lionel Trilling, © 1944 by Lionel Trilling. Reprinted by permission of Diana Trilling and the Hogarth Press Ltd.

"The Italian Romances" by George H. Thomson from *The Fiction of E. M. Forster* by George H. Thomson, © 1967 by George H. Thomson. Reprinted by permission of the author and Wayne State University Press.

"*The Longest Journey*" by John Colmer from *E. M. Forster: The Personal Voice* by John Colmer, © 1975 by John Colmer. Reprinted by permission of the author and Routledge & Kegan Paul Ltd.

"Injunctions and Disjunctions" by Alan Wilde from *Horizons of Assent: Modernism, Postmodernism, and the Ironic Imagination* by Alan Wilde, © 1981 by The Johns Hopkins University Press, Baltimore/London. Reprinted by permission.

"*Howards End*" by Barbara Rosecrance from *Forster's Narrative Vision* by Barbara Rosecrance, © 1982 by Cornell University Press. Reprinted by permission of the publisher.

"Forster: Inclusion and Exclusion" by Martin Price from *Forms of Life: Character and Moral Imagination in the Novel* by Martin Price, © 1983 by Yale University. Reprinted by permission of Yale University Press.

"Forster's Friends" by Rustom Bharucha from *Raritan: A Quarterly Review* 5, no. 4 (Spring 1986), © 1986 by *Raritan*, 165 College Avenue, New Brunswick, N.J. Reprinted by permission.

"The Geography of *A Passage to India*" by Sara Suleri, © 1986 by Sara Suleri. Excerpted from a study of Forster and Naipaul and published for the first time in this volume.

Index